DIRECTING NEW PLAYS

PRAISE FOR
DIRECTING NEW PLAYS

New plays need directors who can translate their passion and creativity into clear plans and thoughtful communication. Evan Cabnet's masterful text on directing embodies just this, seamlessly melding inspiration with structure. This immersive guide, perfect for both novices and professionals, equips directors to bring new work to the stage with artistry and impact.

CHRISTOPHER SHINN, *writer and teacher*

I highly recommend anyone interested in what a theater director does to read Evan Cabnet's smart, succinct and invaluable book.

JAMES LAPINE, *playwright and director*

In *Directing New Plays*, Evan Cabnet offers a clear and candid guide through the process of creating new work; demystifying the process, while illuminating the craft of the new play director.

LILEANA BLAIN-CRUZ, *director*

Evan Cabnet's *Directing New Plays* is necessary reading for anyone who wants to learn the craft or better their approaches. Cabnet provides unpretentious practical advice and real world scenarios, applicable to any rehearsal room. Leading a new play process, or any play process for that matter can be a lonely endeavor, *Directing New Plays* not only demystifies the work but also provides solidarity from the encouraging voice of a colleague.

JENNIFER CHANG, *director and professor*

Few artists know the American theatre and the new play process as well as Evan Cabnet. This book distills his experience, guidance, and wisdom into a crash course for novice and experienced directors alike. An invaluable road map for any director who wants to bring new plays to life!

DAVID HENRY HWANG, *playwright and professor*

Directing New Plays is the most relevant and brilliantly written book on directing new plays I've encountered. A vital guide for directors interested in working on the cutting edge of new play development and production. Cabnet is able to offer keen and clear insight into the often unseen work directors do, and to paint a bigger picture of the qualities that distinguish truly great leaders in the American theater.

LEAR DEBESSONNET, *director*

Though written specifically for directors, Evan Cabnet's spectacular book is a guide that is educational for anyone involved in the new play process.

MICHAEL R. JACKSON, *writer and composer*

DIRECTING NEW PLAYS

Tools for Art and Collaboration

EVAN CABNET

methuen | drama
LONDON • NEW YORK • OXFORD • NEW DELHI • SYDNEY

METHUEN DRAMA
Bloomsbury Publishing Plc
50 Bedford Square, London, WC1B 3DP, UK
1385 Broadway, New York, NY 10018, USA
29 Earlsfort Terrace, Dublin 2, Ireland

BLOOMSBURY, METHUEN DRAMA and the Methuen Drama logo are trademarks of Bloomsbury Publishing Plc

First published in Great Britain 2024

Copyright © Evan Cabnet, 2024

Evan Cabnet has asserted his right under the Copyright, Designs and Patents Act, 1988, to be identified as author of this work.

For legal purposes the Acknowledgments on p. 258 constitute an extension of this copyright page.

Cover design by Rebecca Heselton
Cover image © Ron Dale / Adobe Stock

All rights reserved. No part of this publication may be reproduced or transmitted in any form or by any means, electronic or mechanical, including photocopying, recording, or any information storage or retrieval system, without prior permission in writing from the publishers.

Bloomsbury Publishing Plc does not have any control over, or responsibility for, any third-party websites referred to or in this book. All internet addresses given in this book were correct at the time of going to press. The author and publisher regret any inconvenience caused if addresses have changed or sites have ceased to exist, but can accept no responsibility for any such changes.

A catalogue record for this book is available from the British Library.

A catalog record for this book is available from the Library of Congress.

ISBN:	HB:	978-1-3501-7925-7
	PB:	978-1-3501-7926-4
	ePDF:	978-1-3501-7927-1
	eBook:	978-1-3501-7928-8

Typeset by Integra Software Services Pvt. Ltd.
Printed and bound in Great Britain

To find out more about our authors and books visit www.bloomsbury.com and sign up for our newsletters.

This book is dedicated to my collaborators:
past, present, and future

CONTENTS

Introduction 1

PART ONE BEGINNINGS 3

1 **What Does a Director Do, and How Do They Do It?** 5

2 **Finding and Reading a Text** 14

3 **Meeting with a Writer** 18

PART TWO DEVELOPMENT 23

4 **Readings** 25

5 **Workshops** 37

6 **Pursuing a Production** 50

PART THREE PRE-PRODUCTION 57

7 **Assembling the Creative Team** 61

8 **Casting** 72

9 **The Design Process** 88

10 **The Producing Organization and Production Meetings** 100

PART FOUR REHEARSAL 113

11 The First Rehearsal 117

12 Tablework 122

13 Building a Rough Draft 133

14 Preparing and Organizing a Rehearsal Day 141

15 Actors 145

16 The Stumble-Through and the Next Draft 159

17 Rehearsal Room Challenges 170

18 Rewrites 180

19 Run-Throughs 186

PART FIVE THE SPACE 197

20 Preparing for Tech 199

21 Tech 203

22 Dress Rehearsal 219

PART SIX THE AUDIENCE 223

23 Previews 225

24 Preview Rehearsals 238

25 Final Previews and Freezing a Production 244

26 Opening, the Run, and Closing 249

Conclusion 256

Acknowledgments 258
Index 259

INTRODUCTION

When I was in college studying directing, I read all the luminaries: Clurman, Brook, Foreman, Bogart, and Ball. I loved hearing how one director staged *King Lear* or another *Three Sisters* and it was fun to imagine myself making such monumental art. My actual experience, however, involved rehearsing in small, windowless rooms, sitting next to a playwright as we worked with actors to will a new play into existence. This is a book about the art of navigating that process.

The twenty years that followed taught me there is nothing more challenging or rewarding for a director than bringing a play to life for the first time. I've learned that how a director is—how they lead by example, how they treat their collaborators, how they support and nurture every artist's individual process—has a profound effect on the success of the work they make.

This book is for directors who are beginning a new play process. For those directors who have never done it before, I hope to provide an outline of how to prepare, what one can expect at each stage, and how to identify, develop, and use their creative tools to make their strongest work. For experienced directors, I hope to provide a review of the basics: useful reminders and advice to recall during challenging or confusing moments. With every new production, directors are always starting again: we are perpetual beginners. With that in mind, this book can be used as either an introduction, a guide, a resource, or a reminder of what we do, and how, and why.

What this book is not is a "How To." Each process is entirely different—new text and new collaborators, and with them new questions, challenges, conflicts, solutions, and successes—there could be no definitive instruction manual. Over time, however, a director can begin to notice patterns: familiar moments, recurring obstacles, and recognizable behaviors. It is my aim not to tell you what you should or should not do (how could I know?), but to share what you can reliably expect and how you can best anticipate and resolve the most common challenges as they arise. I will be breaking each step in a process down to its fundamentals in an effort to understand who your collaborators are and what they do, the director's tasks and goals, and how one can define success. Through this process of identifying and illuminating the basics, I hope to provide you with a roadmap of a new play process from beginning to end, one that is useful regardless of the many inevitable variables that will arise.

We will begin by defining what a director is, understanding what they do, and how they go about doing it. We will then step through an imagined process chronologically, toggling back and forth between the basic and necessary tasks of directing as an occupation and the more complex creative ideas that will guide your work as an artist. A director must be able to think both practically and artistically by equal measure, and we will examine this marriage between your creative vision and the logistic considerations of a successful production.

Our focus is on the creation of a world premiere production. We will be exploring only plays: not musicals, classics, established or devised work. The scenario we are imagining presumes there is a living playwright who will be present for the process and that the play has never been staged or produced before. We will examine how a process is different when the playwright is an active part of the creation of the production, and how the design, casting, rehearsing, and overall creation of the piece is affected when the text changes and transforms throughout.

Ultimately, I wrote this book because directing can be a lonely pursuit. Because there is only ever one (or two) in each room, it can be difficult for advice and hard-earned wisdom to pass from one to another. I've written this book to remedy that lack of knowledge sharing. I've witnessed and learned so much in my twenty years in the new play trenches—some through success, just as much through failure—and I want to pass it along to you. The best directing advice I ever received did not come from a classroom or from an assistant position: it came from coffee meetings in times of doubt or through stories directors were kind enough to share with me. I want you to think of this book as my offering the same to you. I hope some of these observations are useful, that they will help you find your way through a process, and will make you feel part of a long tradition of new play directors.

PART ONE
BEGINNINGS

In this part, we will examine what a director does, the tools they use to do it, and the unique challenges of working on a new play. We will explore ways to find new plays, strategies for reading a play for the first time, and how to meet with a playwright to discuss their work.

Definitions

Something as ephemeral as theater can be difficult to describe. We can use many words for the same concept, or one word that can represent many different ideas. In order to avoid confusion, these are some definitions I will use throughout this book.

Play: A text that serves as the blueprint for the production. It is both a stand-alone work of art and a creative prompt for other artists. It is a foundation on which to build.

Production: The designed, staged, and performed incarnation of the play. It is a three-dimensional work of art that an audience will see and hear. The playwright is responsible for the creation of the play, the director oversees the creation of the production.

"New" vs. "Established" Play: Any play that has ever been fully mounted in front of an audience we will refer to as "established." Revivals, classics, and contemporary work that has already been produced. A play that has never been through the production process is "new." Every creative choice that you and your collaborators will make is happening for the first time.

Story: We will use the term "story" very loosely. Even the most avant-garde, non-linear work has a narrative: the piece begins, something happens, and it ends. For our purposes, any live, temporal event that involves a sequence of events (beginning, event, end) is a story.

Finally, we will be defining people, places, and things strictly in terms of how they relate to the director and their process. I am not providing an objective definition of each step, role, or result; rather, we are approaching the process subjectively. Accept any descriptions or definitions in that light.

1
WHAT DOES A DIRECTOR DO, AND HOW DO THEY DO IT?

Directing is an art, the director an artist, but it is also an occupation with responsibilities, tasks, and expectations. If a producer posted an ad for a new play director, it could look something like this:

- The director will collaborate with the playwright to create the strongest possible production of the text.
- The director will, with the approval of the playwright and producer, hire actors and designers and assemble the creative team.
- The director will work with the designer to create the physical production (including, but not limited to, sets, lights, costumes, props, sound, video, etc.).
- The director will work with fight, intimacy, dialect, and vocal directors and consultants to make a safe, clear, cohesive, repeatable staging for actors to perform.
- The director will run the rehearsal room, stage the play, and prepare the cast for technical rehearsals.
- The director will oversee the technical rehearsal process in a safe and expedient manner.
- The director will bear the responsibility of getting the production ready on schedule and will deliver a production suitable for the first public performance.
- The director will run preview rehearsals and facilitate all technical and creative changes between the first public performance and the freeze date.

- The director will make themselves available during the run of the production for notes and general maintenance and preservation of the artistic integrity of the production.

This list is both accurate and incomplete. It does not begin to articulate all of a director's tasks, responsibilities, and artistic contributions. Depending on the process and on the day, I have described a director's job as a field general, a therapist, a cheerleader, or a referee. A director must play many roles and lean on different skill sets at various points in a process, many of which we will examine in this book. As we begin, we must ask: why is the job of a director so difficult to summarize?

The Paradox of Directing

We can understand what a painter does because we can see the painting. This is true for poets, musicians, and dancers: the end result shows us what they do and the tools they used to do it (language, an instrument, the movement of the body, etc.). One cannot look at a theater production, though, and pinpoint exactly what a director has done nor how they have done it. Even the word "direction" implies constant movement: how can we arrive at a fixed definition of something in motion? To direct is to lead, to guide a group from one point to another. A director is deeply involved in every part of a production's creation, and yet if it is successful, it will appear so effortlessly assembled, so organic and spontaneous, it is difficult, or impossible, to see the hand or influence of the director. This is the paradox of directing.

A production is both a single art object and an assemblage of thousands of individual works and millions of infinitesimal choices and decisions. It is a culmination of the efforts of artists, technicians, administrators, and laborers. All of these workers—each with their own skills, needs, opinions, and interests—must contribute to one object, one seamless sum of many parts. The director's task is to lead and to guide these workers, and the goal is harmony.

We can call these disparate contributors "specialists." They cannot teach one another about every aspect of their work or explain each choice: confusion would reign, time would be lost, and the art would never get finished. They all must trust that good, thoughtful work that will complement their own is happening everywhere. This is the great challenge of art-by-committee: each specialist must work without constant knowledge of how their efforts will complement each other. It is the director who must oversee all of these specialists and their work, who will cultivate trust from and between all of their collaborators, and who will evaluate each contribution both as a singular artwork and in relationship with the whole. And it is the director who must develop a vision for this finished artwork, then share it in a way that is clear, useful, and inspiring.

A director does not offer instructions or give orders: they inspire with this vision. They cultivate trust by listening, by asking questions, and by being patient, generous, and thoughtful. They create cohesion among each specialist's work through the expression of their taste so that each piece serves its singular purpose, works in complement to every other, and honors the play.

At the end of the process will exist the production, and this is when the paradox presents itself: if the director has done their job successfully, their work will be both everywhere and nowhere. This is why a director's art is so difficult to describe. We can know they were successful not because of anything we can point to, but because the production is a harmonious, cohesive work of art, assembled from many and supported by a director's vision. The director's hands are on every element of the production, and yet because they were successful, they have left not a single fingerprint.

A Director Is a Translator

An English speaker who cannot read Russian may say their favorite author is Tolstoy, and no one would find that statement peculiar. We can understand that, while this person has never actually read a word he has ever written, they have come to appreciate, admire, even love his stories because of the success of a translator. Does the reader love the work of the author or of the translator? The truth is that they cannot be separated. The same is true for an audience watching a new play.

All translations are adaptations: the taste, imagination, and perspective of the translator will guide their work. A translation could be faithful to the original text, for example, even if it is difficult for a reader to follow. Or it could differ from the original but be easier to read. It could honor the poetry of the original but not the precise meaning. The choices a translator makes are creative ones: in the process of transforming one work of art into another, they must understand their perspective on the source material and decide how they want to share it with an audience. A translator's task is to coax the writer's work and the audience as close to each other as possible. This is accomplished first through a deep understanding of the spirit and intention of the author. A translator must ask themselves what excites them about a text and why their singular point of view can offer a new perspective.

A translator, then, must be both an artist and a technician. An artist because they must understand the desires and motivations of the author and have a deep connection with the text: they must find creative inspiration from the source material. A technician because they must have an understanding of structure, plot, character, language, rhythm, and poetry. They must understand how each element of the text contributes to the whole. A balance must be struck in order for a translation to be successful: if it is too technical, the reader will understand everything that happens but not why the story is worth telling. If the translation is too abstracted, the reader may experience strong feelings but have no sense of the author's intention.

Translation is the ultimate editorial power and responsibility. An audience will experience a new play only through the director's taste, vision, and perspective: the writer's text and your production will be inseparable.

The Director's Tools

Directing is a peculiar job because so many people believe they can do it, and yet it remains an enormously difficult thing to do well. Why does this gap exist between our certainty we can direct and the humbling challenges we face when we actually do it? I believe it is because we already possess the tools to be a director, but it is difficult to understand what exactly they are or how precisely to use them.

Tools are different from traits or behaviors. A director should be respectful, empathic, generous, honest, and fair. They should have a sense of humor, enormous patience, and deep gratitude for their collaborators and their work. A director should move through a process (and the world) with those characteristics, not only because it is ethical, but also because it will naturally encourage everyone's best efforts. Tools are different: they need to be identified, cultivated, refined, and developed through repetition. A tool is something you work with, like a paintbrush or a chisel. The more familiar and comfortable you are with your tools, the more sophisticated your work will be. The five basic tools of a director are **Awareness, Taste, Vision, Curiosity,** and **Communication**.

Everyone has the power of observation, everyone has taste, and everyone has an imagination. Everyone asks questions, tries to make sense of their feelings, and tries to communicate with those around them. These natural processes transform into tools when you become conscious of them: how they are already working inside you, how you can develop and refine them, and how you can use them for the creation of your art.

Awareness: (focused observation)

Every moment you are awake, you are exposed to an endless stream of stimuli: sound, movement, light, and behavior. Humans are incredibly observant of our surroundings: it's our animal nature, a survival technique. But we get overstimulated. Our senses become overloaded and we discard what information we deem not useful. This is natural: it is why you gradually stop noticing sounds that once irritated you, or how you come to ignore the presence of objects that sit in your field of vision every day. This is our editing process: we cannot notice everything, so our subconscious "disappears" what we feel we don't need.

A director must challenge themselves to reconnect with their natural ability to notice. To pay close attention, to remain open to stimuli, to listen, to watch, to observe. Their creative work will only be as strong as their ability to see what is in front of them, and as obvious as that may sound, focused awareness takes practice. Luckily, it is a skill that can be exercised any time. A director must stay awake to their interior and exterior lives. One's powers of observation in the world will inform their work in the rehearsal room. The more aware you are, the more you notice, the better you see, and the deeper, more detailed, more complex your work can become.

Taste: (personal, emotional response)

Taste is one's style, perspective, and point of view. It is their preferences, aversions, revulsions, and attractions. It is one's instinctual impression of the things around them. Taste can be described as one's emotional opinion. It is a combination of lived experiences, conscious or subconscious associations with colors, shapes, objects, sounds, smells … any imaginable sensory stimuli. Everyone has taste, and everyone's is singular to them. There is no such thing as "good" or "bad" taste. It is entirely subjective. Your taste is you.

Taste precedes intellectual thought: it is a reaction. When we become more aware of our taste, understanding why ours are specific to us, we can begin to use it as a creative tool and incorporate it into our work. It is this understanding that is the key: without it, taste is simply an expression, a feeling, and not something that can be used in collaborative art making. Part of a director's work is to make millions of small decisions based on what they see, hear, and read. They will be presented with the creative choices of their collaborators: authorial choices, acting choices, design choices. How does a director decide with version is strongest? They combine their taste with their deep comprehension of the text. A director will see a thing (a prop, a line of text, an acting choice) and have an emotional reaction. This is their taste at work. Then they will remain aware of the reaction, observing it in an effort to understand it. When given two options, a skilled director will not say "I prefer that one," they will say "I prefer that one because …," articulating their reaction in a way that is clear and precise, and easily understood by their collaborators. Everyone has taste, but a successful director has such a clear understanding of theirs that they can align it with a text and make—and share—informed creative decisions with it.

Vision: (or imagination)

The human imagination is slippery. It floats between our conscious and subconscious minds, it exists in our waking state and in our dreams, it triggers our anxieties and desires. Like a breath or a heartbeat, we cannot control it: the imagination is a human mechanism that simply happens. It is a by-product of being alive and of having a mind.

When we say something "sparked our imagination," we are having a natural response to stimuli that has set off a series of thoughts or images. The often murky nature of our imagination becomes suddenly clear: we have an idea.

The word "vision" implies looking ahead to something that may not yet exist. When someone claims to see the future, they say they are having a vision. A director's vision is an idea about how something *could* be: how it could look, sound, or feel. Vision becomes a tool when a director works to understand these images and ideas in a way that can be shared. When we say a director has a "clear vision," it means they have a deep understanding of what they imagine, and why, and the ability to articulate it clearly and succinctly. The clearer their vision is, the more accessible and inspiring it will be to their collaborators. A director's goal should be to share their vision in a way that is so succinct that those around them feel they can also see and imagine something that does not yet exist.

Curiosity: (or questions)

Questions are prompts. They are the beginning of an idea, an opening up of a thought, a call to investigate. Answers are the end of something. They are final. In a creative process, answers are to be avoided until the last moment, while questions are to be encouraged and cultivated.

Directors use questions to understand their taste and vision. They use questions to understand a text. And they use questions as a tool to expand the imaginations of their collaborations. This is why a director is a guide. They direct the group's attention not to answers, but to the most compelling, intriguing, or challenging questions. A well-timed, well-considered question will lead artists to think about, to wonder about, to remain curious about the same things. This is how a director guides a group of disparate artists toward the same direction: by training their attention through asking who, what, where, why, and how.

Communication: (or articulation)

Taste, vision, ideas, and feelings are only as useful to a director as their ability to articulate them. If awareness is the art of remaining open to feelings and reactions, then communication is the art of sharing them.

WHAT DOES A DIRECTOR DO?

A director observes, has a feeling about what they see, which, in an instant, turns into a new idea. Trying this idea may involve changes to the staging, the lights, or the way an actor plays a moment. A director must be able to communicate to the actor, the designer, and the stage manager the same idea in three different ways so everyone can make an adjustment with clarity and understanding. Communication involves two main components: self-awareness, in the form of understanding your thoughts and feelings, and the ability to articulate to each of your collaborators in a way that is clear, concise, and inspiring. A successful director must be able to speak multiple creative languages: they can discuss acting choices in one "language," design choices in another, and technical adjustments to the stage manager in a third.

Communication is the tool that separates directors from most other artists. Many artists, especially ones who do not make work by committee, do not have to articulate what they see, feel, or think: they can simply pour it into their work. A director must be able to put to words, in the most useful way, everything they see, think, and feel so their collaborators, those "specialists," can work with confidence and proceed with trust in the director. Many artists can be unskilled communicators: the work can speak for itself. A director's ability to communicate is inextricably linked to their art-making process. It is the tool that sets them apart.

And so a director's tools are used in the following way:

- You **notice** the thing (a line of text, a shaft of light, an actor's facial expression: this is your **awareness**)
- You have a reaction to the thing (this is your **taste**)
- Your reaction triggers an idea (this is your **vision**)
- You ask questions to deepen your understanding of your idea (this is your **curiosity**)
- You share your idea with your collaborators (this is **communication**)
- They respond by trying a new thing (a new line of text, a different shaft of light, an alternative expression)
- You notice the new thing, experience a reaction ... and begin the process again.

Directing is the process of making tiny choice after tiny choice until the production is created. When you get lost, return to these basics. This is the root, the DNA, of a director's work.

Another way to connect, or to reconnect, with our tools is through asking ourselves questions. These four questions can also help bring our attention back to the basics:

- What do I notice?
- How do I feel?

- Why do I feel this way?
- How best can I share it?

A director's millions of decisions can often feel overwhelming, especially as they begin to accumulate faster than it feels one can consider them. Returning to your tools in those moments will offer you a way to focus your attention, to simplify, and to find a productive path forward. They can center you and return you to your creative task. You may not be able to hold these tools in your hand like a pen or a brush, but the more you pay attention to them, the stronger they will become, and like a brush, the more comfortable you will feel using them.

Learning how to use any tool takes time, practice, and trial and error. Only through repetition can one begin to develop and hone their personal set of tools, and the gap between suspecting you can direct and being able to do so successfully will gradually disappear.

The Empathic Director

None of these tools will be effective without care, patience, and empathy. For yourself and for your collaborators. Making art is hard, making art by committee is harder, making art by committee based on a work-in-progress is hardest.

Encourage everyone to use the same tools. You do this by remaining open and by asking questions. Are you aware of everyone's distinct and personal process and perspective? How they work, how they feel, what their relationship is to you, to their colleagues, to the play and to their task? Are you cultivating an atmosphere where everyone feels free to share their tastes? Where everyone's perspective is valued? Is everyone able to generate their own ideas, and to share them in an open, positive, supportive environment? Awareness, care, generosity, empathy are the ways in which you guide all of these individual specialists with all of their histories, opinions, ideas, concerns, biases, senses of humor, conflict resolution tactics, and artistic processes toward a common goal.

You lead by example.

The New Play Variable

An established play has a fixed blueprint. It has been built before, so you know it can be done: the question a director will ask themselves is what they will bring to the text so that their version, their translation, will be different. A new play has never been staged, designed, or shared with an audience: no one, not even the writer, knows if it will succeed as a piece of theater. To direct a new play is a risky undertaking. A director must elicit great trust from their collaborators, as they are forging a path together that has never been taken. But the biggest challenge is that the blueprint—the script, the foundation on which the production will be built—will change throughout the process. A writer may make changes, sometimes drastic ones, but even small changes will have great impact. Discoveries will be made during the rehearsal process, or even later, that will upend your and your collaborators' understanding of the play. The creation of a new play demands that you proceed with the same amount of organization and confidence as you would with an established one but with the knowledge that, at any moment, the ground will shift under your feet.

A new play director's job is to combine artistic vision, leadership skills, and a technical understanding of the text to build a cohesive work of art for an audience. A director will use their tools—awareness, taste, vision, curiosity, and communication—to do it. They will lead with empathy, openness, generosity, and care. Through clarity of vision, encouragement, and inspiration, a director will guide a group of diverse specialists toward a common goal: a harmonious work.

2
FINDING AND READING A TEXT

New plays cannot be found at the bookstore or at the library. You have to seek out, read, and get to know playwrights.

Where you find them depends on your circumstances. If you are in school, find out if there are writers in the theater program, and also investigate the literature and creative writing departments. Ask poets, filmmakers, actors, and fellow directors. Many aspiring playwrights do not make public their pursuits (this is true at any age, not just with students): you will be surprised by how many people are quietly tinkering with a play. Read them all.

If you're out of school, begin by asking your friends and peers. Reach out to a local theater whose programming you admire and ask if they have a writer's group. Learn if they need directors or volunteers to help organize or oversee readings. If there is no group, ask if they have a literary office that accepts open submissions ("open" means that any writer can submit a play for consideration). If so, volunteer to read some of those plays. Larger theater organizations hire "readers" to manage what is often a large number of submitted plays. Take that job. Chances are good they are always in need of more readers, so this is a mutually beneficial arrangement.

The value of reading every new play you can find extends far beyond finding a script you would like to direct. First, through this work, you will meet many writers, literary managers, and other members of theater organizations. This is an opportunity to introduce yourself to potential collaborators and colleagues as a director interested in new plays. Second, you can approach this process as an exercise. Reading plays is the only practical training a director can undertake alone. Every time you read a play, you are being given a chance to learn about your taste. A play you don't respond to, a play you don't understand, a play that bores you: reading them is not a waste of your time but a valuable opportunity to educate yourself about what you like and what you don't. Challenge yourself to articulate why. The more plays you read, regardless of their quality, the more aware of and connected to your taste you will become. And finally: writers, like directors, can improve over time. Just because you do not respond to a play now doesn't mean this writer will never write something that will excite you. Developing relationships, and getting to know a writer's work over time, can sow the seeds of a future collaboration.

A common misconception is that in order to be a successful director, one must pursue the most famous and decorated writers. This is incorrect for a few reasons. Established writers usually have a group of directors they already work with, and attempting to add yourself to that list is often time-consuming and rarely successful. A director deserves to work with a writer who is equally excited by and passionate about a collaboration: the enthusiasm for each other's work should be shared. Furthermore, if a famous writer does decide to work with you (for example, you offer to direct a reading of their new play and they accept), when the process shifts to the production phase, they may want an established director who can potentially advocate for a larger budget, entice notable actors through their reputation, or generally elevate the profile of the production. Being replaced when a play jumps from its developmental stage to a production can be a difficult reality, and the best way to avoid this trend is to find writers at a similar professional level. This is how true collaborations and long-lasting creative partnerships are built. Bonds are formed, tastes become understood and aligned, shorthands are developed, and alliances are made. New writers and directors are most successful as collaborators when they grow together.

Reading a Play (part one: for yourself)

The first time you read a play is your one opportunity to experience the play as an innocent. You will not have any preconceived notions, biases, choices, or concerns. You are simply the viewer, unencumbered, allowing the experience of engaging with the artwork to unfold naturally and without interference. Every time you read a play you are working on, you will approach the text with different considerations, perspectives, challenges, and needs. This is your first impression, and it will supply you with valuable information that cannot be recaptured or recreated. This is a chance to allow yourself to think and feel whatever the text elicits. There will be many opportunities for analysis later: during the first read you are simply an audience member. The emotional experience of this read is information you will return to throughout your process.

- Approach the script with optimism and the benefit of the doubt. Optimism in that you should leave yourself open to the idea that you will fall in love with this play. The benefit of the doubt in that you should choose to set aside any limiting notions of what the play could or should be. Awareness means being able to see something for what it is, which means an absence of commentary, bias, or pre-determinations.

- Remember also that many new plays are work in progress: meet the play where it is, and resist the distractions of imagining some other, invented version of it.
- Give yourself enough time to read the play straight through without interruption. Turn off your phone, find a place where you can close a door, and eliminate distractions. Your goal is to experience the play as written: taking breaks from the script will interrupt the natural momentum of the text and will compromise your understanding of how the play operates as a complete work.
- Don't start directing it yet. Directors are problem-solvers by nature: we want to roll up our sleeves and begin. Concentrate your attention on what is there, not what you think could or should be. It is natural to get consumed by thoughts of how you would stage this or that moment or scene, especially if you feel excited by the play. You may have design "solutions," casting thoughts, notes for the writer on how to "fix" a moment you feel doesn't work. Your entire process will be spent working in that psychic space: use this time to allow the writer to come to you without intervention. Every impulsive choice now may mean closing a door to some future possibilities later. All good plays are about many things: let as many ideas exist freely and without editorializing.
- Jot down words, feelings, images, and reactions. Try not to interrupt your reading, but note moments that prompt an emotional response. These will help you recreate the experience later, when you reflect on the play.

After you've finished reading, give yourself time to connect with your gut reactions. Write down how you feel. Document your visceral responses. All thoughts are valid, so avoid self-editing. Anything that comes into your mind should be recorded. These observations are for you: they aren't notes, they don't need to be communicated to the writer: you are creating an emotional map of how it felt to read the play.

The farther you get into your creative process, the more challenging it will be for you to access this sense of innocence. During the work of directing the play, you will be bombarded with the thoughts and opinions of your collaborators. You will have practical, technical, and logistical choices and decisions to make. The mind can always recount facts, refer back to old drafts, or remember questions: it is the emotional experience of the first read that you must record. Weeks and months later, it will be difficult, or even impossible, to remember how it felt when you read the play for the first time. You can return to this emotional map again and again throughout your process. It will serve you when you feel overwhelmed by the logistical concerns of the production, or when you risk losing touch with the emotional center of the piece. The work you do during this first step can serve as a touchstone, a place to return to agree or disagree with, and to remember.

Give yourself a few days to think about the play before you discuss it with anyone. This private rumination time is for searching your gut and deciding if you want to direct this play. There may be external considerations influencing your decision: you want to work with the writer, you want to work at all, you need the money, you think the professional credit will help your career, you need the experience, you prefer to be busy, it's flattering to have been asked, a great production could open professional opportunities. Before entertaining any of those thoughts, you must ask yourself, as an artist, if this play is a work that will inspire something of your own that you will feel excited to make and proud to share. Very rarely have I felt ambivalent about a play and passionate about it later: if a script inspired me when I first read it, that feeling will remain. If it didn't, that feeling is impossible to manufacture. All professional considerations must come after your artistic impulses. If the play does not touch or inspire you deeply, if you do not feel it is a strong and enticing blueprint on which to create your work, then the finished result will inevitably be lacking. A production will not help your career, or your relationship with the writer or producer, if your heart was not in it. Better for you both as an artist and as a professional to keep looking, to keep reading, to keep searching for a text that truly inspires you.

You do not need to think the play is perfect, or even finished, but you do need to understand how it affects you on an emotional level. Directors are always, through their work, making a case for the play: why it should be done now, in this time and place, and why it is worth an audience's attention. The very first step is answering those questions for yourself, and it begins with your gut reaction to the first read.

After you have read a play, no matter how you felt about it, reach out to the writer to thank them for sharing their work. If you are not interested in pursuing a collaboration, respectfully let them know. Remember that sharing a new work of art is an enormously brave and vulnerable-making gesture, and you owe it to the writer to acknowledge how significant it was to send you the play. Saying no to directing a play can be difficult, but as a writer once told me, it's better than no answer at all.

3
MEETING WITH A WRITER

The Playwright/Director Relationship

If an established play's process is linear (play is selected for production, play enters pre-production process, play is produced), then a new play process is anything but. The writer and director are both present and working simultaneously: they must ask each other potentially difficult questions to create clear lines of communication. Who is the creative leader, and when? Who will have the "last word" on a major creative decision? How far can a director's choices veer from the text before they have gone beyond the writer's wishes? How imposing can a writer be about the choices of the director before they are limiting the latter's creative agency? How are these boundaries drawn, upheld, revised, and enforced?

Working on a new play means you will be collaborating with a writer who will be a presence in your creative process, as you will be in theirs. Every change they make will affect your work, and often vice versa. Two pieces are being created with a significant overlap: you are both lead artists, creating works that are inextricably linked and reliant on the other. You and the writer are equals and partners, sometimes the leader, and sometimes the follower. It is as easy and impossible, joyful and frustrating as it sounds. To navigate a successful relationship with a writer-in-process is its own skill with singular challenges and rewards.

Both artists need freedom to make their work. The writer needs to trust that their text will be honored, especially when it is being staged for the first time. The director needs the trust of the writer so they can lead and create with confidence. This is a dance that you and your writer will begin at your very first meeting. It is a successful duet when no one is overpowering the other. A director has not been hired to do the writer's bidding, nor is the play a prompt for the director to do whatever they please. The quality of this relationship will dictate the tone of the entire process.

Preparing for the Meeting

You have identified a play that excites you, and now you need to secure the opportunity to direct it. The hiring of a director is almost always the writer's

MEETING WITH A WRITER

decision to make, and so a meeting with a writer is two things: it is an opportunity to test out a potential artistic collaboration, and it is a job interview. The goals of this meeting are for you to share your ideas about and vision for the play, and for you both to learn if you have a complementary creative language and artistic sensibility. Like all relationships, the central question is one of trust: does the writer trust your ability to stage the first production of this play? Are you excited about the same ideas in the text? In agreement about the same potential problems? Do your tastes overlap? Are you a professional match?

A playwright's priority will be to understand how you responded to their play, to learn how you work in a process, and how you would approach their script specifically. The writer will want to understand you as an artist, not in a general sense, but within the context of their play. Your task during this meeting is to achieve a balance: to share your vision in a clear way while still maintaining the openness necessary at the beginning of any new play process. This is a conundrum: a director must articulate ideas about how the play could look and feel while remaining open to change. How can a director describe their future production in a compelling way when they have only just begun to engage with the text? The balance we seek is achieved by sharing images and ideas that illustrate taste and vision, asking thoughtful questions to spark discussion, specifying what excites, inspires, interests, and confuses you in the text, and articulating what kind of process you would oversee for the strongest possible production. A writer needs to understand what you see, think, and feel when you read their play and grasp what your future production could look like without having prematurely "figured it out." If a director is too vague in this meeting, a writer will not have a clear understanding of their style and vision and may not trust them; if they are too specific, the writer may feel like the director has already staged the play in their mind, leaving little room for collaboration.

Prepare for this meeting by revisiting your notes from your first read. Collect the feelings, images, and reactions that most accurately and succinctly capture your experience. Decide which of these impressions could summarize your reading of the play and be prepared to share them. This is how you will communicate your taste, and will help the writer understand not only your perspective on the story, but also what experience you might eventually share with an audience. The more specific you can be in articulating the emotional journey of reading the play, the better a writer will understand your artistic point of view.

Choose a few moments from the play that were especially evocative for you. Why did they stir your imagination? Attach those moments to sound, color, light, texture, rhythm, movement. Embrace any inspirations that you connected to an outside source. Did the text make you think of a style of music? Does a character remind you of another literary creation? These comparisons can spark a conversation, allowing you to share your nascent vision and to invite the writer to do the same.

While preparing these thoughts, avoid categorizations. Genres have rules, styles, aesthetics, and histories. Let the text be free from potential constrictions. The play is not yet a comedy or a drama; it is not noir or slapstick or agit-prop or a choreopoem. It is a brand new work and categories can limit the brainstorming process.

List and prepare some basic questions you have about the play. Do not worry about answers or analysis: you will not be presenting a thesis about the play and you will not try to solve a problem. You want to arrive curious: eager to share and to listen. Your most incisive questions will provide you and the writer with an opportunity to have a deeper, more complex conversation about the text, as well as the writer's intentions. They can be technical (about the plot, the characters, the setting, the stage directions) or more abstract (theme, tone, meaning). A good question will elicit more information than any observation, so the better prepared you are with what you'd like to ask the writer, the richer and more in-depth you can expect the conversation to be.

If you are excited about the play but feel it needs a significant amount of development, you will want to be honest with the writer about that. A director needs to speak frankly about where they believe the play is in its process. This is an important conversation to have early: many writer/director disagreements and conflicts arise from miscommunications about what needs more attention and revision on the page. Be prepared to ask the writer about moments you found confusing, character behavior you didn't understand, jumps or gaps in logic, and listen closely to their responses. You are not offering them a list of instructions but inviting them to describe what they have made, to offer their perspective on what they wrote. If you speak of the play as though it needs "fixing," you will imply that it does not work, that it is broken. A new play is a work in progress, it is not a car in a shop, and you are speaking with its creator, who may not yet completely understand what it is that they have made. Be honest but be respectful: if you don't feel you can truthfully express your thoughts without insulting the play, this may not be the right project for you.

The meeting itself must reflect your desired balance of creativity and professionalism. Treat both the writer and their play with professional respect by setting up the meeting in a way that conveys your seriousness about the project. Do not text them, do not reach out via social media or any other informal approach. Choose a location that is informal enough that you can speak freely and openly, but not so casual as to be distracting. Cafes and theater lobbies are great, bars or apartments are not.

The Meeting Itself

When I was a young director, I was sent a play by a very successful writer. I did not care for it, but felt I should still take the opportunity to meet with such an esteemed artist. I began by sharing my thoughts in the most diplomatic way possible. I was not interested in directing the play, but wanted very much for this important theater figure to think I was brilliant. A few minutes into my clever monologue, she stopped me and said, "Listen: you sound very bright and that's wonderful for you, but did you like my play?"

Because these meetings are primarily about laying a foundation of trust, you must lead with honesty. A common pitfall of these meetings is that, because everyone is so effusive and polite, neither artist gets a true sense of the other. If you aren't eager to direct the play, don't take the meeting. If you are excited and inspired by it, begin the meeting by saying so. A writer will not hear anything else until you express your enthusiasm for the work.

Once your excitement for the play has been made clear, encourage the writer to speak about the history of the play. Why did they write it, where did the idea come from, how long have they been working on it, how many drafts have there been, what are they happy with and what do they have questions about, what future changes are they considering, and where do they think the play is in its developmental trajectory. Until now, you have been responding only to the text without either context or background, so listen closely, and cross-reference it with the questions you prepared for the meeting. Maybe you felt the play was promising but needed a lot of future development and the playwright will say they think they are finished. Maybe you feel the play is ready for production, only to learn you've read what the writer considers to be a first draft. Maybe they are unhappy with the ideas in the play that excited you most, or that they want to center the story of a character you felt could be cut. Listening to the writer will help you contextualize what you've read, will give you the chance to reevaluate what you'd like to discuss at this meeting, and will begin to teach you if you are in creative alignment.

After they have shared the story of the play's journey, recount your experience of reading it. Share your ideas, articulate your feelings, describe the images the play conjured in you. Then outline for the writer some of the moments that struck you and explain why. By working in this order, you are walking the writer through your process as a creative thinker. This explanation will help the writer understand your vision with more clarity than a description of some imagined future production.

Then proceed to ask the writer questions. Lead with prompts such as: "I'm curious about …" or "Something I want to know more about is …" or "I'm interested in hearing your thoughts on …" Avoid statements like: "I didn't understand …" or "I think you should try …" or "My problem with this is …." Remember to keep your questions simple: the profundity will come from the conversation they elicit. How the writer responds and how you begin to trade ideas and observations are the heart of this meeting. It is how you begin to learn how you might work together as a team.

Disagreement is a natural part of the process. Do not be alarmed if you and the writer are not in complete alignment: the success of the meeting will be based on the quality of your communication, not on total agreement. A director should have a different perspective and point of view than the writer, or else the writer could simply direct the play themselves. What is being evaluated is not whether or not you always agree, but the nature of your communication style. Do you feel heard and understood? Does the writer? How do you resolve disagreements: with someone overpowering the other, with someone relenting on their idea, or by finding a shared new thought you can both be excited by?

Like your experience of reading the play, you will probably know during this meeting if you are a promising fit with the writer. The connection does not have to be perfect, but it should be promising. There are many reasons a writer and director are not a match—different tastes or visions for the production, different ways of working and talking about the work, and simple personality incompatibility. Their play compelled you to have this meeting, so both respect and admiration have already been established: perhaps another opportunity will present itself. Thank the writer for their time and ask them to keep sending you their work. Not every director is right for every play, but a writer who makes work that inspires and excites you is rare and should be valued.

If you and the writer suspect you are a creative and professional match, you are ready to move beyond conversations about the text. The next step should be to find or create an opportunity to hear the play aloud.

Two Additional Tips

Schedule enough time so you do not have to rush. Your behavior at this meeting will teach the writer about your commitment and interest in the work as much as anything you say about it. If you have to cut the meeting short in order to be somewhere else, you are teaching the writer a lesson about your seriousness about their play.

Avoid gossip. Discussing theater you have seen or artists you admire is a very effective way to determine shared tastes. If you speak ill of an artist, though, what you are teaching the writer is that you may not be trustworthy. This is also true for the writer: if they complain about other directors they've worked with, I can sadly assure you will be on that list eventually. Gossip can create the illusion of closeness, but it conveys an unprofessional attitude that will not work in your favor.

PART TWO
DEVELOPMENT

In this part we will step through the process of directing readings and workshops. How to prepare organize, oversee, and learn from them.

Readings, workshops, or any event that involves actors performing the text before the rehearsal process begins will fall under the category of "development." The primary purpose of this step is for the writer and director to learn about the text by hearing actors speak it, or by watching them perform sections of it on their feet. The information gathered from development will teach the writer about how their play sounds aloud, and will provide the director with new information to respond to and to draw inspiration from. The goal of development is to prepare the script for a production process.

Reading a Play (for development)

The first time you read the play it was to experience it as an audience member would, to remain aware of your reactions and record them, and to prepare to discuss the piece with the writer. Now, you are reading the play with a mind toward development: what you hope to learn and how you plan to learn it.

Communicating with actors is a new challenge of the developmental process. A director should read the play and think of how they would like to articulate the thoughts, feelings, and ideas they have been carrying since they first read it. Until now, these musings have existed only in your head, in your notes, or shared directly with the writer. Now you must take them and transform them into thoughts you can share with a larger group. The development process can move quickly, and often a director will need to provide guidance to an actor who has only hours or moments to prepare to read a role. Can you be helpful to them in one sentence? Can you express your feelings and ideas about the text in just a few thoughts, and in a way that will be useful for an actor to play? A director's advice or perspective in a reading or workshop does not need to be perfect, but it needs to be clear and concise enough for an actor to use. The more succinct you can be in your communication with the cast, the stronger the performances will be in readings and workshops, and the more useful those events will be for you and for the writer. As you reread the play, revisit your notes and think of how you might articulate them to an actor.

Begin by solidifying some of your thoughts and feelings into clear expressions of your point of view. As you reread, consider your reactions and expand on them. Ask yourself questions about your experience of the first read. This is how your taste will transform into a vision. What do you think the play is about? What would you say are the central themes? If you had to describe the story in a few sentences, could you? If you had to share a few words about the feeling of the world of the play, what would they be? The more familiar you are with a text, the more freedom you will have engaging with it, and the more extemporaneous you can be when communicating with actors. A deep and solid understanding of a text will open you up to more useful conversations and better support for actors in a developmental setting. You do not need to hold yourself to these thoughts: what you are trying to define is what the play is about for you now, at this moment, and at this point in the process. Actors will need this information, and so you should work to feel comfortable sharing a clear point of view, even one subject to change.

Read to create a list of questions. This can take the form of questions you want to ask the actors, questions you want to ask the writer after you have heard the play, or questions to challenge yourself with to better understand the text. These questions will be your prompts: from them you will build your development worklist.

Your list of questions will be unique to each play, but the underlying ones are always similar at this point in the process: how do you expect the experience of reading and of hearing the play to be the same? How do you expect it to be different? Why? What do you hope to learn from a reading? From a workshop? What are your specific questions about this play? Ask yourself about story, character, tone, logic, momentum. Pay attention to when you feel lost or confused. Everything you are confused or curious about should go on to your list in the form of a question.

Read to understand the play's practical needs. Casting, any technical needs for a reading or workshop, and whether a reading (i.e., hearing the play) or a workshop (i.e., working on your feet) would be more useful to address your questions. If the goal of development is to hear, to learn, and to work on the text, then the decisions you make based on this read will determine the success of your developmental process.

4
READINGS

A reading is an un- or minimally-rehearsed event where actors read the play aloud. "Reading" is a literal term: it is a recitation, not a performance. You are seeking an auditory experience, not a visual one. For you and the writer, this is your first step away from the page. It is a new way to experience the text: your first opportunity to hear instead of to read it.

A reading is rarely, however, a time to work on the play. You are setting up this event so you and the writer can be audience members, not because you want to rehearse or make changes. This process must begin with a discussion with the writer about your goals, and you must be explicit about what is and is not possible. If you both want to hear it, plan a reading. If you want to work with actors, experiment with new pages, or see some of the play performed, schedule a workshop.

One virtue of a reading is that they are relatively easy to produce. They are the most time and cost-effective way to hear the play, and the shorter the time commitment for the actors, the more casting options will be available to you. Not all readings are the same, however. The purpose will change depending on the intended audience, so you, the writer, and any producer or theater company must have a clear consensus on the goal of the reading before you begin.

- A private reading is for the writer and director. It is a chance for you both to experience the story and emotional trajectory of the text as it is spoken. This is the ideal scenario for a first or early reading.

- A public reading is hosted by a producing organization. It is usually a fundraiser, a donor event, or part of a new play festival. The intention is either to raise money or to create what theaters refer to as "additional programming." Decisions surrounding casting, location, and schedule will favor the needs of the producing organization over the artists.

- A programming reading is an opportunity for the artistic director or producer to audition the play. The play will or will not be "programmed" or offered a full production based on the success or failure of this reading.

- A casting reading is a chance to hear specific actors in the roles. These typically happen in place of a formal audition process. Conversely, a casting reading can also take place when an actor of note wants to hear themselves in a role or the play in its entirety. In that scenario, it is the actor who is auditioning the part, the writer, the director, or the play itself.
- A backers audition is a reading meant to entice potential funders (backers = investors) to participate in a commercial production. It is a fundraiser.

Only one of the above scenarios can exist for each reading. A backers audition is not an ideal opportunity for a director and writer to learn very much about the play. A public reading is not productive for a play that has never been read aloud. A writer and director must protect a play from situations that will not serve it, or from scrutiny it is not ready to withstand. You should only agree to hear the play in front of an audience (donors, producers, theater companies), when you feel it is ready to be considered for production. For our purposes, we will concentrate only on the ideal scenario for developmental work: a private reading.

If you ask yourself who or what a reading is for and do not have a clear answer, you should not do it. A reading for the sake of a reading, especially after you and the writer feel you have learned all you can from hearing it aloud, can be a mistake. A writer can only listen their play so many times before repetition can become counter-productive. There is such a thing as over-development, and writers can begin to make changes for the sake of changes, or revise so a scene or moment makes more sense in a reading scenario. Stay attuned to when readings no longer answer your and the writer's questions. That is how you know it is time to end this part of the process.

Casting

Directing a successful reading means understanding that you don't: you *prepare* the event thoroughly and meticulously, then experience it as though you are an audience member.

Until now you've been responding to the text. Your primary focus has been understanding your emotional response to the page. A reading marks a significant shift: it is the first time you will have to make creative decisions, and most of those choices concern casting.

Casting marks your first transition from abstract thinking about the text into concrete choices. It is the journey from a character as an idea in your imagination to a role inhabited by an artist.

Pivot your thoughts about each character to actors who align with how you imagine the role. Think about objective truths like age, race, physical attributes, and other concrete considerations. Then contemplate the nature of the character as written: their energy, their sense of humor, their attitude and behaviors. Make a long list of potential actors and do not be afraid to dream: include those who are no longer living, include animated characters, include actors who are decades too old or too young for the part. You may not be able to articulate why yet but include all ideas. This work is partially an exercise: you are pushing yourself to articulate your taste in the form of actors who feel right for the world of the play, and for a character in particular. Ask the writer to do the same. Compare your ideas and surprise yourselves by the ways you align in your thinking and how you differ. These discussions are about casting, but they are also dramaturgy: they challenge you to match real ideas with your taste, and to clarify further how you think about the play.

This exercise will unlock a different way of thinking and of talking about the characters. Everyone responds to actors differently: who you may find completely charming, the writer may not. These conversations will force you to understand your vision for each character and give you a newfound clarity of the writer's imagination. Argue! Debate! Casting a reading is your first collaborative decision-making process. Do not rush this conversation. Resist the urge to choose a "favorite" idea and immediately make an offer. The dreaming portion of this process may seem frivolous, especially for ideas that could never be realized, but the information you will gather—what you will learn not only from the writer but also about your own taste—will serve you well beyond this reading.

Once you and the writer are in agreement, begin narrowing down your idea lists, focusing your attention on actors who are local and available to you, who you can reach, and who you feel will realistically commit to a reading. Have a few ideas for each role: sometimes the first actor you approach will say yes, sometimes the first four actors you ask will be busy. Hope for your first choice, but prepare a list of actors for each role that you're excited about.

Schedule

There are generally two types of readings: cold readings, in which the cast reads the play aloud without any rehearsal (cold = no warm-up), and a one-day reading, in which you rehearse for a few hours before the actual event. Assuming you have the choice, ask yourself which scenario will allow you to hear the play best. Do you trust that the play will make sense to the cast without any rehearsal? Then a cold reading can suit you. Do you anticipate actors will need a rehearsal in order to ask questions? Then a one-day reading will be useful. Take an educated guess how long the play will take to read aloud and then double that amount: that should be your minimum rehearsal time. Expect to take a break between the rehearsal and the reading itself so the cast can relax and prepare.

Choose a date that will increase the chances of actor's being available to you. If you're asking actors who are in rehearsals or performances, aim for a day you know they will be free. Cross reference with a calendar and avoid holidays, long weekends, or any other time actors are less likely to be free. Once you've settled on the date, begin reaching out to actors no earlier than six weeks in advance nor less than four. If you cast too soon, you risk losing someone to another commitment. If you cast too late, you may find yourself scrambling.

Location

Your location is your setting. There is a huge amount of information and storytelling in where you choose to host the reading. A couch in a friend's apartment tells one, an agent's office another, a rehearsal room another. Think of the emotional experience of being in each space: is somewhere formal an appropriate setting for a first draft? Is a dorm room the right place to invite a professional actor? Where you choose to do the reading will set a tone for the play, the cast, and for you and the writer: consider your options to give the play the best possible environment in which to be heard.

Audience

Keep a private reading "closed:" no guests. Any additional listeners, even supportive friends, will split your focus. You might think because you're working on a comedy you want to hear some laughs, but if the script is still very new, avoid putting that pressure on the text and the actors. A private reading is for you and the writer to hear it, nothing more. You both are audience enough: any other listeners are potential distractions from your own experience.

Preparation for Yourself and the Writer

In the days before the reading, revisit your lists of questions, thoughts, and ideas. Remind yourself of what you're most curious about, confused by, and excited to hear: then put the list away. Remaining fixed on what you want or expect to hear will limit your ability to hear the play simply as it is. Any preparation should be in service of receiving the auditory experience with an open mind.

Ask the writer what they are curious to learn, and what they will be listening for. This will help you organize your brief rehearsal time, if you have any. What you hope to avoid is a situation where the writer tells you after the reading is over that they were particularly interested in hearing something specific that you did not address with the cast.

Request that the writer not make any drastic changes just before the reading. An actor may ask for the script days before the event so that they can prepare (some actors need time to read in advance), and the version you send them should be close to what they will read aloud. You must be able to speak knowledgeably about the play and to answer basic questions for the cast, and that is not possible if you're not familiar with the most recent draft. Remind the writer that this is not an occasion for the play to be perfect, or "right," or any other unfair system of measurement. Relieve them of the pressure to "finish" a draft in anticipation of the event. This is a chance to hear the play just as it is: it is reasonable, and expected, for sections to not yet "work" or to make perfect sense. To learn what does and does not make the leap from the page to the spoken word is a primary purpose of a reading.

Preparing the Event

- Contact the cast a week before the reading to relay all of the logistical information (time, place, etc.) and let them know who will be in attendance. You do not want to surprise a cast that is expecting to perform in a private reading with a few dozen potential investors. The cast should then be reminded again the day before.

- Confirm that the space has all the necessary supplies (pencils, highlighters, pens, binders, and the right amount of scripts of the correct draft) and make sure there are bottles of water for the company. The success of a reading can often be determined by your attention to detail. Copies of the wrong draft can instantly derail an entire day. Decide if you want the cast to sit at tables, in front of music stands, etc. and make certain they are at the space, that they are what you had imagined, and that there are the right number. You do not want to spend any time on the day of the event looking for more chairs.

- An artist should expect to arrive at a work space that is ready for them. Preparedness conveys professionalism. It is a show of respect for their time, talent, and effort.

- Make copies of the reading draft at least a day in advance. It should have numbered pages and be formatted in a way that is easy to read. Once the script has been copied and is ready for distribution to the cast, there should be no further revisions. This is to avoid confusion among the cast and using precious rehearsal time inserting new pages.

An often overlooked task is deciding in advance which stage directions should or should not be read. This cannot wait until the rehearsal, and you cannot ask a cast to read a script without this clarity. It is confusing, it can interrupt the timing of the actors, and it can make the cast tentative in their delivery. You and the writer cannot hear a clean read if there is not a shared consensus of what non-dialogue text will be read aloud.

If the reading is only for you and the writer, the decision is simple: no stage directions at all. If there are other listeners, keep only those stage directions that describe an action that cannot be understood through dialogue ("She pulls out a gun," "They kiss," "She enters wearing a mask"). Descriptive stage directions rarely have a positive impact on a reading. They interrupt the rhythm of the dialogue and can be difficult to follow.

When possible, send the actors the script with stage directions that will not be read already struck-through. This will save an enormous amount of time during any rehearsal, and will be even more helpful for a cold read.

Rehearsal (if any)

Asking an actor to participate in a reading is asking them to take an enormous leap of faith. With little to no preparation, they're being asked to read aloud and perform a role they're not familiar with, to invent a fully realized character in real time. Remember their bravery as you work with them. Also remember that any actor, paid or not, is volunteering their time and talent.

Begin your rehearsal time—no matter how brief—by offering a context for the event itself. Why you are hosting the reading, how many times you have heard the play, and reiterate who will be in attendance. Articulate where you and the writer are in the play's process, and what your expectations are of the reading itself. If the play is still very much a work in progress, for example, make that clear. Context will put the cast at ease: remember, they are walking into a situation with very little information, so the more you can offer about the who, the what, and the why, the more comfortable the company will be.

Set up the basic scenario of the play. The setting, the circumstances, any necessary backstory. Share a few overall thoughts about tone and style. Conjure the feeling of the world of the play with a few specific descriptions. Share your perspective on the characters in a way that summarizes the essence of each role. Ask yourself in advance: if you want each actor concentrating their attention on one objective, thought, or idea, what would it be? Think about the character's status, their wants, their energy, their relationships with the other roles. Keep these thoughts as simple as possible: clever or abstract observations that can confuse an actor are worse than none at all.

If you have enough time, read through the play:

- Ask that the cast hold their questions until after you've read through the entire script: starting and stopping can lead to discussion that may take too long and you'll struggle to get to the end of the play.
- Follow your own instructions: only interrupt an actor if they appear lost.
- Make a note of moments and sections that seem confusing to the cast: they may need some clarification or guidance. These notes will become your worklist for any extra time you have available.
- Listen for basic storytelling. Does everyone seem to understand what is happening in each scene? The tone and rhythm? If there seems to be confusion, choose a few particularly complicated moments to adjust and use them as examples of the whole.
- If you don't have time to read the entire play, choose a few scenes:
    - Make sure everyone in the cast gets a chance to read something.
    - Choose sections that are evocative of the overall tone and energy of the play.
    - Include parts that might be confusing for an actor to read cold.

After this read-through, you may have some time left to work with the actors. Here are some ways to organize it:

- Meet privately with your writer after the rehearsal read to get their thoughts. Ask: "What did you not hear that you want to?" and "What did you hear that you don't want to again?" You do not have time to make big changes or to engage in scene work, but you should know the writer's point of view as you spend your final moments working with the cast.
- Ask yourself what you hope to achieve with the time you have left and prioritize. What is realistically possible? Consult the notes you took during the rehearsal and organize them in order of importance (to you). If you're giving acting adjustments, be succinct: you must be precise and economical.
- Decide on a simple seating arrangement for the company. The relationships of the roles should teach you fairly easily how the cast should be arranged. This is not an occasion to make a creative statement: put the actors in the best possible position for them to give their strongest read.
- Resist staging, even a few moments. A director or writer may think some minimal blocking will be useful to a listener, but staging in these

circumstances always takes longer than you can spare, with often confused or confusing results. Honor and embrace the auditory nature of the event.

- If the piece has an intermission and you can cut it, do. Intermissions can let the energy out of reading that is difficult to regain after an act break. Preserving the momentum will teach you more about the text and should be a higher priority.

Notes to Give the Cast

- Ask the company to read the script verbatim. Even if they trip over their words, there is valuable information in their effort. Actors are experts on making challenging text sound natural: relieve them of that responsibility. You are trying to hear the play as it is: improvisation or changes of any size means an actor is making authorial decisions that will interfere with your learning process.
- Avoid pauses where they aren't specified, honor overlapping dialogue, and avoid adding extra words or vocalizations ("um, uh, like, yeah"). Like paraphrasing or improvising, these gestures effect rhythm and timing. The playwright included these rhythmic signposts for a reason, and you must hear them as written.
- Remind your stage direction reader that their performance is just as important as the rest of the company's. Encourage them to be clear and concise. They shouldn't telegraph the emotion of the scene. They are the unbiased narrator of the play and should lead with clarity and purpose: they serve the momentum of the story, they should not editorialize.
- Reiterate to the cast that any physical action will be read by the stage direction reader. This includes kisses, hugs, embraces, slaps, or any violent actions. Make this explicit so everyone is clear and no one feels compelled to make a last-minute choice that is either dangerous, inappropriate, or confusing.
- If there is an audience and the cast is not seated around a table, ask the actors to stand when they're "in" the scene and sit when they're "off." This can help a listener track who is and isn't in the scene and help boost the energy of the proceedings. If the reading private, there is no need.
- Encourage the cast to continue, even if there are line mistakes or someone loses their place in the script. The closer the company can get

READINGS

to providing a clean read without interruption, the more information you and the writer will receive.

- If you are not able to read the entire play in advance, warn the cast of any surprises in the text, sharp turns in logic, or anything technically difficult like a section with a lot of overlapping dialogue. Let the listeners be shocked by an unexpected moment, not the cast.

- Reiterate your basic thoughts on the shape of the story, the tone, and the desired momentum. Point out what you felt was successful during the rehearsal, articulate why, and encourage them to follow that energy.

Listening to the Reading

Now your work is done and you can assume your role as the audience. In the way you once read the play with fresh eyes—without interference or preconceived notions—so you should strive to achieve that same feeling of openness here. This is an opportunity to let the play come to you in this new form. Put your script away and listen: don't trouble yourself with writing down all of your thoughts, simply pay attention to your experience.

Hearing a play aloud for the first time can be an unpredictable and very different experience from reading it. The cast's pace will not be the same as the rhythm in your head, there will be a huge amount of creative decisions made by the actors that differ from the ones you might have made, and the tone and style will be dictated by the cast: it is not yours to control. In short, your awareness, your taste, and your imagination are being given a massive amount of new information to respond to, some in complement with what you had already felt or thought, some of it in opposition to, and some entirely new that you could not have imagined. Remain aware of and open to it all: everything is useful. Not only are you hearing the play in this new form, you are receiving a new set of artists' perspectives and choices.

As you listen, remember the context of the reading. The company has spent only a few hours at most with the script, so you are not going to hear performance-level reads and it is unfair to assume you will. Part of your task as a listener is to identify the difference between an actor's choice and the circumstances of an unrehearsed performance. Listen and learn, but do not judge either the text or the actor without recalling the context. A perfectly cast company can smooth over parts of the play that don't yet work, and a cast that isn't quite right can make the play sound like it needs revision where it may not. A transcendent performance does not alleviate you or the writer from continuing to be rigorous about changes and improvements, nor does an unsuccessful read that mean something on the page is all wrong. Leave room for healthy doubt: a great reading doesn't mean the play is "done" nor does a terrible one mean you need to start over. A reading is a wealth of new ideas, lessons, and inspirations, but it is still simply a recitation with very little preparation: while the information you gather will be helpful, you should not consider it definitive.

Post-Reading

A successful reading is not one that sounded great, or that made everyone laugh or cry. The immediate response to the event itself can be a thrill (or a letdown), but it is secondary: a reading can only be considered a success if it provides you with new ideas, thoughts, challenges, and clarifications. How did it feel to listen to the play? How was it the same experience as reading it? How was it different? What was unexpected or surprising? What did you learn? What did you find exciting? Confusing? Troubling? Confirming? Reflect on these questions and any others that spring forth. The depth and richness of your thoughts after the reading will determine the event's value. If your mind is racing afterwards, it went exactly as it should have.

After the reading, ask the actors if they have any immediate reactions to share. You've just introduced new artists to the piece, so take advantage: their experience and perspective will be unique. When asked about a performance they just gave, an actor will usually describe the emotional journey of their role as well as what "worked" for them or didn't. They will be reflecting on the ease of the text to speak aloud, on the emotional trajectory of their role and the ways it did or did not make sense or feel natural, and on how easy or difficult it was to recite without practice. You may agree or disagree, but they will be reporting from within the piece, a point of view no one has ever experienced, and that alone is of enormous value.

As you did after reading the play for the first time, give yourself time afterwards to reflect. Eventually, you will have to describe your experience to the writer, but the longer you can observe and contemplate your feelings, the clearer they will become and the easier to communicate. Avoid talkbacks, discussions, or any other scenario that forces you to listen to outside opinions or to have to articulate your thoughts before you're certain you understand them. The time after a reading should be used for reflection, not for receiving notes or for winning arguments.

After some time, document your experience. Note when you were engaged, when your mind wandered, when you were confused, when you were moved. Revisit your notes from before the reading: how was the experience what you expected, and how was it not? Pay close attention to both: positive similarities teach you something is undeniably successful, differences mean you've been gifted new information. Pay attention to your most pressing questions. Those will become your worklist for a workshop.

Post-Reading with the Writer

Meet with the writer only a few days after the reading. There is such a thing as too much time for reflection: the mind will begin to separate from the actual experience of the reading. You'll want to discuss how you're feeling and what you're thinking without struggling to remember. Begin by summarizing your experience of the event: general thoughts, observations, and gut feelings. Think of this first part as a meeting between two people who just saw a play for the first time: what did you both think? Step out of your position as director, distance yourself from your professional tasks and considerations, and discuss the piece as an observer.

Then, gradually, let the conversation become more specific. Talk through your opinion of each actor's performance. Who did you respond to favorably? Why? Who did not feel like the right fit? Why? Like the casting conversations, this is a discussion of actors but it is also text analysis: you are learning about the play through your responses to the performances. Disagreement is common and useful: if you and the writer have very different opinions about an actor's work, you will know that a gap exists between your visions for the role. Your tastes are not in sync, and communicating why you did or did not respond to an actor will present a new way to think and talk about the text. Challenge yourselves to explain in detail what struck you as particularly strong about an actor: this can be the most productive approach to text analysis you can find at this point in your process.

Let your review of the actors' work lead to an even more detailed conversation about how the text sounded aloud. Share your impressions about scenes, moments, and lines of text that felt powerful, effective, confusing, moving, etc. and ask the writer to do the same. Try to connect your small observations to your overall thoughts (we will call them the "headlines"). A moment you loved or did not understand should be related to a larger thought or question about the play, and these "headlines" should be supported by highlighting specific moments. Understanding the direct correlation between the "headlines" and the details will help you both develop a more comprehensive and nuanced understanding of what is working, what is not, and why.

End your meeting with a review of everything you've discussed. Some of these thoughts will go on future worklists. Some you will want to listen to again, some you want to continue to reflect on, some you want to experiment with in a workshop, and some the writer will want to address in a rewrite. Get clarity on what the writer wants to edit and change and set a deadline so you know when to meet again and can preserve a sense of momentum. You should know what the writer intends to do so you can know what to expect. The writing process is fluid: an idea that seems promising after a reading may drift into some other idea, or it may disappear altogether. A rewrite worklist can be useful as a record of what you were both thinking and feeling after the reading.

The rewrite following a reading is your first opportunity to learn about the writer's process. How fast they work, the amount of changes they'll consider, how radical they are in their revising, how focused their attention is, how closely they follow their own to-do list, and how much they'll want to include you in their process. Some writers will share ideas and edits with their director regularly, some will disappear for weeks or months and emerge with a new draft. Pay attention not only to what they are writing, but also to how they are writing it. This is information that you will need throughout your process. It is a lesson about how you communicate, what changes or adjustments you might need to make to be effective, what timelines may be most realistic, and how that will affect the speed of development and the work during production. If you learn at this stage that a writer takes months to make small changes, for example, you know you need a draft that is as close-to-finished as possible before rehearsals begin.

5
WORKSHOPS

A workshop is a series of sessions in which the director conducts experiments on the text with actors. A workshop may resemble a rehearsal but it is not the same: the goal of a rehearsal is to prepare the *cast* for public performances whereas the goal of a workshop is to prepare the *script* for the beginning of a production process.

Many theater artists call workshops "labs" or the work "experimental" because the process mirrors a scientific one. A scientist will begin an experiment with a hypothesis, and a director will do the same in a workshop. A theater hypothesis might sound like: "If we try this scene in this way, we suspect this reaction/feeling/behavior/story may result." And then the director and actors will make changes, play the scene with them, and examine how it is different. In a laboratory, experiments are not random: they are thoughtfully planned with room for improvisation. The same should be true for a workshop. You and the writer arrive with a worklist: experiments you want to try and hypotheses about how they might transform the play. Scientific processes are like workshops because we begin with a clear idea of what we want to learn, what we are curious about, and what we don't yet understand, but without an assured destination. If we already knew the answers, a workshop, like any scientific pursuit, would not be necessary.

Many, or most, established plays go into rehearsals without a workshop. A new play, however, may contain questions about the text that are too large or complicated to address during a rehearsal process. This is why workshops are helpful, or even necessary. Experimental work during a rehearsal will take up too much time, and there is no guarantee a clear answer will materialize before performances. Furthermore, a huge amount of creative decisions need to happen *before* rehearsals even begin. An effective casting process and an informed design process cannot happen if the script is still in a nascent, experimental phase. How can a role be cast if the writer isn't sure who the character is? How can a set begin construction when entire locations are still subject to change? A workshop is not only useful for you and the writer, all of your future collaborators will benefit from the clarity that will come from these experiments. If your questions about the play are so substantial that you cannot go into a casting, design, or rehearsal process with confidence, then a workshop is the necessary next step.

Preparing a Worklist

In rehearsals, everyone understands there is a deadline: the audience will arrive on a certain date and will expect to see a play. Because a workshop simply ends when you run out of time, the schedule inherently lacks structure. It is a director's responsibility to give a workshop its shape and objectives. This shape is dictated by your worklist. What you want to work on, what you consider a priority, and what you hope to learn will be the prompts that will give your workshop its form. Think of your workshopping time as a fluid: it must be poured into a container (your list) in order for it to have a well-defined shape. The clearer the structure, the more freedom you will have within it.

Begin by revisiting your notes from the reading, identify your most pressing questions, and ask the writer to do the same. Ask them to articulate what they are interested in seeing (in addition to hearing) and what experiments they would like to try. It is likely, since you have been in conversation for some time, that you and the writer are already in alignment about what you are curious about.

Some common items on a worklist could be:

- Experimenting with reordering scenes
- Making drastic cuts
- Reimagining or changing the emotional trajectory of a character
- Reviewing, rewriting, or rearranging scenes or sections of consistent confusion
- Trying to fill gaps in story logic, missing pieces of information
- Trying multiple versions of the same scene
- Staging moments of the play on which the writer and director disagree

A workshop—because of its experimental nature—is the ideal environment to try an idea, a moment, or a rewrite in a number of different ways: any big question or idea is fair game. Another way to approach the creation of a list is to ask yourself this question: what must be clarified on the page before rehearsals begin?

Conversely, here are a few examples of items to leave off your worklist:

- Staged moments of violence or intimacy
- Moments that require scenery or design not available to you
- Minutiae: tweaks, trims, and small edits

Any play that does not have structural problems or dramaturgical questions that must be addressed through rewrites does not need a workshop; it needs a rehearsal process. In the same way endless readings may encourage the writer to make unnecessary changes, so a workshop can lead both you and the writer toward arbitrary experiments that can damage what already works, or cause confusion where there was none.

Preparing a Schedule

Once you have your worklist, determine how much time you will need to complete it. Begin by considering the amount of rewrites you expect, and how quickly the writer works. While it's useful to think of how much time you will want with actors, remember that the writer will be working in between those hours. Three days of workshopping, for example, means two writing sessions. Five days means four rewriting sessions. The difference between three or five days may not seem drastic, but if it means you are doubling the writer's working time, you can see how it can affect your scheduling decisions. Another option, when possible, is to "stagger," working with the cast every other day, giving the writer a full day between to work. You'll already have a sense of the writer's natural rhythm from watching them work after the reading: that information will be useful here.

Too much workshopping time can be physically and mentally exhausting for you, the writer, and the cast. You can only ask a company—who are not working towards a performance—to experiment for so long before fatigue sets in, and there is only so much information you and your writer can absorb. Saying "we need as much time as we can get" may seem advantageous, but that attitude can exhaust a group physically and mentally. Think of the minimum amount of time you will need, then remain close to that number as you plan.

After the schedule has been set, discuss the worklist with the writer and arrange it in order of priority. Be mindful of which experiments may generate rewrites. These sections should be addressed on the first or second day. This maximizes the writer's time to revise, and will give you an opportunity to experiment with new pages later in the workshop. While you cannot predict how long each experiment may take, you can estimate which are the most potentially time-consuming. Prioritize those as well, as they may take more than one day to address. Keep the latter part of the workshop more flexible: your priorities and new pages will bleed into subsequent days, so you need to leave scheduling space for that inevitability. Experiments are unpredictable: discoveries will lead you away from your to-do list, and while you should follow them, also be mindful of why you built your list in the first place. Balance improvisation with your priorities.

Your Producer or Producing Organization

It is likely someone is producing the workshop. Make clear to this party (a producer or producing organization) what your plans and goals are, and ask about their intentions. If they are paying, what precisely do they expect in return for their investment? Because a workshop can take so many shapes, you and the producer must not assume the same goals or outcomes: seek clarity before the workshop begins. You may intend to use the time to run experiments while the producer expects the workshop to end in a programming reading. Understanding the intentions of the producer will demystify any of their choices (if they want a say in casting, for example, or if they want to determine the schedule). Afterwards, they may want to host a notes session and you should have clarity about whether those notes are conditional. Is the producer saying "make these changes or we won't produce it"? You and the writer may or may not choose to take those notes, but you should know even before the workshop begins what the circumstances are, as well as the expectations.

Casting a Workshop

Revisit your casting lists from the reading and ask that the writer do the same. Would you describe the character differently now? Why, and how? Revise your lists accordingly, adding new ideas and removing those that no longer make dramaturgical sense.

Because a workshop demands a specific way of working, do not assume all actors will be enthusiastic about experimentation. Seek out actors who are not only ideal fits for the role, but who you also trust to be enthusiastic collaborators. A workshop may not be the appropriate time to approach an actor you don't know or haven't worked with. It may not be the moment to ask that famous actor you have been dreaming of casting. The focus of this time is on the play itself: too much attention spent learning how to communicate with actors you don't know with will take a significant amount of time you may not have to spare.

Location

The needs of your worklist will teach you about the physical requirements of the space. Do you need a lot of room to move? Do you expect actors to be stretching out and warming up on the floor? Will you need a piano? Speakers for music? A lot of tables and chairs? Will you need immediate access to a printer for new pages? Imagine each item on your worklist playing out in space: what must you have in order to be successful? Confirm with whoever is arranging the space (if it isn't you) what is and isn't possible. A space that cannot meet all of your needs is unfortunate, but learn in advance what can be achieved so you can plan accordingly.

Preparing Stage Management

We will be speaking in detail about the role of and the director's relationship with stage management later, but for now we will assume you are working with one for this workshop. Contact them at least a week in advance to make sure they have the most recent draft of the play and all the necessary information about the cast, the location, and the schedule. Share your worklist with them and arrange a meeting to discuss it in detail. The stage manager will oversee all the scheduling, so they should not only have your worklist, they should understand on a deep level what you want to work on, and in what order, and why. That information will help them make decisions about how the workshop schedule will be structured, and can help you organize, strategize, and improvise as necessary.

Share with your stage manager what you've learned about the writer's process. Do they generate a lot of pages? Are they very organized? Or not? Do they send changes at the last minute? A stage manager will be the one handling the formatting and distribution of rewrites, so the better they understand how the writer works, the more prepared they can be. Nothing can derail the momentum of a workshop faster than confusion around inserting new pages. You, the writer, and the stage manager must have a system for inserting rewrites in place before you begin.

The First Day

Begin the workshop by offering the actors context and setting expectations. Keep it simple: this is what we are here to do, this is how we plan to do it. Explain to the company how you expect to use the time: will you be around a table reading? Should they expect to be up on their feet? Will there be a constant flow of new pages, or will the rewrites be more surgical? Articulate what you want and need from the actors, and what your expectations will be: some workshops need a lot of discussion and the sharing of opinions, others need less dialogue and more trial and error. You want to invite the company into this process as colleagues, partners, and fellow-scientists, and they can only participate in that way if they understand your objectives from the beginning. All of this is subject to change depending on what you learn in the room, but a company that understands the goal of the workshop and their role in it will feel empowered, confident, comfortable, and able to do their strongest, bravest work.

Make explicit that this workshop is an experimental space. The cast should be encouraged to share their thoughts and to ask questions—all ideas are welcome—but make clear that a worklist has been developed in advance and that there may not be time to entertain every idea. Share this before you begin so actors feel welcomed to contribute, but not offended if their ideas do not make it onto your list.

Frame the workshop as a place for inquiry, not a place to "fix" the play. It is full of promise, that is why we are all here! The goal is to make a good thing better, or a great thing excellent. Actors will have suggestions for the writer, but they should be shared as questions or observations, not instructions or demands. A rule should be that the text should be spoken verbatim, and all changes, cuts, and edits are the writer's decision. We are here not to tell the writer what they should do, but to reflect on our experiences performing the text.

Make it a rule that nothing will be discussed before it is tried. Workshops can quickly pivot into long conversations with very little experimentation, and that rhythm can be difficult to break. Always read the scene, get the actors up on their feet if that's useful, try it, then discuss the result. Let the writer see how it plays instead of explaining it to them.

A workshop is not only a chance to experiment with the text, it is also an opportunity for you to experience rehearsal conditions with actors and see what approaches are and are not effective. Until now, most of your communication has been with the writer: in this setting, your pool of collaborators has expanded, and you must learn how to share your thoughts with a different group of artists in a productive way. A workshop is your opportunity to experiment with the tone you will want to set in rehearsal and how best to articulate your ideas to actors. The goal of a workshop is to prepare the text for a rehearsal process, but it is also your time to prepare and refine your directorial approach.

On Your Feet

Start with a complete read-through of the most recent draft. Hear it aloud, with this cast, and be reminded of the aural experience. Learn about this new company (some may have read it before, others may be new) and pay attention to the performances of their roles. They will teach you a lot about each actor's point of view before you even begin, and that will be useful information as you get on your feet. This reading is an opportunity to give the group a shared point of departure. It is a chance to observe the entire play before conducting experiments on specific parts.

A director's first task is to encourage an atmosphere of bravery and without judgment. Like readings, workshops can be vulnerable environments for actors because they are thrown into experiments with little to no preparation. It will be your job to set this tone: "trial and error" can be difficult because no one likes to feel like they are making an "error." Your explanation of the motivations and goals of the workshop will go a long way. While you are working, teach the cast that no choice is "wrong," and that experiments demand strong choices that may not work. How respectfully you speak to the cast and respond to their choices will determine how confident the company will be.

Your worklist will structure your day, but if you are struggling to find a way to begin, here are a few approaches. The more you experiment, the easier the process will become, and the more options and ideas will reveal themselves.

- Stage the problem: if a scene or a moment feels stuck, put it on its feet, just as it is. Don't try to "do" anything to it, just put it up for you and the writer to observe. This is an awareness exercise: very often the "problem" has become an intellectual one, and seeing the moment exactly as it is can refocus your attention and allow you to see it with fresh eyes. Stage it and look at it. Try it a second time, or a third. You don't need to conjure some genius staging, you're not trying to find what's "right," you're simply looking at what it is, sitting with the feeling that something is not working, and asking yourself why.

- Repetition can be your ally in a workshop. Directors and actors can feel an obligation to make different choices every time a scene is attempted. This is a result-oriented response: we feel pressured to prove we are smart, talented artists who have an endless stream of good ideas. You must guide the room away from that way of thinking. In a workshop, you have the time to play the scene, contemplate, discuss, and then play the scene again without having solved anything at all. Watching a scene not work, in exactly the same way, over and over may help you and the writer find more clarity than if you tried it different ways each time.

- "Strong and wrong" is a tactic to break a room from struggling to find solutions or answers. It is a freeing gesture: you suggest a deliberately terrible choice—the worst, most absurd, ridiculous way of playing the scene—so that by running as far as possible from a "good" choice, the actors are liberated from the pressures of being "smart" or "good." This shift in perspective can give you and the writer a chance to see the scene with fresh eyes, and the actors are eliminating any feelings of self-judgment or pressure to succeed. A tense room can also be loosened up by the fun of intentional wrong-ness.

- Reading around the table can be just as useful as getting up on your feet. Some pages are too new, or too complicated, to stage immediately. It can also be difficult for actors to walk through a scene with their eyes on the page. So long as you are continuing to try and not to discuss, working around the table can be just as productive and informative.

Remaining aware of what seems to be useful will determine the value of working in these ways. "Useful" can mean many things, but your primary system of measurement should be whether you and the writer are learning from what you're seeing, and if one experiment leads to another. You and everyone else in the room will know when you've hit a dead end and need a new tactic. Be prepared to throw out one approach and replace it with another. If incremental changes aren't addressing your questions, try something drastic. If "strong and wrong" is just confusing everyone, repeat a simple version a few times to refocus your attention. One way to know if you've exhausted your work on a scene is if you've done all you can and now the writer needs time to rewrite or to revise. Remember that only half of the workshop unfolds in the room: the other half will happen when the writer takes the day's information and makes changes accordingly.

If you find yourself stuck, remember that the problem with one scene could be caused by an entirely different moment in the play. Perhaps an emotional climax late in the story does not make sense: it's possible the necessary changes can be found in a much earlier scene. If you and the writer are struggling with a moment, first identify the problem (in this case, the emotional reaction feels confusing), then retrace the dramatic steps that lead to this moment. It's very possible something elsewhere in the play needs your attention in order for the problem at hand to sort itself out.

As you work, remain aware of the way you are speaking about the play and the characters. Make mental notes of what seems to resonate with the actors. Because this is an opportunity for you to workshop how you will eventually lead a rehearsal room, paying attention to the effectiveness of your language now will serve you later. Make adjustments to how you share and see how different ways of speaking about the play can elicit different results. You are sharpening your tools of communication. Be mindful also of the questions you are asking yourself as you watch. Return to the basics: can you follow the story of the scene? Are you asking yourself what happens next? And after that? The simpler the questions you pose to yourself, the easier it will be to identify your next step.

Ending the Day

Thank the cast, release them for the day, and then meet with the writer to hear their thoughts. While you'll be checking in with them throughout, the end of the day should be spent comparing notes, thoughts, ideas, and questions, and also planning the worklist for the following day. These conversations should cover overarching story observations as well as detail-oriented thoughts. Ask the writer to expand on what they noticed and how they responded, and get clarity on what they plan to work on overnight and what you can expect to read in the morning. Your worklist for the next day will depend on that information, so encourage the writer to be as honest and clear as possible about what they expect to accomplish.

Once you know what the writer wants to do, combine that information with your list and make a schedule for the following day with your stage manager, who will share it with the cast.

Not all writers generate a lot of new pages in workshop settings. Many may not know how they will react or respond to seeing their work reflected back to them, so it may not be until the morning of the second day that you will understand what kind of rewrites to expect. If it becomes clear that they will not be generating a lot of new material, don't push them. There are many ways to experiment successfully without rewrites, so if the workshop becomes less about the integration of new text and more about learning as much as you can about the current draft, it will still be enormously productive.

Schedule a few more experiments than you might be able to achieve. This is not to rush, but because it is impossible to predict how quickly work on a scene will go, it is better to have other experiments at the ready than to finish with nothing else to work on. Stagger your call times and be respectful of the actor's time, but err on the side of a packed schedule so that you can use every moment in the room.

Subsequent Days

Before the cast arrives each day, meet with the writer to read through any new pages. Always see the rewrites before anyone else: you need some time to reflect, to prepare, and to develop a plan. Read the pages together: you can ask the writer questions and they can help you understand what they were hoping to achieve with their changes. Even though you are working quickly, remain aware of the experience of reading something new: pay attention to your reactions, ideas, and feelings. Sometimes you will respond negatively to a rewrite, and that will have less to do with the words on the page and more with their newness. Are you resistant to a rewrite for artistic reasons, because you're not used to it, or were you expecting (or hoping) for something different? If you are unsure, add the pages to your worklist and hear them aloud.

Whether or not you have new pages to incorporate, approach the beginning of each day in the same fashion. Choose a scene, a moment, or a section, and try, assess, adjust, try, assess, adjust. Avoid spending too much time on one experiment. You and the writer may need time away from a section that remains confusing, and spending hours on a single section can exhaust your creative energy. Sometimes looking at another, perhaps unrelated section of the play will inform and inspire solutions to the other. Don't force yourself to stay with a scene just because it is on your schedule: if an experiment is not revealing anything helpful, move on and come back to it.

At some point, you may feel like you have lost sight of the play. Too many experiments, too many new pages, too many lingering questions. The play has been disassembled so completely that it has become impossible to remember how it all fits together. This is natural, especially when there are many big rewrites. If you find yourselves in this situation, stop your work and read the entire play again, including the new pages. This will take up time, but by bringing the room's attention back to the play as a single work, it will give all your experiments a clearer context.

Ending the Workshop

On your final day or days, prioritize those sections you must see, or see again. You may not get to everything on your list, and that's to be expected. Your last hours should be spent working on what you can and at the same rate: a rush to the finish line will not yield helpful information. Ending with another reading can be a helpful way to review your experiments. A full read will allow you to see what sections have improved, and which require more attention. Think of it as a summary of your scientific results: this work was successful, this was not, this remains incomplete.

Make time after the workshop to review notes with the writer, and come to an agreement about any upcoming rewrites. Because you and the writer have been in constant communication throughout this process, it is probable you have shared opinions, but do not assume: make a new list together. Ask yourselves: which questions have you answered? Which remain? Do you feel as though you have solved as much as you can without a full rehearsal process? Why or why not? It is your responsibility to summarize the results of the work in a concise and helpful way for a shared clarity and to keep developmental momentum.

The question of whether or not the play is ready for production is, ultimately, a personal and creative one. All plays have questions (we will discuss that later), so you must ask yourselves: do you feel you now have the text you want to build a production on? Do you feel confident it can support that work? Is the story on the page the one you want to share with the world? If *you* are ready, then the play is ready.

Overdevelopment and the New Play Industrial Complex

It is possible to over-develop a play: it happens when a text has been workshopped so much everything singular, mysterious, and idiosyncratic has been written out of it. The writer is left with a text that is so over-explained, so thorough in answering every question, that an audience has nothing left for them to do. The work has been done for them, and what they are watching is one long explanation of events. We may not understand this intellectually as we watch a play, but we know it intuitively: the play's pace may be fine, but it still feels slow. This is what we mean when we say we "were ahead of it the whole time." This sensation occurs when a creative team has cheated an audience out of the pleasure of wondering, of asking questions, of being curious. They detach not out of confusion, but the opposite: there is no room for them to participate. The audience has been encouraged to be passive, and they have no choice but to comply.

Too many readings and workshops, and not knowing when to put an end to development, are often the cause of this type of play. Artists invited into a development process are encouraged to ask questions, offer thoughts, and share opinions. But are all questions created equal? Are all of them worthwhile? Or necessary? A workshop can be overwhelming for a writer because of the amount of feedback they will receive. No artist comes to a workshop to *not* offer their opinion. A writer can become oversaturated by too many suggestions, and it can be difficult to discern which are useful and which can be dismissed. This becomes even more complicated if the notes are coming from a producer, or anyone who may play a role in the play's future.

Many of these observations may seem like a note but are actually a sign that the moment in question is working perfectly. An actor could say "I want to know more about my character's father." That may not be a note, it may be excellent news: you *want* the audience to be asking themselves the same question. A producer may say "I don't understand why she leaves him at the end," and that may be exactly the open-ended finish you were hoping for.

It is part of a director's job in a workshop to separate helpful notes, thoughts, and questions from those that should be set aside. You must serve as the filter, sorting out which ones are worth considering, which are not and which are simply proof that you are on the right track. Everyone in a workshop wants to be helpful, they want to contribute, and they want to sound intelligent. You should encourage their input and cultivate their curiosity, and also help the writer identify the difference between "smart" and "useful." They are not always the same thing.

Plays are sticky: they pick up new things wherever they go. How many stops should a play take on its developmental journey before it is too many? There is only so much workshopping and only so many questions a writer can handle before the mysteries of their work are noted out of it. Because workshops are relatively inexpensive, a new play is often given numerous development opportunities. A writer can be tempted to accept every invitation, especially new, young, or emerging writers for whom a workshop can feel like an honor; however, pursuing them can take an enormous amount of time and effort. Artistic statements, applications, proposals, resumes, bios, play descriptions, recommendations, application fees … the time and mental energy, and sometimes money, it takes to submit a play can be significant. Promising plays are chosen for these opportunities, but are then overwhelmed by well-meaning notes, which may require more workshopping. A play may find itself in a developmental loop.

A writer can only be asked the same questions for so long before they may doubt the quality of their work, or give up trying to defend their choices. Recurring questions get spelled out in the text, the idiosyncrasies of the writer's voice are written out for clarity's sake, rough edges are sanded down, sharp turns are made smooth, everyone in the workshop feels like all their questions have been answered, and the future audience is cheated out of their opportunity to engage with a singular voice and a complicated work.

It can be scary to reject the opportunity for more workshops, but development for the sake of status, or to stay busy, or because you think an affiliation with these organizations will increase the play's profile, can be potentially play-damaging miscalculations.

Developmental Momentum

To paraphrase the great playwright and teacher Marsha Norman: a writer has about two years to finish a play, otherwise they will have grown so much from who they were when they started that it is an entire different writer, and person, who finishes it. Once a writer has begun to develop a play, it should not sit in a drawer too long between drafts. Some time away from a script can allow a writer to see a play with fresh eyes, but too much time will cause the writer to forget where they left off.

I was once developing a play with a writer who suddenly found himself with a number of production opportunities on other projects. He took them, and the play we were working on together sat untouched for about eight months. When we reconvened to hear the play after all that time, he decided he no longer liked the direction he had been taking the play, so he threw out the second act and wrote something entirely new. Then more opportunities for other plays came up, and it took another year before we could meet again. This time, he was confused by what he had done during his previous rewrite, felt (correctly) that he had written two different plays, and didn't know how to reconcile them. He gave up on the play, and it was never heard again.

What the writer had done was not edit the previous draft, he had begun an entirely new play based on the old one. The writer who created the first draft had grown into a different artist, and this new one wasn't interested in the creative work of the first.

New plays can take a long time. They should not be rushed to completion, nor should they be neglected for long stretches.

6
PURSUING A PRODUCTION

The process of getting a play produced can be perplexing, frustrating, and confounding: the variables, obstacles, and unknowns are infinite and vary from project to project. In an ideal situation, the path looks like this: the script is sent to a producer or producing organization to be read and considered. If the organization is interested, they will option it for production, and if they are not, they will "pass." We already know this is not always the case, as sometimes a play is in development at an institution, or it has been "auditioned" by way of a programming reading. What I will be explaining in this section is a very—perhaps the most—common route to securing a production, the submission process.

In order to best understand this step, I will make one assumption: that you and the writer are working as a team, and that you have been empowered by them to help get the play produced. This journey from development to production can be a complicated one for a director, because in spite of all the effort you have put into the development of the play, it is not yours. It is and will always belong to the writer, and so your role in the submission process will vary, and will depend largely on the writer's desire. Some will want to work with you, others alone, others with an agent or manager if they have one. For our purposes, we will imagine the director and writer are proceeding as equal collaborators.

Begin by creating a list of organizations where you would like to send the play. Research institutions, organizations, and companies. Learn about their history: find a list of titles they have produced, look at archival footage or photography of their productions, promotional artwork, the language they use to describe them, and their mission statement. If you don't know where to begin your search, look to the plays you admire and see which theaters have produced them. Working in this way will assure you there is a shared taste and artistic sensibility.

Some prompt you can use to begin your research are:

- Do they produce new work?

- Does the play you will submit match their mission?
- Have they produced work of a similar size and scale as the play you will send?

  Can you get a sense of their audience? Do you think this play would resonate with them?
- Who selects the shows they produce? Can you get a sense of their taste?

When a play is submitted, it is immediately clear to the producing organization if the writer or director has an understanding of the company: their mission, size, and taste. If you are asking a theater to dedicate the time to read and consider a play, prove that you have also spent time learning about them in advance. There is no better way for a submission to demand serious attention than to have chosen to share something that is in aesthetic, thematic, and budgetary alignment.

Before you send the script, learn who reads and chooses the plays for each organization and make sure your submission lands in their hands. I once spent a long time in conversation with an associate artistic director at a reputable theater company. They raved about how much they loved a play I had sent and described how wonderful the production was going to be. They told me there was a space available in their next season and to expect an official offer soon. The offer never came. I learned many years later that the artistic director and their associate did not get along, and that the former did not care for the latter's taste. That the associate had taken an interest in the play was actually a guarantee that it would never get produced. How could I have known? The only way to avoid a similar scenario is to learn first who receives and reads the submissions, and also who make the producing decisions. Not every organization is structured in the same way, and not all titles (Literary Manager, Director of New Works, etc.) mean the same thing everywhere. You can find out this information by seeking out the advice of people who have already worked with the company. I have found great success and valuable information from contacting directors, even ones I had never met, to ask questions about a company: almost every time I have reached out to a fellow artist with an advice question, they have answered. This is one of many ways I have found theater colleagues to be enormously generous.

Taking a Meeting

If a theater has read and responded favorably to the play and to the possibility of working with you, the next step will be an interview with the producer or artistic director. During this meeting, you must make a case that you are both a professional and an artistic fit: a competent, responsible collaborator who can be trusted to work within the technical and financial parameters of the organization, and an artist with a clear, compelling vision for the play and an infectious passion for bringing it to the stage.

Like any job interview, consider the following:

- Be on time. It is an easy way to prove your enthusiasm and respect for the project.

- Arrive prepared to speak about the play and your vision for it. Be ready to summarize what attracted you to the play, why it speaks to you as an artist, why you think audiences will respond favorably to the work, and why you are the best person to direct it. What do you consider the script's strengths? What are the production's potential challenges, and how are you prepared to meet them? Can you describe what your production would look, move, and sound like? Revisit your notes from the development process and refine them into clear and concise thoughts. You are teaching the producer to see the play through your eyes, so the clearer and simpler you can be, the more compelling your argument.

- Be open. artistic directors and producers are creative people and will have their own opinions. Listen closely, as their thoughts will help you understand how your ideas might align (or not) with the creative leader of the organization. You aren't obligated to agree with everything they suggest, but you should pay attention to how your visions do and do not match: the ways in which you and the producer agree and disagree about the play during this meeting will most likely continue throughout the process.

- Make your case, not theirs. There is a subtle distinction between explaining why you want to direct the play and why you think the artistic director should produce it. You cannot know or guess what planning, budgeting, or other considerations are unfolding behind the scenes of any company. Make an argument for the quality and intrinsic value of the play on its own merit without assuming to know what is the best for the company.

- Convey respect for the company and the staff. Most artistic leaders are, or should be, protective of their staff and are careful to avoid artists who they suspect might mistreat or behave disrespectfully toward them. If a director appears dismissive of the people who run the institution, it will give a leader pause. Prove yourself as a generous and conscientious collaborator and a future positive addition to the company.

- Prioritize professionalism. Producers and artistic directors do not need more friends; they need trusted colleagues who are going to make strong, compelling work. A director can certainly be warm and welcoming, but do not use the meeting as an opportunity to try to win an AD's friendship.

You cannot know why a company makes its hiring decisions. It is, and will remain, a mystery. What is within your control is how prepared you are and how you conduct yourself during the meeting. If you present your vision in a clear and convincing way and yourself as a professional and generous colleague, then you have done all you can.

A Note on "General" Meetings

There will also be opportunities to meet with producers, artistic directors, agents, and other decision-makers without a specific project to discuss. These are called "general" meetings: a chance to introduce yourself, to talk about your art and your work, and to build relationships for potential future collaborations.

Follow the same advice for these meetings but be mindful of two key differences. The first is that you must prepare to describe your work and your style in a general sense, not in relation to a specific project. Your goal during a general is to be broad enough that you can make yourself employable for many different types of projects, but specific enough about your work and style that the listener can imagine what you might be right for. In my position as an artistic director, I once met with a director who told me they're only interested in magical realism. That's very limiting from a hiring perspective: would they not be interested in or able to direct anything that doesn't fall under that category? And who can create a fixed definition for that genre, anyway? I also met with a director who said they made "dangerous and boundary pushing" work. Very difficult to get a sense of their taste with that description. Your objective is to describe your work with such clarity that, when they will be looking for a director in the future, they will remember how you described yourself. If you are too specific or too vague, you limit your chances for consideration.

The second difference is that you must arrive prepared to recommend plays for them to read. Your research about companies will have taught you about their taste, so select a few unproduced plays you are developing that you suspect will align with their style. Try to make certain these are plays they have not yet read (the best way to confirm that information is by asking the writer). During a general meeting, you will inevitably be asked what writers you love, and if you have read anything you'd like to share. If you have a clear answer to both of those questions, your chances of this general meeting leading to a job will become exponentially higher. A turning point in my career came when a producer asked me to send her a play I was developing. I had done a lot of research about the plays she had produced in the last few years, and felt confident I had an understanding of her taste. I had just directed a reading of a new play I suspected she would admire by a writer who did not yet have an agent, so I sent her that script. Even though the play was eventually produced by another organization, she identified me as someone with intriguing taste, and we worked together soon after and for many years following. If I did not have a play ready to share, that general meeting would not have led to a next step, and our professional relationship would not have blossomed as quickly and significantly as it did.

Auditioning the Play

If the meeting goes well, the next step will likely be a programming reading or workshop. This event is a pure audition: you and the writer will go through the same process of preparation—casting, planning, and rehearsing—but without any "development" in that you won't be working on the play. Afterwards, you may be asked to meet with the producer. They may give notes, and it may be very tempting to take them if you feel there's a production waiting for you if you get the rewrites "right." Ask yourself if you are taking the notes because you believe they will improve the play or because you suspect an offer is dependent on it. If it is the latter, be careful. Not only will you be shifting the play away from your vision and toward a producer's, you will also be teaching the producer that any changes they suggest will be taken. Once that dynamic has been set, it can be difficult to reverse.

If you do not agree with their notes, you must make the difficult decision to part ways. It can feel like madness to turn down an opportunity for production, but if a theater is giving notes you do not agree with now, you can trust that a collaboration will not be a fruitful one. The writer will not be able to tell the story they want, you will have to fight for what you feel the play needs, and the organization will inevitably be unhappy with the production. Signs that the collaboration between the artists and producing organization will be successful or not are often revealed early, but there is usually so much excitement and desire for the production to happen they go ignored. Pay attention to warning signs that you do not see eye to eye: they will not disappear with time. Usually it's quite the opposite.

Obstacles

Fantastic new plays are difficult to find, and there are often obstacles standing between you and an opportunity to direct them. A theater organization may prefer to work with a director they know and have worked with before, especially if the playwright is new to them. If the writer has agent, they may want one of their director clients to work on the play. Then there are other, perhaps more accomplished directors who are looking for a new play and they've heard the one you have been developing is worth their attention. If a writer is influenced by these factors, there is unfortunately little you can do. If a producer tells a writer they want to do the play, but with a director of their choosing, that can put the writer in a difficult position. To get passed over or replaced on a project you helped develop is something that happens to all new play directors eventually, and it is a very painful experience. You've spent a significant amount of time and energy on the play, your wisdom and creativity exist on those pages, and it may be in a favorable position for production because of your contributions. This is unfair, but this is an unfortunate part of any directing career.

The good news is that this will not often be the case. There will always be writers who advocate for you, and who value your collaboration and your contribution to the development of the play. They will demand your involvement, and a producer will honor it. And then you are on your way.

A Note on Inviting People to See Your Work

You will often hear people in positions of power say "invite me to your work." This is especially true during general meetings. How is a director supposed to make work to invite people to see when these producers will not offer you an opportunity to make it? It can feel like an endless cycle. The solution is to seek out opportunities to work on quality texts that you believe in, regardless of the size, scale, or prestige of the production. One acts, ten-minute plays, scene nights in basements, rehearsal rooms, or bars … a producer, artistic director, or agent will be able to see your talent and understand your taste even in the lowest budget situation. As long as you are working on promising material that you feel shows your creative skill and technical ability, the setting and scale of the event is irrelevant.

PART THREE
PRE-PRODUCTION

In this section, we will examine the assembling of a creative team and the beginning a design process, the casting of a production, and the building a relationship with the producing organization. We will understand the tasks and contributions of each of your collaborators as well as how to communicate with them successfully.

In the development phase, your process was largely chronological. One meeting, one reading, one workshop at a time. It was also very intimate: most of your work happened either alone or with the writer, with brief periods among a company of actors.

The two new challenges of the pre-production process will be the sudden increase of collaborators and the subsequent splitting of your focus. A director must oversee multiple facets of the production as they take shape, many of them beginning at the same time. The number of collaborators will expand exponentially: what was previously a team of two will grow to ten, then twenty, then maybe fifty or more in only a few weeks. These changes will test a director's communication skills: how you introduce your vision to these creative partners will set the tone and trajectory of the entire process.

Many different kinds of machinery will lurch into motion during pre-production, and you will need to guide everyone toward common goals with clarity, generosity, and inspiration.

Reading a Play (for pre-production)

Because of the many collaborators you are about to meet and plethora of decisions you will need to make, your primary goals during this reading will be a clarification of your vision, a synthesis of your creative ideas with your logistical needs, and a list of your priorities. You must prepare yourself to speak the many different languages of a production: budget, design, press releases, casting, and many more. During this stage of the process, you will be sharing and advocating for your vision of the play while simultaneously uniting disparate groups together under your guidance and leadership.

The most immovable decisions of your production—creative and technical—will be made during pre-production. The set will be designed and will begin construction. The cast will be chosen and hired. The publicity materials will be sent out into the world. A budget will be finalized, as will a calendar. These are concrete decisions that are very difficult, or impossible, to reverse. This is why rereading for the sake of clarity and confidence is essential.

You have now read the play through multiple lenses. You have been in deep conversation with the writer, you have heard the text aloud, and you have begun to feel what it is like to be in dialogue with actors. Combine all of your lists of questions, gut reactions, images, and ideas. Revisit and review them as you read, deciding which still resonate and which are no longer relevant. Approach this reading as an *editing process*: some of your questions will have been answered, some will no longer feel necessary to ask, some will remain urgent. Some ideas will still excite you, some will fall away. Pay close attention to those first reactions that persist: they are your strongest guides because they have proven durable. Trust your taste: it is what will make your production singular to you. It is during this busy period of pre-production when you can become overwhelmed by the logistical concerns of building the production and lose sight of those initiation impulses. Remind yourself of them and hold them close.

Your goal is to edit and refine you thoughts until you arrive at simple conclusions. A director needs to dig to the very root of a text until they are able to say: "This is what the play is about" or "This is why the play speaks to me" or "This is how I see it" in a way that is clear and useful to all of your collaborators. If, as you read, you feel the play is about so many things, or that your thoughts remain scattered, keep peeling away layers of meaning until clarity emerges. You do not need to throw out ideas you find interesting, inspiring, or intriguing: this work is not about elimination but about refinement. A thought can be worth keeping in mind but isn't at the very heart of what the play is about to you, and that is the purpose of this work. You cannot guide a group without first finding that simplicity for yourself. The language you use will be personal to you: it is the ability to speak succinctly about your vision that is necessary.

Your other goal for this read is an understanding of priorities. As you crystalize your vision for the play, consider what will be most important to you in its realization. Soon you will be asked to make decisions about casting, design, budget, and scheduling. Your ability to make the most successful ones depends on how well you can meld your creative ideas with the realities of a production. Reread and imagine your future production: what elements are necessary to realize your vision? How do you rank them in order of importance? What traits *must* an actor have in order to play the role as you envision it? What design elements *must* the production possess to tell your version of this story?

This process involves reconnecting with the basics of the play, then filtering them through your vision. Let's imagine the writer has described a character as sixteen years old. Hiring a minor can be complicated and expensive: it may mean making cuts to other elements of your production. Do you need an actual teenager, or would someone older playing sixteen suffice? Why or why not? What is it about the character's behavior or personality that must be preserved in order for the actor to fit your vision? Dialogue with yourself and be rigorous and relentless: the more specific your questions, the more precise your answers. You will have pushed yourself to articulate what and why, making it much easier to communicate your findings with others later. You will have broken down any barriers between your creative thinking and your logistical concerns. You will be able to speak the language of both artistic and technical needs in the same breath. That fluidity is your goal, and the depth and rigor of your preparatory work at this stage will provide it.

A director cannot be expected to keep all of their ideas, questions, inspirations, and concerns in their head in an easily accessible way. There will be times during pre-production when you only get one opportunity to communicate your thoughts, so you must be prepared to be concise. As you reread, create a document that will help organize your ideas, needs, and wants. The simultaneity, the many considerations, and the sudden influx of outside opinions you will face during pre-production can be overwhelming: having your thoughts written out and on-hand will allow you to be clear and thorough, regardless of the meeting, circumstance, or subject under discussion.

This document can include:

- A plot summary (What happens?)
- A thematic summary (What is the play about?)
- A scene breakdown:
    - List of characters
    - Setting
    - Other details (time of day, weather, etc.)

- Event of each scene (plot)

A simple way to locate the event of the scene is to identify one action or line of dialogue that changes the course of the play. The Greeks called this peripety, a turning point in a story. Challenge yourself to summarize the scene for yourself in one sentence: "This is the scene in which _____ happens." If the scene does not seem to have one single event, that is something you should discuss with the writer: it may be dramatically inert.

- Necessary technical and design elements

Technical and design elements can include fight choreography, blood, a specific piece of furniture, a wig, a door that needs to fall off its hinge, open flame: any need that will involve the contributions of multiple artists or departments. Do not assume that everyone has the same understanding of what they read on the page: what may seem obvious to you may not be to someone else. If you have not articulated what you see and what you need, you should not assume everyone is aware.

This organizational work is more necessary during a new play process because your collaborators will not be familiar with the text. No one would need you to explain the plot of Hamlet, for example, but they will need to know how you hope to stage the Ghost. With a brand new play, a director's collaborators need a wealth of information, from the basics of the plot to their creative vision of the world to the small components that will make up the whole. The more precisely you can answer those questions for yourself now, the easier it will be to share them later.

7
ASSEMBLING THE CREATIVE TEAM

A primary task of pre-production is the assembling of your creative team. As you begin interviewing and hiring collaborators, here are the central questions that must guide your process:

- Do you feel you can have a creatively successful collaboration with this person?
- Do you trust them as a professional colleague?
- Do you have a shared appreciation of the merits and challenges of the text?
- Do your tastes align?

You must find collaborators that are an emphatic yes to all of the above. These questions provide a basic criterion for who will make a strong member of your team.

Your designers, stage manager, and other collaborators will most often be a combination of people you have worked with before, people you have admired from afar, and people recommended by colleagues and by the producer. Very often you will have to interview potential collaborators. It can take a significant amount of work for a potential collaborator to prepare for these meetings, so do not treat them as generals: this is a job interview, so only meet with collaborators you are considering seriously. Reach out to these prospects to find a time and place, and send them the most recent copy of the play. You must ask everyone to read the play in advance. These conversations are about alignment: with one another as colleagues and with the text. A designer you love speaking with but who has a wildly different interpretation of the play will not be a fit, and a director can only learn that if they are able to discuss the play together in detail.

You may know exactly who you want to work with and prefer not to interview anyone. Before you make an offer, ask yourself the same four questions. Not every designer will be ideal for every project no matter how positive your previous collaborations have been, and not every frequent collaborator will feel inspired by every play you choose to direct. Previous positive experiences do not automatically translate to successful future ones: ask questions, be rigorous, and make sure every artist you make an offer to meets all of the professional and creative needs of this singular project.

Every project will also involve collaborators that are assigned to you by the producer: your process of introducing yourself and your vision should unfold in the same way as if you had hired them yourself. Ask about the way they approach their work, their perspective on the play, and about how you will most successfully collaborate. Just because you did not choose them does not mean you should be less curious about their thoughts on the play or less committed to developing a strong creative relationship.

Designers

The best way to evaluate designers is to see their work live. Not still photography, not audio tracks, not costume sketches. You need to see their work in its intended context: how it moves, how it serves the story, how it conjures the world of the play. Design elements need to be understood by how they behave over the duration of the play. A beautiful photograph of a set or of a lighting effect will teach you very little about the designer's understanding of pace, rhythm, and story. This is why attending the theater and seeing your colleagues' work is part of a director's job.

Set

A set designer is responsible for the design and realization of the physical production. Anything onstage you can see and touch that cannot be picked up (props) or worn (costumes) is the responsibility of the set designer. They develop the design in collaboration with the director, draw technical plans to share with the other designers and the shop that will build it. A set designer will work with the Production and General Management offices to stay on (or close to) budget, and the Technical Director to collaborate on the set's construction.

The most successful interviews with any designer do not begin with a discussion of scenery, transitions, or logistics. They are an opportunity for two artists to talk about a piece of art: the play. No need to get specific yet, no brainstorming or problem-solving. Just share your feelings about the text, and ask what excites, intrigues, and fascinates the designer.

Bring some images that you associate with the play. Photographs, paintings, or anything that evokes an emotional quality you receive from the script. These are illustrations of your taste. Ask the designer to bring the same. Nothing literal yet: you are trying to use images to capture a feeling and to generate a discussion about the *emotional life* of the play. The subsequent discussion of the image and how it does or does not connect with the text is a way to understand the designer's thought process and a way to share your tastes with each other.

By conducting the meeting this way, you are approximating a collaboration. How do you respond to this image? How does it make you feel? Does some element of the image—the color, the mood, the composition of its contents, etc.—conjure the world of the play? Why or why not? So much of your process with a set designer will be looking at things together: how you do that as a team in this context will help you understand what a future collaboration might feel like.

After looking at images, lead the meeting toward more concrete questions. What is an ideal process for them? How fast or slowly do they like to work? Do they spend a long time in the brainstorming phase, or do they move quickly to drawings? How often do they like to meet with a director throughout the process? How often do they like to watch rehearsals? At this point the theater should have given you a production calendar: do they have scheduling conflicts? Ask them to tell you about a process they loved and why: does that experience sound similar to how you like to work?

Reflect on how you suspect this process will unfold and see if it aligns with how this designer prefers to work. If they work slowly, could that be a logistical problem? If they work quickly, will a steady flow of rewrites mean they will have to make constant changes? Do you like to know what the set will be well before rehearsals begin so you can plan accordingly, or do you prefer to learn more about the design as you work with actors? Cross-reference your style of working and the needs of this particular project with what the designer shares with you. Articulate any concerns about how their approach may conflict: better to voice them now when they can be discussed openly and without any looming deadlines.

Lights

A lighting designer is responsible for the design of the production's lighting and the creation of the light plot (a drawing of the lighting instruments and their location in the space), for overseeing the hanging and focusing of those instruments, and for the building of light cues during the tech process. They will work with Production and General Management to fit the design within financial and logistical parameters.

What is more difficult to talk about than light? Light is like pure emotion: almost impossible to put to words. Before you discuss light itself, begin with a conversation about the play, just as you did with the set designer, and again share images to prompt a conversation. Notice the language the designer uses, and then ask them to use an image to describe what they mean. Two people can have very different ideas of how the word "mysterious" could look, for example, so you must pair words with images to see if you and the designer are in alignment. Any conversation that does not use both language and image will not teach you if you are compatible artists.

Discuss style, mood, and tone, and also pace and rhythm. Lights change and move over time like music. Even one long, unchanging light cue is an artistic decision about the shape of the story. Ask them to describe the emotional journey of the play as they imagine it, and if there are multiple scenes or locations, discuss how those transitions might look or feel. Remember that light is not only visual, it has an enormous impact on momentum and story: be sure to understand their perspective on both.

A lighting designer's process is singular because they not only use the text as the foundation on which to create their work, they also use the set design. Their task is to paint with light, and the set is their canvas. Learn in advance if the set and lighting designer have worked together or know each other (and like each other), and if you suspect they will be a good aesthetic fit. A set designer will share all of their drawings with the lighting designer, will provide locations for lighting instruments, and will engage in conversation with them about elements like color and texture. Set and lights will be working together closely throughout the process, so as you build your team, be as mindful of their relationship with each other as you are about your relationship with them both.

Sound

A sound designer is responsible for the sonic life of the show. That includes building cues like phones ringing or offstage noise, ambient or abstract sound, music played during scenes or in transition, designing the sound system, deciding whether or not to use microphones on the actors or in the space, and creating a sound plot (a drawing of what type of the speakers, microphones, and other equipment will be needed and where they should be located). They may provide cues for the rehearsal process, they will oversee the placement of sound equipment and a sound balance: a session in the space where every speaker is prepared for tech rehearsals. During tech, the sound designer will build cues, set volume levels, and adjust them for timing. A sound designer may create original music for a production, but that is a different creative position.

Like light, music and sound are so emotionally powerful because they conjure feelings we have no words for. Because of this, your meeting with a sound designer will mimic the one you had with your lighting designer. Begin with the play, listening to their thoughts and reactions. Even though you are discussing sound, bring images anyway: any ways in which you can make such an abstract topic concrete (even by way of pointing to pictures and describing them) will teach you how the designer thinks, how they use language to articulate their taste, and can serve as prompts for discussion. As you did with images, bring sonic examples to listen to together. Make sure you have multiple options and ideas. Two people can hear the same song, for example, and what appeals to them can be difficult to describe. With many examples of music or sound, you are sharing and discussing a number of options, and your conversation will be less about what you did and didn't like about a particular song and more about connections between them. By comparing songs and discussing how they are and are not in emotional conversation with one another, you can understand whether there is a shared language and sensibility between you.

Costumes

A costume designer is responsible for the design and creation of everything that is worn by the acting company. They purchase or build what each character will wear onstage, they meet with the cast during the rehearsal process for a series of fittings, in which the actors try on the costumes and creative decisions will be made about style and storytelling, as well as technical decisions about measurements and fit. The costume designer will attend tech rehearsals to see the cast onstage and under light. They will then make any artistic or technical adjustments accordingly.

In addition to discussing the play, tone, and style of the world with a costume designer, you must also discuss in detail the characters that inhabit it. Of all of your collaborators, it is the costume designer who must think most about every role as well as the actor who will be playing it. After a discussion of the play and the sharing of images, ask the designer questions about who they feel the characters are: their style, their taste, their class. How well they take care of themselves, how modest or how vain, how self-aware or how oblivious. Speak of the characters as though they are real people: what do you both think of them? Very often the costume designer will be hired before the production has been cast, so you can focus this conversation only on the character: there is not yet a person to dress.

Pay attention to how the designer talks about their process. The costume designer will have an intimate relationship with the cast because of fittings, and because choosing what clothes an actor will wear onstage can be a very vulnerable process. Do you trust this designer to be kind, patient, and respectful with the cast? You will not attend these fittings, so you must have confidence that the designer has the attitude and approach you want for the company.

This meeting can be an exciting challenge, as it will ask you to speak in detail about the characters in a way you haven't yet had the opportunity. This sharing of ideas and observations can help you clarify your thoughts and have a positive impact on your casting process. The clearer and more specific you can be in this meeting about who you think the characters are and how you imagine them in the world of the play, the better you may understand them in advance of auditions.

Other Designers and Collaborative Hiring

There will be other artists on the project, some of whom will be on producing team's staff, some who will be hired by the designer, and others who will be hired "by committee." This last group could be video designers, puppeteers, composers, magicians, props fabricators, wig designers, or make-up artists. Video or projections are part of the scenic design of a play: does the director hire the video designer, does the set designer, or do they find and interview them together? Does a composer choose the sound designer, or does the sound designer choose the composer?

There is no "correct" sequence of events for these scenarios. You must build your team in the order of how it best serves your creative process. If original music is your priority, then hire the composer first and let that collaboration teach you both what you are looking for in a sound designer. Ask yourself if projections are the most prominent visual element of your production or one piece of a larger environment your set designer will create. Always be transparent with designers about who you have already hired: they will want to know who is involved, and they will learn about your priorities by the order in which they are approached. A set designer, for example, may not be interested in working on a piece in which the creation of projections is already underway. Let your artistic priorities guide these decisions, and remain honest with your prospective colleagues so they can make informed decisions about whether or not they want to be involved with the project.

Fight and Intimacy Directors and Dialect Coaches

A fight director is responsible for any staged physical interaction that creates the illusion of violence and has the potential to put the performers at any type of risk to themselves and to each other. In collaboration with the director, the fight director will stage moments of violence, train the actors to perform these choreographed sequences, and teach them the appropriate movements, behaviors, signals, and safety mechanisms to play these moments in a safe, convincing, and repeatable way.

An intimacy director is responsible for the creation and choreography of any staged physical interaction between two or more actors that will simulate any intimate contact. They will create a code of conduct between collaborators for safe and open communication. In collaboration with the director and the cast, the intimacy director will build a set of behaviors, actions, and movements that will be agreed upon by all involved and then staged in a way that is safe, comfortable, and repeatable.

A dialect or vocal coach is responsible for the accuracy and dramaturgical appropriateness of the company's speech. They teach accent or dialect work, support actors with their breath, projection, enunciation, and oversee all technical or creative concerns surrounding how an actor speaks.

As an audience member, you have probably witnessed a moment of intimacy, a flash of violence, or an accent that broke the illusion of the play. It is easy to blame the actor, but very often the problem is a lack of seamless work between the director and their collaborators. The actor's incongruous performance is the end result of a gap between two different directorial tastes and styles. Your goal is to find partners who you feel so aligned with that it will be impossible for an audience to know they're watching the work of two different artists. A fight director, an intimacy coordinator, or a dialect coach should have their own ways of working and their own point of view, but the end result should be so seamless with the rest of the production that their contributions will be indistinguishable from the whole.

Revisit your pre-production lists and identify what you think the production requires. Do you anticipate the need for accent work? Is there violence? Are you performing in a large theater that will require strong voices?

During the interview, ask about their process, specifically their style with actors. These colleagues will shape and guide the most emotionally charged and vulnerable moments of the production. The safety and leadership they provide to the company will be critical. Do they seem to be a natural fit with the rehearsal environment you want to cultivate? What kind of energy do they bring to the meeting? Are they strict, serious, funny, disorganized, eager, relaxed? Which do you want in the rehearsal room?

New plays will inevitably change during rehearsal. Moments that do not appear violent or intimate on the page may become so during the process. The writer may add a moment that requires a fight or intimacy director's attention very late in the process. You cannot know precisely what dialect work you may need until the casting process is complete. Hire these colleagues based on the needs of the play at the time, but pay attention to how well you fit as collaborators in general: it is possible, even likely, they will be called on to contribute in unanticipated ways.

Assistant Director

The role of the Assistant Director will be different for each project. Their duties will depend on the needs and style of the director and of the project itself. Some assistants pick up lunches, make coffee runs, and generally tend to the director's non-creative needs. Some are observers, primarily there to learn by watching. Some are note-takers and deliver information to actors, stage management, designers, and departments outside of the rehearsal room. Some are artistic partners, reflecting on the work as another pair of creative eyes there to offer a different perspective.

Think about what you need from an assistant, and what role you expect them to fill in the rehearsal process. Consider cast size and if another directorial mind and voice in the room would be useful. Think about the producing organization and the complexity of the project: maybe someone who can act as a liaison would be ideal. It's difficult to predict what a show's obstacles and challenges will be, but to the degree that you are able, let that be your guide in the hiring process.

Be transparent with prospective assistants about your expectations. Some potential assistants are happy to get coffees, while others would never. If that is the job you are offering, make that explicit: give the potential assistant enough clarity about the position so they can make an informed decision about whether they want to participate. What do *they* want to do? What are *their* expectations for the job? What do *they* hope to learn from this opportunity? Ask them, and use that information to help make your choice.

Dramaturg

A dramaturg is a position that eludes clear definition. We can accurately call them academics in that they conduct research, work primarily with texts, and contribute to a process by being well versed in the history of an established play, its author, and the period in which it was written. We can also call them artists in that they generate ideas, ask questions, work as editors, maintain an active presence in a rehearsal room, and contribute to the creation of the production. For a new play by a living, present writer, their role will depend on the type of attention the play needs, the amount of work that will be done on the text, how they will participate in the rehearsal process, and what type of research may be useful.

In America, dramaturgs for new plays can be a rare and welcome presence. If you are lucky enough to work with one, it is likely they will be a staff member of the producing organization. If you have the chance to interview and hire one, focus on these three questions:

- How can a dramaturg help the writer?

What kind of research is necessary for the play? Where is it set (time and place), and what types of information could a dramaturg provide to inform the writer's work? Does historical, geographical, or cultural accuracy matter to the play? Does the writer want or need that type of support? When is the dramaturg entering the process, and what is necessary and useful at that point in the play's development?

- How can they contribute to your work with the text?

Is there still significant work to be done on the script? What larger questions still need attention, and can another point of view help you find answers? Can a dramaturg work closely with the writer while your focus is elsewhere during the process? Can a dramaturg work closely with you as you analyze the text in anticipation of design meetings and rehearsals?

- How can they contribute to the rehearsal process?

As your attention gets pulled in multiple directions during the process, would it be useful to have an additional creative mind thinking primarily about the text? The deeper you get into the rehearsal process, the more your attention will be focused on performance. Ideas can build on one another naturally, but this way of working can occasionally lead to a drift from authorial intent. A dramaturg, who pays close attention to the script while the production takes shape, can be a valuable asset to remind, refresh, and guide you and the entire creative team back to the text if your rehearsal discoveries have pulled you away from it.

Use these questions to help clarify for yourself what you need from a dramaturg, then meet with candidates. Some dramaturgs are more experienced with research, others with new work, others with being an additional creative voice in the room. Be transparent about what the job will entail, and describe what you anticipate the process will be like. Ask the candidate how they like to work, what kind of processes they find most fulfilling, and what role or roles are they most comfortable playing. A great dramaturg will illuminate a text in ways you couldn't have imagined: during this interview, do you feel they have the potential to expand your understanding of the play? More insight, more wisdom, more ideas … this is new play dramaturgy at its most successful.

Stage Management

A stage manager's duties include:
- Creating a rehearsal, tech, and performance calendar
- Scheduling and organizing rehearsals
- Coordinating call times for actors, including fittings, as well as call times for necessary artists like fight/intimacy/dialect work, etc.
- Running the rehearsal room, keeping the director and company on task and on schedule
- Tracking script changes
- Notating blocking
- Writing rehearsal and performance reports
- Acting as liaison between the rehearsal room and all design, technical, and administrative departments
- Running tech rehearsals
- Calling cues in performance
- Rehearsing understudies
- Maintaining the staging and acting performances after the show is "frozen"
- Overseeing the creative integrity of the production throughout the run

This list is only an introduction to everything a production stage manager will do.

A stage manager is the central nervous system of a production. Every change, every decision, every choice travels through their department. They are your counterpart in the process, and your equal in the production's creation and success.

There was a time when the director and stage manager were more closely connected. As theater became more technologically complex, the stage manager's job expanded to include overseeing crews, calling increasingly elaborate cues, and managing the many disparate specialists responsible for the production's creation. Even though the roles have drifted apart over time, you must remember that your and the stage manager's positions constantly overlap: if you are an artist who must think logistically, they are a manager who must think like an artist.

Your ideal stage manager should be complementary to your creative and leadership style. Reflect on your own process: do you struggle to remain organized and on time in rehearsal? Are you able to prioritize? What kind of

ASSEMBLING THE CREATIVE TEAM

tone do you prefer in a rehearsal room: more casual or more rigorous? What atmosphere will be best for this play? Anticipate the needs of this production and imagine the best type of manager to oversee them. Do you expect there to be many cues and that the show will be challenging to call? Is the play an emotionally delicate one and will require an empathic presence? Are there children in the company, or older actors? Will there be a lot of rewrites that will need impeccable organization?

Ask candidates about their style: how they like to run a rehearsal room and a tech rehearsal, how they prefer to give notes to an actor after the show has opened. You need to know if the stage manager is compatible with you and with the process you think this play will demand. They can be very different from you in terms of style and skill. In fact, that might be ideal: if you get so into the work you lose track of time, you want a stage manager who is strict about staying on task. You are seeking someone you can work well with, not someone who is exactly like you. How do your skills, approaches, and personalities complement one another?

The stage manager will be responsible for maintaining your production after opening. Do you believe this candidate can watch a performance and see it through your eyes? Do you trust them to give actors notes that will help them preserve the integrity of your vision? It can be easy to interview stage managers while thinking primarily about rehearsals and tech. Remember that they must be creative thinkers and communicators as well: they will speak for you and your work long after you're gone.

8
CASTING

The number of books written about how to audition could fill a library. How to *run* an audition, however, is far less discussed, but equally important.

An audition is a job interview in which the applicants (actors) will perform a short section of the play for the creative team's (writer, director, and producer) consideration. It is also a mock rehearsal where the director and actor will work together on the text to learn how they communicate. The more organized and professional an audition room, the better work you'll see from the actor. If an audition process is disorganized or disrespectful, you will be putting the actor at a disadvantage. They won't be able to do their best work, and ultimately it is the production that will suffer the consequences: you'll wind up casting the actor who weathers a difficult process best, not necessarily the one who is the strongest actor for the role. The better organized an audition process, the stronger the work, the more informed the casting choices, the more successful the production.

The Casting Director

A Casting Director oversees the audition process. Their duties include:

- Creating and circulating casting breakdowns
- Vetting applicants and collecting headhots/resumes
- Contacting actors and/or their representatives to arrange audition appointments
- Providing the applicants with sides and other audition materials
- Acting as the liaison between the actor and the producing team
- Scheduling appointments
- Hiring readers
- Arranging an audition space
- Keeping the process professional and organized

All of these logistics could lead a director to think a casting director is a managerial position; however, a director should think of the casting director as a specialized dramaturg. They read the play with an emphasis on character to understand the behaviors, motivations, complexities, nuances, and idiosyncrasies of each role. Their goal is to apply that knowledge to the audition process. The more rigorous they are when reading the play and contemplating the nature of the characters, the more useful they will be in generating promising ideas and making astute creative decisions. It will be your job to guide their reading so they can proceed with a clear understanding of your vision.

While casting decisions will ultimately be made by you, the writer, and the producer, it is the casting director who will decide which actors will get appointments to audition. In this way, they have an enormous impact on the process: curatorial decisions about which actors are appropriate for a role will happen well before you see anyone read. Ask the casting director to read the play and schedule a time for you and the writer to meet with them before they begin their work (the writer must be present to share their thoughts). Engage with them as you would a designer or any creative collaborator: start with an open dialogue about the play, then get more specific. Pay close attention to the ways in which your tastes and opinions on each character align and the ways in which they do not. Discuss those differences in an effort to reach an understanding: if the casting director has a different perspective on the play or a role, they will choose actors who will match their point of view, not yours. Have a conversation about each role, even the smaller ones. Every character is being brought to life for the first time, so no role is too small and nothing should be assumed. Who does and does not get an audition appointment will depend on the clarity of this meeting: you must be as thorough and comprehensive as possible and feel certain you have been heard and understood.

Offering Actors from Readings and Workshops

It is possible you have already heard an actor read a part and would like to make them an offer, or you and the writer have always had a specific actor in mind for a role and don't feel they need to audition. Before you make an offer, consider the following:

- Whether or not you have ever heard the actor read the role. Imagination is a powerful thing: just because you can picture how perfect an actor would be, or you know the writer created the role with this person in mind, the reality will inevitably be different. Casting an actor without

- their ever having read it aloud can put both you and the actor at a disadvantage if the fantasy and reality do not match.
- Whether or not the producing organization agrees. If they have heard the actor in a reading or workshop, that makes the decision easier. If they haven't, they may want the actor to audition, regardless of your excitement or certainty about them.
- Whether you are confusing familiarity with "rightness." Are you positive this is the perfect actor to realize the role, or are you so comfortable with an actor that you do not want to investigate further? Are you nervous you will not find a better option? If you suspect your decisions are being influenced by familiarity and not rigor, host auditions for the role: that is the only way to proceed with total confidence.
- Whether you can separate the circumstances of development from a production. Some actors thrive in readings or a workshop: that does not guarantee you will be good collaborators in a rehearsal room. It can be uncomfortable to ask an actor you've developed the play with to audition alongside actors who have no history with the piece, but it is always preferable to cast with clarity. Seeing an actor audition that you have already heard in the role will offer you the ability to hear them in the same conditions as other actors, and to compare their choices. This perspective can be necessary to make informed decisions.

Offer-Only Actors

If an actor is "offer only," it means they will not audition for a role but will entertain an offer. Usually, this is an actor who feels—or their representation feels—their work is well known enough that auditions are no longer necessary for them to get work.

If you and the writer are familiar with an offer-only actor's work and feel certain they are the most right for the role, make an offer. If you find yourself in a situation where casting a famous actor is necessary to elevate the profile of the project, you may feel pressured to make offers to actors you don't know. When the play is new, offers are riskier. This is because nothing is known about the role in performance. Offers are never without an element of chance, but matching a well-known actor to a well-known role is different than bringing a character to life for the first time.

When faced with a decision about an offer-only actor, you will have three options:

- Host a reading for the actor, which can double as an audition by another name.

- Ask if the actor will meet one-on-one to discuss the play and the role.
- Make an offer.

A reading will teach you how the actor sounds in the role, but not how you might collaborate. A meeting is the opposite: you may get a sense of how you would work together but not know how the actor sounds in the role. Some offer-only actors will only do a reading or take a meeting after they've been made the offer, in which case it is the actor auditioning you.

When possible, cast actors who are willing to audition. The amount of changes to a new play in process are far too great, and the ways in which a role will grow during rehearsals too unknown. Making offers exposes you and your production to many unknown factors.

Casting Breakdowns

The first step in an audition process will be the creation of a casting breakdown: a brief description of each character that will be shared publicly. It is a job description for actors, agents, and managers to decide if they want to apply. It is also a way for actors to understand the director's interpretation of the role as they prepare for the audition. The breakdown is your description of the character, not a description of the type of actor you would like to play it. This is a subtle but critical distinction: the task is to describe the attributes, behaviors, and personality traits of the *character* so actors can decide for themselves if they feel they are a potential fit. A breakdown says: "This is who I think the character is." It is then the actor's decision whether or not they agree and believe they are the right actor to play it.

Begin with a list of descriptive adjectives. Then edit them down into one sentence that you feel fully describes the character. You cannot assume an actor will see the role as you do, so offering your point of view will help them prepare. Because it's likely the entire script will not be available to applicants (they cannot pick it up in a bookstore), breakdowns are the actors' only introduction to the play and to your vision. Be brief, succinct, and careful with your word choices. Language that is playable is best: ask yourself if the words you are using might be useful for an actor preparing alone. Your casting director will help you edit them, and ask the writer to contribute, too. A clear description will not only supply actors with the tools they need to prepare; it will also serve as a guide to the casting director as they receive audition requests and make decisions about who will get an appointment.

Choosing Sides

A "side" is a short section of the play an actor is asked to perform during an audition. A director will choose a part of a scene that prominently features the role the actor is auditioning for. It should provide the actor with an opportunity to show the creative team their perspective on the character through their choices. A director's task when choosing sides is to provide the actor with ample material to express their point of view. A side must also provide a moment or scenario that the director and actor can discuss, change, and experiment with as collaborators. A thoughtfully chosen side will have an enormous impact on the success of the audition for both actor and director.

Often, a director will select two sides from different moments in the play. This is to give the actor a chance to show their "range," or ability to play different qualities, emotions, or stakes. Always keep sides short: no more than four pages total, no matter how many different sections you want them to prepare. Asking an actor to prepare more than that is a huge time commitment and a short, carefully selected moment will teach you more than any large section of the play. You want the actor to think as deeply as possible about the role, so the less material they have to consider, the more likely they are to be thorough. Because the sides are also a prompt for collaboration, it will be easier for you to try a small section a few different ways than to make sweeping adjustments to an entire scene.

Avoid sections with many characters, with a lot of action or stage direction, or any physical activity. You want to encourage the actor to think about who this person is, how they think, how they feel, how they move through the world. You also want them focusing on the text and how they speak it (that is certainly what the writer will be listening for). You don't want them working to understand how a scene could work in an audition or how to "stage" a complicated moment in this context. The side should encourage an actor's creativity and imagination: clear away any obstacles that could confuse or divert their attention.

Choose sides that allow the actor to excel at the role's necessary skills. If the part is funny and requires excellent timing, you must supply the actor with a side that encourages them to show their abilities. If the text calls for an actor to play multiple roles, make sure you see them read a selection of each part. You must be certain an actor has the skills needed to perform the job effectively. Make it easy for them to show you their best work.

Choose sections that encourage the actor to be emotionally available. An audition is not a place to learn if an actor can cry on command or fly into a murderous rage. That will teach you very little about the actor beyond their ability to approximate those emotions on cue. There is no need to ask them to prepare the most intense emotional moments: look for sections of the play when the character is open, vulnerable, revealing of their "true" selves somehow. Is there a moment in which the character's public mask slips and they can be entirely themselves? A moment of honesty will teach you more about an actor's alignment with a character than any emotional pyrotechnics ever could.

Look for moments when a character must change, when they are given new information that upends their point of view: these are the types of scenarios that can give an actor a lot to work with as they prepare, a lot to play in the audition, and a lot for you to experiment with as collaborators. Providing them with a moment of change will encourage the actor to make strong choices and will give you a clear prompt to play with together as you learn how you communicate. A vague adjustment to an actor's performance can leave you both in murky terrain: the actor will wonder if they are doing what you've asked for, you are wondering if you've been clear, and you both will wonder if you are good potential collaborators. Choose sides that you know in advance you can play with: it will put both you and the actor in the best position to succeed.

A Note on Memorization

Actors will want to know if they should memorize the sides. That is a question of the director's taste, but in my experience, it is not worth the effort. They may rush to learn their lines and then paraphrase in the audition, and you will not have time to undo those choices. You and the writer need to hear the text verbatim in order to make an informed decision. On the other hand, the virtue of an actor being off-book is that you can see the actor fully present: attention off the page and on the reader. If the sides are short, an actor can be active and alive in the space while still consulting their pages. That scenario is preferable to an actor pressuring themselves to memorize and making mistakes in the process. You want an actor thinking artistically and analytically as they prepare: memorization is a task they should not concern themselves with.

Audition Space

The location needs to be suitable for a job interview. Consider what you will need in the space to do your work. Do you need a lot of room to move? How many people do you expect to be in the space watching the actor: will it be crowded? What about the area outside: can the auditions be heard through the door? Is there space for actors to wait comfortably? Often, the room will be chosen for you in advance, so articulating your needs should be done well before the process begins.

Scheduling

Begin the audition process by leaving enough time to conduct a thorough search. As was the case with casting a reading, you do not want to start so far in advance that you risk losing actors to other jobs, nor so late that you feel hurried. Strike a balance of timing, and be mindful you don't begin a process while the script is in the midst of a large revision. A large rewrite can effect a character breakdown: only start a casting process when you have confidence the recent draft is definitive enough to share with actors. All readings and workshops should cease while casting is underway. Actors should not be asked to participate in development while they (and others) are being asked to audition. Overlapping those steps can make the actors not involved in development feel they are at a disadvantage, and those actors who are in development as though they are undergoing a long audition.

The casting director will schedule auditions by timed appointments: every actor will be given either ten, fifteen, twenty minutes, etc. Think about how long you will want to work with each actor, and also if you want or need time in between each appointment. A lack of communication about timing can lead to a logistical headache: actors waiting forever to be seen, you rushing to try to catch up, and both of you learning very little about a potential collaboration. Casting directors will err on the side of shorter appointments so you can see as many actors as possible, but that system only works if you have enough time to evaluate all the actors respectfully and properly, in a focused and unhurried way. Be honest with your casting director in advance about the time you will need.

Think also about how many hours you can do at a time. Auditions are mentally exhausting and overstimulating for you and a writer. It can be difficult to remember everyone you saw and even the most copious notes may not be helpful after a long day. Don't put actors at a disadvantage because you're exhausted. If it is possible to do shorter days over a longer period of time, do.

Readers

A reader is an actor who has been hired by the casting director to serve as the auditioning actor's scene partner. They will perform the other role(s) on the side.

While the reader is a part of the team running the auditions, they are first and foremost an artist who has been hired to act and must be treated as such. A director's focus may be so drawn to the auditioning actor that they may not engage with the reader, which is a lost opportunity. Sides are scenes, which means both actors need your attention. Treat the readers as another artistic collaborator: the more confident they are in performance and clear on their objectives, the stronger the auditioning actor's work will be. Like any artist, their choices are not fixed: offer suggestions and adjustments to the reader's performance when you feel it would be helpful.

No two actors will read the scene the same way, so encourage the reader to avoid repeating their choices. Encourage them to respond to the energy they get from each auditioner, which will in turn help you see the applicant's choices with more clarity.

Arranging the Space

There is storytelling in how you arrange an audition room. Are you, the casting director, and the writer lined up behind a table, or are you free to get up from your chair as you work with actors? Where is the reader located, and do you feel that location will make the actors most comfortable? Do you want to provide the actors with space to move, are they positioned at an appropriate distance from you, and do they have anywhere to sit if they'd like? These questions might seem insignificant, but they can have a profound effect on the actor's work: consider all your options to make the space most actor-friendly.

Speak with your casting director in advance about how many people will be in attendance. A smaller room is always more comfortable for an actor, so the fewer people watching, the better. Does the assistant director need to be there? What about the casting director's assistant? Does the producer need to be present? It's amazing how quickly an audition session can become crowded: be as strict as possible about keeping the room intimate.

Beginning the Audition

As the director, you set the tone. Lead by example: no whispering or talking while the actor is working. Give everyone your undivided attention and focus. Make sure all phones and devices are off and put away. Treat every applicant with great respect and dignity.

- Welcome the actor and introduce everyone in the room. Auditions can be intimidating: do not make the actor guess or wonder who is watching their work.
- Give them time to settle in. Ask them how they are, thank them for coming in, provide you both with a moment to connect.
- Ask if they have any questions about the sides or the character. Unlike established plays, there is no way for them to do any research. Technical

questions about the text—pronunciation, for example, or the action that precedes the start of the side—are welcome, but anything more complex should wait. The first read is your chance to see the actor's choices. Asking complicated questions can signal to you that the actor would prefer to do it the way they think you want, which is not the goal. Assure them there will be time to discuss later, then begin.

Observing an Audition

The word "audition" comes from the Latin "audire," like "audio" and "auditory": it means "to hear." An actor's primary task is to speak the text in a way that can be understood: an audition, then, is primarily about listening. How does the actor speak the text, and what can it teach a director about their interpretation and understanding of the role? Almost everything you need to learn about their "rightness" for the role will come from your ears, not your eyes.

I use the word "rightness" in place of measurements like "good" or "bad." Asking yourself if an actor is more or less "right" is a question that will lead you back to the text and to your taste and vision. It is about proximity to your understanding of the role, not about an actor's talent. An actor can be objectively "good" but not "right" for the role as you envision it. "Right" can mean "close," in that the actor—their presentation, demeanor, behaviors, choices with the text, and understanding of the role—feels *closest to your vision*. Close, however, is not the same as perfect. When a director says an actor is "perfect," what they may mean is that the actor is "perfectly" aligned with what they had in mind. Perfection, though, is not the auditioning actor's goal. They are autonomous artists: their job is not to guess correctly what the director is imagining. They are creating a work of art based on the text (just like you), and their different observations, tastes, and choices are what will make their work unique (just like you). While it's inevitable that you will compare an actor's audition to what you had in mind, remain open to the ways in which they make different choices, how they expand your understanding of who the character is and what the role could be. While "right" and "close" are valid ways to consider an actor, it is their creativity and singular point of view that will deepen a performance beyond anything you could have imagined. Casting only those actors who seem most "perfect" may be a safe choice, but probably not be the most interesting.

Release what you think the actor should or shouldn't be doing and take in what you see and hear. These are the same tools of awareness you used when you first read the play: remain open and notice how you react and how their performance makes you feel.

A few questions you might ask yourself:

- Can you understand the actor in a literal sense? Can you hear the words and follow the basic logic of what they're saying?
- Can you understand the narrative trajectory? Does the actor seem to understand the character's circumstances and convey them in a truthful way?
- Do you sense an emotional comprehension? Simply put: do you think to yourself "they get it"?
- Does this actor's way of speaking align with the music of the text? Notice pace, timing, pauses, rhythm, and intensity: the tools all humans use to convey emotional meaning with language.

As the actor works, jot down some notes to use as a reminder to yourself. Do not try to capture every thought or observation: you can give yourself time between auditions to note your reflections on each actor's work. These are just flashes of feelings and fleeting reactions you may not remember when the moment has passed.

Adjustments

After the actor has finished, begin your work session. Your task is to try a few brief experiments with the goal of understanding how you communicate and collaborate. You are trying to learn how well you understand one another, not how well the actor can mimic what you say.

Compliment the actor on what you liked and what you want them to "keep" for the next read. Asking an actor to hang onto something they were playing will allow you to see how aware and in control they are of their performance. Repetition is a necessary skill for a stage actor: see if the actor can repeat some of their work while incorporating changes.

Offer some adjustments. Keep the adjustments clear and playable. Use the basics: what does the character want in the scene? What are they trying to do to the other character? Offer a different tactic of getting what they want. Choose one or two adjustments that are a departure from their first read to see if they're able to stretch themselves and experiment. Try something completely different that will get them away from the version they prepared. Avoid notes that involve mood or tone: that can be difficult for an actor to achieve on the spot. You are understanding how the actor listens, so give them something playable.

As you watch the actor incorporate your adjustments, ask yourself if the actor is delivering the same performance or are you seeing new things happening? Have they managed to keep what worked from the first read? Do you feel that your ideas and suggestions were listened to and understood? Give the actor another adjustment: what happens then? Giving an actor more than one opportunity to play an adjustment will help you understand how you dialogue as collaborators.

If you have determined whether the actor is "right," "close" or in alignment with your ideas, and if you feel you can communicate well, the audition is over. Thank the actor for their time and effort and move on.

Ending the Audition

Use the time between appointments to write down your reactions and responses in more detail. Be thorough: you may think you will remember, but at the end of a long session, your memory will not be as reliable as you may think. How did you feel watching the actor perform? These are strictly emotional responses. Keep a record so you can refer to it later.

Wait until the day has ended to discuss each actor. Not only will conversations about each actor between their appointments use up valuable time, you may put the reader in an awkward position. You cannot ask for total confidentiality: maybe they know an actor who auditioned, maybe a friend will ask what was said. The appropriate approach is to remain discreet until the end of the session.

A Note on the Writer in Auditions

The writer may want to give their own direction to actors, or they may disagree with your adjustments. They will have an opportunity to see more from an actor during callbacks: the first round is for you. That your adjustments may veer far from what the writer has imagined can be confusing for them to watch, but it is a necessary part of your work. Your goal is not to show the writer a fantastic version of their scene, it is to learn how you and the actor communicate. An ideal read of a scene is a concern for another time.

Post-Audition Meeting

After the session is over, meet with the writer and casting director to decide who will be asked to return for a callback. You will be dividing applicants into three groups: those who you agree not to see again, those who you want to call back, and those who you are unsure about. Discuss every actor you saw, including those actors you feel were not right. You will learn as much by articulating why you felt someone wasn't right as you will by explaining who is ideal. Those you will and will not see again are lists that will take shape easily. Discuss anyway: do not assume you are saying "yes" or "no" for the same reasons. The third list will make up the bulk of this meeting, as disagreement is common. It can be alarming when you learn the actor you loved most the writer did not like, or vice versa. How can you have been working closely for so long and responded so differently? How can your tastes be so divergent after all of these deep conversations about the play? Does the writer not understand their own characters? Have you misunderstood the play all along?

These meetings are another opportunity to clarify and articulate your vision. Explain what exactly you did or did not respond to, and ask the writer to do the same. These moments provide a wealth of new information about how your tastes apply to the work of other artists. You are not trying to convince the writer to see the actors as you do, you are simply articulating what you noticed, and how you responded.

If you cannot reach a consensus, bring the actor in for a callback. See them again through the eyes of the writer, or share with the writer what you saw. If you are unsure about any actor, see them again. Don't overwhelm yourself by bringing back too many people, and do not waste an actor's time if you feel confident you will not be casting them, but give them every opportunity to earn the job.

A Note on Directing Auditions

Auditions can be as stressful for the director as they are for the actor. You have a limited amount of time to watch a performance with your full attention, remaining open to receive the work, while simultaneously preparing adjustment ideas. You must give spontaneous, precise, and active notes, and you must be certain these adjustments will illuminate your potential collaboration and their rightness for the role. All while the writer and casting director watch you work. There can be moments when it seems unclear who, exactly, is under the microscope: you or the actor.

It is possible the adjustments you gave the actor were not as effective as you had hoped. It happens, so don't rely only on your memory: ask your "audience" what they saw and if they observed a miscommunication, give the actor another chance: it is unfair to expect your every adjustment to be brilliant, or for an actor to understand a less than ideal note.

Callbacks

Callbacks are a subsequent series of auditions in which a smaller group of actors are brought back to work in longer sessions that are more similar to a rehearsal atmosphere. You and your team have already agreed these actors are technically and artistically "right," and you have surmised they are strong potential collaborators. Now you are working with the actors again in order to determine who will be cast in each role.

Before you begin, review the list of returning actors with the writer. Decide in advance what you both need to see from each in order to make a final decision. Your questions or reservations about each actor will vary, so discuss what adjustments you'd like to try before callbacks begin. Your goal is to arrive with a worklist tailored to each actor and what you need to see. You want to finish callbacks with absolute clarity: the worst case scenario is to work with an actor again and still have no idea if you should make them an offer for the production.

New Sides

In addition to having the actors prepare the original sides, select a new one. It should also be very short and should highlight what you need to see that you feel you haven't yet. You do not need to give every actor the same callback side: each actor can be given a different one depending on what you're hoping to learn. A callback side should provide the actor with an opportunity to go deeper into the psyche of the role. That will give you a stronger sense of their intellectual and emotional alignment with the character. If every actor you have called back is right in some way, investigating emotional depth and connection is often the answer to who is the *most* right.

Directing Callbacks

A main difference between auditions and callbacks, besides the amount of time you will have with each actor, is the presence of the producer or members of the producing team. If callbacks go well, offers will be made based on these sessions, so a representative of the producing body will want to be there.

Begin by reading a side—the new or old—to reacquaint yourself with the actor's take on the role (do not rely on how you remember it). Get up on your feet, start and stop the scene as you would in rehearsal, offer adjustments to the reader if needed, and answer any questions the work may bring up. Because you have more time, encourage discussion. Ask them to articulate the virtues and challenges of playing the role, and let their observations influence additional adjustments. You and the actor are working to reach a place where your questions about their rightness have been answered and reservations addressed. Learn everything you need to in order to cast them with confidence.

Once you've worked with the actor, and once you feel you've incorporated the necessary adjustments, ask the actor to play the scene straight through so that everyone watching the callback can see one clean, complete performance of the side. After the actor has finished, ask them to step outside, along with the reader. Ask the group if they have seen all they need or if they have any additional questions or adjustments. Do not assume because your questions have been answered that is true for everyone. Release the actor only when everyone in the room feels decided. If reservations remain, bring the actor back into the room for another round of adjustments, focusing specifically on addressing them. Once everyone feels confident they have seen enough to make a decision, the callback is over.

Casting Decisions

Casting will affect your production as much as any decision you will make, so do not rush, and do not succumb to outside pressure or influence. Begin this meeting by removing those actors that the group can agree are no longer under consideration. Lay out the headshots of the top choices for each role, and begin to imagine them as an ensemble. Who might fit best with whom? You are not casting each role in a void, you are creating a company. Different creative energies can be exciting, but everyone in the cast must feel like they're of the same world. Often, when an artistic team is torn between two actors who are very right for a role, it is how each actor relates to the emerging ensemble that a consensus can be reached.

Producers will expect to have a vote in who gets cast, and everyone may have a different top choice that they feel passionately about. A director must remember in these moments that while they did not write the play, nor are they producing, it is their job to create and oversee the production and it is their responsibility to elicit the strongest possible performances. No one will be working with the actors as closely as you will be, so your confidence in them and your faith that you will collaborate successfully is paramount. You must work with the actors you feel are the best suited to your production, full stop. This is a situation in which you must get what you want.

One way to resolve conflicts is by bringing the group's attention back to the question of who is "right." Rightness can be argued by citing the text and by using specifics from the callback to make your case. Who is "best" is purely subjective, difficult to argue, and often personal. Conflict among the creative team is rare if the process has been thoughtful and thorough, and if you and the writer have prepared the callbacks well. If you cannot reach a consensus or remain unsure about a decision, give yourself time to contemplate and understand where any reservations lie. The impact of these choices is too monumental to rush or to finalize without time for reflection.

Offers

When consensus has been reached and you are ready to proceed, the casting director will call the actor or their representatives to make them the official offer. An offer is not an acceptance: there will be conversations about schedules, contracts, and other logistics before an actor will become a definitive "yes." This is an exciting moment in the process but also a potentially confusing one: just because the actor has worked hard to get the role doesn't automatically mean they do not have a conflicting television commitment, or a family wedding on opening night. The producer will bring those conflicts to you for your consideration, but in the meantime, wait until these issues are resolved before you contact the actors directly. The casting director will tell you when an actor is officially on board, at which point you can reach out. If you choose, once an actor has accepted, you can also reach out to those actors who did not get cast to thank them for their time and effort.

When making offers, prepare second and third choices. Never assume an actor will say yes: they pass, they have second thoughts, they have conflicts, they drop out, they choose a different project. As you discuss actors with the group, agree on who you would offer to next, should your first choice not accept. Have this list ready so the process can proceed quickly should you need to move on.

Accepted Offers before Rehearsal

The period of time between when an offer is accepted and when rehearsals begin can be days, weeks, or months. What kind of contact or relationship should a director have with the company during that time? Some directors choose none, others will host a reading so the cast can meet and everyone can hear the play, and others meet with each actor individually to begin a dialogue about the role, the play, and the upcoming process. While hosting a reading is wise whenever possible, individual meetings are ideal for a new play.

Plan to meet with the actors as soon as they have accepted. An actor will have thoughts, questions, ideas, and concerns, and will seek to address them on their own if you aren't available to offer your support and perspective. Choices about the role will be made by the actor well before rehearsals begin: make sure you participate in that work.

These meetings should be professional but informal. They are an opportunity to get to know one another as collaborators and artists, a chance to share your ideas about the play, and to hear their thoughts and questions. Not only are you sharing your vision, you are providing a history of the play's development and preparing the actor for what the process might look like. Do you expect a lot of rewrites, for example? Letting an actor know will allow them to prepare with more clarity, and therefore more confidence. This meeting is also a chance to share your style as a director: how you approach a text, how you like to oversee a process, what kind of questions interest you. Based on this meeting, the actor can come into the rehearsal room with an understanding of both your perspective and your approach.

Suggest a few thoughts for the actor to consider while they read the play on their own. Share your vision of the world and some ideas for your production so they can read with an understanding of the tone you are aiming to achieve. Prepare some questions to share with the actor: what would you like them to be curious about? Your questions during this meeting are prompts for their contemplation in the days and weeks ahead. They are meant to serve as guides as they begin to imagine the play and their place inside of it.

You chose the audition materials based only on how useful they were to that process, but those sides are an actor's entire introduction to the play and to the role: they may place a great deal of meaning on them. It is also possible you offered notes in the audition that were appropriate for that context, but aren't relevant to how you see the role in production. I have heard actors in rehearsal say "In the callback you told me I should play it like …" months after the audition process was over. An actor will remember these adjustments and may consider them definitive, not experimental. Sitting down with an actor early will allow you to clear away audition work that is not relevant to the next steps.

Remind each actor that a new play exists in a state of flux. Aspects of a character can be rethought or rewritten between the audition process and the first rehearsal. An actor will prepare their role based on the materials available to them: what if the side that got them the role is cut from the play or drastically rewritten? That can be deeply confusing for an actor. Let them know changes are inevitable and that you will keep them up to date on any rewrites. A cast should not be reading pages they have never seen before on the first day of rehearsal: that can be disorienting on an already emotionally intense day. Continue to share any revisions and make yourself available to discuss what those changes may mean for the actor's role.

9
THE DESIGN PROCESS

The physical production will be dreamt up, developed, planned, revised, and finalized over a series of design meetings. These are either one-on-one conversations between the director and designer or a larger meeting as a group, and they begin as soon as the creative team has been assembled. The number of meetings will depend on the size and complexity of the project, your relationship with the designer, and the creative process you feel is necessary to develop the strongest design. How the meetings will be organized (one-on-one or as a group, how closely together they will be scheduled, etc.) will also depend on the project's needs. No two design processes are alike, even with designers you have worked with before.

While one-on-one meetings are useful, scheduling time for as many designers as possible to meet together, particularly as you begin the process, is ideal. Encourage them to learn from and be inspired by each other in real time, to dream and to problem solve, and to build upon one another's ideas.

A director already knows the most basic logistical concerns of an established play such as the order of scenes, number of locations, and specific design necessities: a design team can begin solving Hamlet's ghost with confidence the moment will never be rewritten or cut. A new play requires a balance of commitment and flexibility: a director and design team must work with the same effort and rigor as they would with an established play, but remain nimble enough to change and adapt as the play grows.

Emotional Fluency and Brainstorming

The first step in any design process will be to identify shared tastes, a shared perspective of the play, and a shared language to discuss it. Think of this process as a funnel of ideas. Gradually, they will become more focused, specific, and practical, but as you begin, you and your designers must remain as open as possible. This first meeting is an abstract brainstorming session: an opportunity to share all of the disparate thoughts and feelings the play conjures. The more ideas you can consider at the outset, the stronger your

THE DESIGN PROCESS

choices will be later, as time, budget, and other necessary considerations must be taken into account and the funnel narrows.

These early meetings will be a natural extension of the interview process, where you learned you have overlapping sensibilities and a shared enthusiasm for—and point of view about—the play. Begin by discussing the journey of the play in purely emotional terms: where you as the reader begins and ends, and what you feel in between. Remember that design is about movement through the piece: consider how each section of the play feels, and discuss how it feels to travel from one to the next. Postpone literal thinking and problem-solving: you are building an emotional map which will serve all your subsequent choices. Even if the play is set in a realistic space, you will have decisions to make about color, size, light, sound, and scale: those creative decisions will be based on a foundation of taste and vision.

I once worked with a set designer who wanted to meet many times at the beginning of a process. The set was the living room of an affluent young couple. Because it seemed very straightforward, I was eager to look at research and drawings, and to decide on a ground plan. The designer was resistant: we had meeting after meeting where we discussed the nature of the couple's relationship, the emotional journey of the play, and the writer's sense of claustrophobia and anxiety that was apparent on every page. After the third or fourth meeting, I could feel myself growing frustrated: it was just a living room, I thought, why are we still talking about our feelings?

The next time we met, she finally took out some paper and began to draw. In just a few minutes, we had some very promising ideas that we were both excited about, and by the end of that meeting we had a ground plan we thought captured the spirit of the play perfectly. Very few changes happened between that meeting and opening night, and the production was a success in no small part because it had a visual container that served both the technical needs and emotional heart of the play.

On another occasion, I worked with a set designer on a play set in a politician's office. The first time we met, he had already made some preliminary drawings, and the second time I was presented with a fully constructed set model. In the early days of rehearsal, the cast and I made some discoveries about the play that lead to rewrites, which in turn had a dramatic effect on the scenic design. Because the set designer and I never had any discussions about the emotional life of the play, we did not have any ideas that went deeper than our research. We had to start our work over, with very little time to do it.

Understanding a text from an emotional point of view is critical for a new play, where changes can be assured. A strong, clear grasp of how the world feels can withstand any amount of rewrites. A director and designer can return to the emotional heart of the play for inspiration, which is impervious to the addition or subtraction of a location, the changing of the time of day, or an actor's costume.

The longer you extend this period of abstract thinking, the greater your collective confidence will be when it is time to make decisions, and the easier it will be to adjust them. This is true for each designer's process: much of their work will happen in your absence, so the more attuned you are to each other's feelings about the play and the better you can communicate with them as a result of this work, the further you both can stretch your ideas, trusting that you will remain in artistic alignment.

Shared Vocabulary

Every successful design process I have ever participated in was the result of seamless communication among artists. And every unsuccessful one lacked a shared vocabulary. During these early meetings, spend time learning to understand one another.

Imagine a meeting in which one of your collaborators describes a climactic moment of the play as "Intense." You all enthusiastically agree: it *is* intense. If there is no further attempt at understanding that word, however, everyone in the meeting will proceed with their own definition, and later you will see four of five different and disconnected artistic interpretations of "intense." Finding a shared vocabulary is simple: ask your collaborators what they mean, and encourage a search for a common definition. After the designer elaborates on what "intense" means to them, you may reach a consensus that a more accurate word could be "frightening." That term is slightly more evocative of tone, but keep searching for a clearer language. The pursuit of clarity *is* the work, and that specificity will be reflected in every element of the physical production. A cohesive design relies on how well you understand one another, which is entirely reliant on both emotional consensus and a shared vocabulary as you begin your process.

Ideas, Research, and Choices

There will come a moment in your process when describing how the play feels and your reactions when reading it will no longer provide new information. This natural creative fatigue is your sign to pivot your meetings to the physical and sonic design: begin to imagine how your production will look, sound, and move.

Start by considering every possibility. Make outlandish, playful, ridiculous suggestions. Draw pictures. What seems interesting or intriguing? Hang onto it. What does not grab your attention? Throw it out. Every idea is worth investigating, nothing is set in stone. Reflect on what you find inspiring and challenge yourselves to articulate precisely why. There are no right or wrong answers, only choices that have potential and those that do not.

THE DESIGN PROCESS

Let these early ideas inform your research. Look up the work of artists who you suspect have some emotional connection with the world of the play. Find paintings, photographs, films: anything that speaks to your nascent ideas. Revisit the images you brought to the interviews: keep what still resonates and jettison what doesn't. Take another step: if the play is set in a specific location or locations, research images of them and choose the ones that have potential, even if you cannot yet articulate why. To be excited or intrigued by an image is enough. Share your research with the design team and ask them to share with each other. Listen to music, look at clothes: share music with the set designer and scenic research with your costume designer. Which pieces of research remain interesting? Ask yourselves why and push yourselves to be specific. This will lead you to choices: what you like, what you don't, and shared understanding of why.

Practical Design

As your ideas become more concrete and you begin to make choices, you and your designers must meld your creative desires with logistical considerations. You are at a juncture where you must consider how your design can be functional, practical, safe, and easy for actors to navigate.

- **Read and reread the text for information about the setting.** Begin with the basics, then become more detailed: What can you learn from the stage directions about what may be necessary for the set, the lights, the sound, the costumes, the props? Make a list of what information the writer has made explicit. Then take another step:
    - What do the characters say that provides more information or a deeper understanding of what is seen and heard onstage?
    - What can you discern about the circumstances of the play: time of day, time of year?
    - Is it set in the past, present, or future?
    - Are there interior locations, exterior locations, geographical locations, real or fictitious locations?
    - How much time passes between scenes (minutes, days, months, years)?
    - What clues does the writer provide about how the world changes over that time?

Let's say your play is set in a "contemporary kitchen in Los Angeles." Challenge your designers to ask basic questions:

- When was the kitchen built?
- What was the style of that time?
- Has it been well maintained since?
- When was the last time it was remodeled?
- How wealthy are the current occupants?
- How neat are they?
- How often do they cook?
- Who decorates it?
- Who cleans it, and how often?
- Who uses the kitchen, and to make what?
- Who does the grocery shopping (if anyone)? What do they buy, and for whom?
- Are there windows? What's on the other side of them?
- In what neighborhood is this kitchen? What street?
- Is the kitchen in a home or apartment? If an apartment, what floor?
- What sounds from outside would someone hear from this kitchen?

The list of potential questions is endless. Push yourselves: the specificity of your design will relate directly to the rigor and quality of the questions you ask. These are dramaturgical questions, not only technical ones. What kind of space someone inhabits, how they choose to maintain it, what happens in it, and how others interact with it are all revelations of character. These design choices are storytelling about every detail of the world and of everyone in it. The more precise you can be when interrogating the script, the more opportunities for specificity, texture, and creativity you will be generating for yourself.

- **Consider the logic of your entrances and exits:**
    - From where will your actors come and go?
    - Do you have strong locations to reveal actors as they enter?
    - Can you get actors on and off quickly?
    - Can actors make surprise entrances, if necessary?
    - Notice how quickly the play moves on the page. Does the placement of entrances and exists support that momentum?
    - Are there large props or items that have to get on and off stage? How and where will that happen?

THE DESIGN PROCESS

- **Consider the shape and size of your playing space:**
    - Is there enough room for the play to unfold?
    - Is there too much or too little room? (A wide open space will disperse energy, a claustrophobic space will limit your ability to create stage pictures.)
    - How much moving scenery do you envision needing? Is there enough room for it in the wings?
    - How many actors will be onstage at once? Is there space to accommodate them and give you room to block them?

- **Consider the visual and storytelling logic of any transitions:**

How the story moves from scene to scene is as much a part of the experience of the play as the scenes themselves. Transitions must be built into every part of your design. To consider transitions is to think about movement: the play's rhythm and momentum. They must accommodate both the technical needs of moving from scene to scene and the director's desired pace of storytelling: if you are making an audience wait, it should be because the natural shape of the play demands it. Solving transitions after the design has solidified is too late.

Lead with the basics, using your growing list of information as support:

- Who is onstage at the end of one scene and who at the beginning of the next?
- Does the location change?
- Are there props or furniture that need to move?
- Who do you imagine will move them?
- Will the costumes change?
- Will there be a mess onstage that need striking/cleaning?

Based on your increasingly specific understanding of the setting, imagine how long each transition will take. Now think of the momentum of the play at that point: is a long transition desirable? Do you need to jump immediately to the next scene? This work will teach you where you need to streamline or uncomplicate the design for the sake of the forward motion.

Consider also what the audience will *see* in transition:

- Will the audience see the actors moving in darkness?
- Will actors move scenery or strike their own props?
- Will the crew come onstage and be visible?
- How do these choices affect the experience of the play?

These are questions about time, movement, and pace. Once scenery is built it is difficult to make changes and you will be at the mercy of the objects and the people moving them. A scenic design that has not taken into account how the piece moves from scene to scene is still incomplete.

- **Consider your light sources**: Who controls light in this world?

    - The characters?
    - Nature (the sun/moon/stars)?
    - The outside influence of a designer?
    - What does each possibility teach the audience about the world of the play? What story does each potential choice tell?

If you decide that light will come from onstage sources (lamps, overhead light, open flame), will the lighting designer decide to enhance them with stage lighting? Should that choice be obvious to an audience, or are you creating the illusion that there is no "theatrical" lighting? If the play is set in a heavily abstracted world, what are the rules and logic of light? The root of all these questions is source—where the light comes from, and who controls it—and the first decision must be if we will see the hand of the designer or if every light should appear motivated by something organic to the circumstances: a lamp, a streetlight through a window, or the sun overhead.

- **Consider the source of both sound and music**: from where is it coming?

    - Does a character put a song on during the scene?
    - Is there sound/music illustrating a character's interior life that only the audience can hear?
    - Is there sound/music illustrating the emotional quality of a scene or moment, like cinematic underscoring?
    - Does that choice continue throughout the play, or do the rules change? When is it and is it not necessary or appropriate?
    - Is the music coming from an outside source: the hand of an unseen designer?

Like light, your first decision is from where the sound and music comes. Is it motivated by onstage action, like car horns, phone rings, gun shots, or putting on a record? Is this a play where sound or music can be added from "outside" by the designer? Challenge yourselves to understand the story you would be telling with each of those choices.

THE DESIGN PROCESS

Unlike some other design elements, sound can be listened to and decided on well before you begin tech. This is design through trial-and-error: listening to choice after choice and responding to how each makes you feel. This will be a four-step process:

- First, you and the sound designer will listen to a cue (an effect, a tone, a piece of music) and agree on what feels most right.
- Second, you and the designer will hear the cue in rehearsal, within the context of the scene or moment, and make adjustments accordingly.
- Third, you will hear the cue during tech in the theater, responding to the choice in the space and within the context of all the other design elements.
- Finally, you will hear the cue in front of an audience, noticing their responses and making necessary changes or adjustments.

- **Consider the sources of the costumes:**

    - Do the characters dress themselves?
    - Where did they get their clothes?
    - How well do they take care of them?
    - How new/old are they?
    - How conscious are the characters of how they look?
    - How vain or unaware?
    - What do these answers reveal about the interior life of each character?
    - What is each character's relationship to the others in each scene?
    - What do they want from them and how might that information affect how they choose to present themselves?
    - If the characters don't choose their clothes, what does that say about the world of this play?

Ask questions about how the characters change over time. Costuming is a central—often *the* central—visual indicator of a character's growth and transformation throughout the play: make a flowchart of each character and discuss their emotional trajectory, their status, power, and money, their triumphs and tragedies, and consider how that information influences how they look.

For a production in which the costumes are built by a shop (often an abstract or period piece), decisions need to be made early so the designs can be constructed. This also leaves you fewer opportunities later for significant changes. When the costumes are purchased (often a contemporary play), you and your designer will have more flexibility for experimentation.

- **There is no such thing as an entirely abstract or fully realistic design**. The most avant-garde design still needs a way for actors to get on- and offstage, and the most realistic set is still a collection of thousands of creative and editorial decisions. "Abstraction" and "realism" are words that require agreed-upon definitions: what do they mean to you as a group? Once defined, play with how far you can push the design in one direction or the other. Can a realistic setting be abstracted: how? And why? What do you learn about the play? How realistic can an abstract world be? And what do you learn by trying? Abstraction and realism exist on a continuum so there can be no fixed point: you must find a space where this design can live through experimentation with extremes.

- **Beware an over-designed production**. It will over-explain, spoil the plot, steal focus away from the cast and the text, and telegraph to an audience how they are supposed to feel. An over-designed production cheats an audience out of their experience by doing the work for them. A set that screams horror as soon as the lights come up will tell an audience exactly what to expect. A set that is so bright and silly as it pushes for comedy will answer an audience's questions before they even know what to ask. A successful design is an invitation for an audience to enter into it, to be curious about it, and to pay attention. An over-designed production forces an audience to be passive: they are being told everything has already been figured out so there is no need for them to participate.

  It can be tempting to try to answer every question the play poses through design, and it can feel as though you are losing something when you scale back your ideas. Ask yourself and your team if you are telling an audience what the play is about or if you are creating an environment in which the tone is clear and appropriate for the story to unfold. Strive to be specific about the world, then invite the audience to wonder what will happen inside it. A design that overshadows a play, especially a new play that audiences are hearing for the very first time, can cause it to disappear among big and illustrative gestures.

- **All theater is site specific**. The stage itself, but also the number of seats, the way they are configured, the lobby, the architecture of the building … everything that will contribute to an audience's experience. Work with the physical theater space you'll be performing in, not against it. Embrace its challenges and its virtues.

THE DESIGN PROCESS

All designs begin with two sources: the text and the space. You've devoted a lot of thought and creative energy to the text, now apply that same thinking to the space:

- What is the general energy of the building? What will an audience feel when they enter?
- What about the building is tonally appropriate for the play?
- What about it is not?
- Consider the scale, the architecture, the acoustics: what story do they tell?
- Imagine yourself in the audience: what about the space do you notice?

Take note of relevant technical considerations:

- Is there wing space for scenery to come on and off?
- Does the theater have a fly rail to bring pieces in and out from above?
- How raised is the stage, and how will that affect sightlines?
- If the seating is wide, how will that affect sightlines?

No matter what you create onstage, the audience will never be able to ignore the space they are in. You and your team need to recognize that the theater itself will have a profound effect on their experience of the play: incorporate those realities into your choices. Resist fighting or rejecting the space: use it to your advantage in every way possible.

Think about the audience's entire experience from the moment they enter the theater. The space itself will set up expectations.

- Is it formal or informal?
- Is it new or old?
- Is it clean or dirty?
- Does it feel polished or relaxed?

An audience coming into a small space will have different preconceived notions of what they're about to see than if they are entering a grand theater. How will your production work with those expectations? Will the play feel like an intimate discovery if you stage it in a basement, will it feel exposed if you stage it in a Broadway theater? Take the audience's expectations into account when designing your production. The most successful designs are mindful of context.

Whenever possible, bring your designers to the theater and meet in the space. Is it a proscenium? Then you can think of the physical production like a painting. Is it a thrust, or in the round? You can think of the piece as sculpture. Is the seating fixed or flexible? If you have a choice: where do you put the audience, and what story does each audience-performer relationship tell? How would each possible configuration affect the audience's experience?

Decisions, Deadlines, and Changes

There will come a point in your process when your ideas are transformed into drawings, models, budgets, and equipment requests that are then shared with the producing organization. The production manager will have provided each designer with a series of deadlines for when they need to submit their designs and requests: for scenery, lights, sound, video, and costumes. This timeline is created by counting backwards from tech rehearsals: in order for the scenic elements to be ready, for example, the design must be approved a certain number of weeks in advance so it can be built, rented, or otherwise prepared.

A set designer will submit architectural drawings based on the results of your meetings, and the lighting and sound designers will submit a "plot": a blueprint detailing what equipment they want and where it would be placed. A costume designer may also submit a plot: a breakdown of what will be necessary for each character. The sharing of these materials is not the end of the design process but the beginning of a negotiation. The production manager will decide what is and is not technically and financially possible, and will return to the designers with an estimate of what the current design plans cost. This number is almost always higher than the budget.

Your subsequent round of design meetings will be spent evaluating your options: honoring your vision for while making cuts to fit within the budget. This is the moment when the priorities list you created at the start of pre-production will be useful. These meetings can be difficult: parting ways with ideas you love is always frustrating, but so long as you and your team are able to return to the emotional roots of the play, you will find solutions. While it may feel discouraging to be told "no" about something you feel strongly about or put a great deal of thought and effort into making, cutting back on the design can spur creative problem-solving and birth an even better, clearer idea. The simplest option is often the strongest, and stripping down a design to reach a budget goal can reveal unexpected but exciting new choices.

The next step will be a series of back-and-forth conversations between your designers and production during which cuts and changes are proposed, a new number is returned to the designers, who will continue to edit until the necessary number has been reached. A good production office will make suggestions and work collaboratively, but ultimately the responsibility to make the production "fit" falls on the creative team. Occasionally, an institution will raise the design budget, especially if they see genuine effort to make substantial cuts, but you cannot expect or rely on that possibility.

The Writer and the Design Process

Some writers are visual thinkers with a clear idea of what they want the physical production to look like, others less so. Both will have strong responses to design ideas, so incorporating the playwright into the conversation early will bring another valuable perspective into the design process: they will see things no one else can, and they will have questions no one else could have thought to ask.

Inviting a writer into the design conversation is different from inviting them to participate in the meetings. Like every artist working on the production, your designers should be provided with the freedom to brainstorm, to come up with ideas without judgment, and to find their own creative path into the play. A writer is capable of generosity in these meetings, but they are also the creator of the world, so their presence alone can make a process feel less open to experimentation, to trial and error.

Share your design ideas with the writer as they develop, ask for their feedback, and then bring those thoughts back to the design team for discussion. Your task is to open the lines of communication. The writer should feel included and as though their vision is being taken into account, while the designers should enjoy the freedom of their own creative journey. This way of working will give you an opportunity to inch all of your collaborators closer to a unified vision while also encouraging experimentation.

10
THE PRODUCING ORGANIZATION AND PRODUCTION MEETINGS

Producing Organizations

There are two basic models for producing theater in America: commercial and institutional.

The commercial model is for-profit: a producer acquires the rights to a play, forms an LLC, raises money for the production, and then relies on ticket sales to make their money back, hopefully at a profit. The institutional model is usually not-for-profit: an organization, overseen by a board of directors, has a full-time staff, including an artistic director, who will program a season of plays. Their income is comprised of a combination of ticket and subscription sales as well as tax deductible donations.

A commercial venture means creating and selling a product: your production. The money the producer will raise goes into the building, advertising, and maintaining of the product. They must keep costs low enough that ticket sales alone will pay all of the salaries, bills, and expenses. An institutional project is part of a season: an artistic director plans and curates a year's worth of projects, of which your production is one. The virtue of a commercial production is that your project will have the undivided attention of the staff that has been assembled to make it. At an institution, the staff must think of your project within the context of the entire season: decisions may be made that will prioritize the needs of the organization or another project in their season. The virtue of an institutional production is that because their income derives from multiple sources, the fate of your project is not dependent on turning a profit.

There is a third option, which is to self-produce the work, but that is a different skill entirely and the subject of another book.

The Staff

Many, or most, new American plays are first produced at institutions. This is primarily because audiences are less likely to pay commercial theater ticket prices for a play they aren't familiar with. Institutions customarily have lower prices and have a vested interest in encouraging audiences to see new work, especially if that is part of their mission. Because every production at an institution is part of a larger mechanism, a director must understand who works there, what they do, what they are responsible for, and how they can best work together throughout the process.

The staff members of an institution are your collaborators and they—like you—are employees of the organization. They are charged with producing your work to the best of their ability while also considering their other projects and the general health and efficiency of the institution. The staff has worked at the organization before you arrived and will be there long after your production has closed. You must be a leader who understands you are also a guest. This will cultivate a sense of generosity and understanding, and will earn the respect and gratitude of the staff.

Artistic Director

All artistic directors are not alike. Some are more similar to commercial producers: their focus is on budgets and on ticket sales. Some are artists: more invested in great work than in financial concerns. Some are primarily fundraisers: their focus is on the board of directors, donors, patrons, corporate sponsors, and foundations. Some are more similar to literary managers: their attention is on the plays themselves.

Most ADs are some combination of the above. Learn which type of AD you are working for and where their priorities lie: it will provide you with an understanding of their thought process, a context for their notes and decisions, and it will allow you to anticipate what kind of relationship you can expect. Will they want to give you a lot of notes on your work? Will they ask you to attend donor events? Will they pay close attention to your budget? Will they encourage casting decisions that may help boost ticket sales? Will they want to meet after every preview to discuss what they saw? How they define their job will help you communicate with and understand them.

Artistic Directors vs. Producers

Artistic directors and producers are similar in that they are always searching for projects that they feel inspired by and believe in, that they trust they can support and make successful, and that they suspect will attract an audience. While a commercial producer must think about making a profit through sales, they are also invested in making great art they can feel proud of. And while an artistic director must serve the organization's mission, they can be just as focused on making money as any commercial producer. To a director, they are similar because both positions will be your boss. They are the ones who hire you, who have approval over the hiring of designers and actors, who will give you notes on your work, and who will approve or deny designs, budgets, and scheduling requests. While their models, motivations, and concerns can be different, how you interact with them will be largely the same.

General Management

The general manager is the central organizational role of the institution.

- They determine the overall budget for each production.
- They create a season calendar for the entire institution and set the dates for each production.
- They handle all contracts and uphold and honor all union agreements.

It is their responsibility to keep each project on schedule and on budget, and they work closely with production management to do so. Your offer to direct the play will come from general management, and they will represent the organization during the negotiation of your contract.

Contracts and Sub-Rights

Your contract is an agreement between you and the producing organization. You will be their employee, hired to perform a task (to direct the play), and when the play has opened, your contract will be considered fulfilled. Most director agreements are simple and straightforward: they articulate the schedule, the fee, how you will be credited, and at which points in the process you will be paid. Review all of the paperwork and make sure the contract offers you appropriate compensation and make a note of any questions.

Often, your fee will be determined by a union agreement or by the size of the theater. Learn (usually by asking directors who have worked there before, not the organization) if there is flexibility in the fee. Often there isn't, but do your research before you sign.

"Crediting" simply means how and where you will be listed in the program and on any other public-facing materials:

- Will the director's name be on all advertising and marketing materials?
- Will the director's name appear next to the writer's in front of the theater?
- Where will the director's name appear on the title page of the program?
- Will the credit read "Directed by (your name)" and is that what you want?
- What size will the director's name be in relation to the other artists'? *(This may sound like a silly question, but how you are acknowledged matters and your value needs to be recognized appropriately)*

Do not assume that your name will appear on marketing materials. Your contract will make explicit where your name is obligated to appear, and you should assume any advertising or public listing that is not included in your contract will not include a director credit. If you feel the list of mandatory crediting is incomplete, you need to address that before you sign.

Royalties are a percentage of the box office that are sometimes—not always—paid to some of the creative team. Usually, royalties go to a director if and when the play extends beyond its scheduled closing date. If you have a hit, and the theater decides to keep the production running, you should be entitled to a portion of that money. In a contract, royalties will be articulated as a percentage. Identify both the percentage and when royalties would begin, and decide if you are comfortable with both. It is not presumptuous to prepare for the possibility that the play will be an enormous financial success and to secure your participation in the profits.

This production will be known as the "world premiere." An organization will hold the rights to the play (the writer's intellectual property) and to your production (your intellectual property) for a set amount of time after the production has closed. This will give them a protected window of time to decide if they want to remount the play during which no one else can produce it. The organization cannot remount your production without crediting and compensating you. Once the institution releases the rights, however, the play becomes the sole property of the writer again, and other organizations can produce the play without your involvement. If you want to direct future productions of the play, that is between you and the writer: you have no legal attachment to the play itself.

One exception is something called "sub-rights." It is a contractual agreement between a writer and director in which the former will guarantee the latter a percentage of all the money generated by future productions. The argument for sub-rights is that a new play director helped develop the piece and deserves some financial recognition for their creative contributions. If the play becomes a hit, the director should share in the financial reward. The counter-argument is that the play is the writer's work, and a director's contribution to the play's development does not make them a partial-author.

Asking for sub-rights can be complicated: not only are you asking for a portion of the writer's income, you are asking for confirmation that you helped create the play. It's impossible to know how a writer will respond, but if you plan to approach the writer, do so before your process begins.

Production Management

The production manager is responsible for all physical aspects of the project. The building, installing, and maintaining of all design elements, hiring and overseeing a crew, renting lights, sound, or other equipment, hiring and/or overseeing the shop that will construct the set, and managing the design and production budget, which will be given to them by general management. They are also responsible for making sure the physical production is safe, properly constructed, and on schedule for tech rehearsals. They run all production meetings, they schedule all work calls during tech, and they prioritize what work is done, and when, and by whom. Anything you can see, touch, or hear in the space, and anyone responsible for making, renting, loading it in, loading it out, and running it falls under the purview of production management.

Company Manager

The company manager is responsible for handling the needs of the actors, designers, writer, director, and any freelance staff who have been assembled to create the production. They manage housing and travel, field ticket requests, coordinate with general management to distribute paychecks, and act as a general liaison between the institution and the artists. If someone in the cast has a question, concern, request, or complaint, they speak with the company manager.

No member of the institution's staff will have as much direct interaction with the cast and creative team as the company manager. For many of the artists, they are the face of the organization. They shoulder a significant amount of responsibility and can have a profound impact on the comfort, happiness, and morale of a company. How supported and listened to they feel by the organization, the degree to which their needs are or are not being met, how valued they feel as hired artists: much of that can be influenced and determined by the attentiveness and care of the company manager. They have the power to set the tone for the entire process.

Marketing

The marketing department creates and manages all public facing aspects of your production, including the promotional artwork and any language describing the play. They are responsible for enticing audiences to buy tickets: they articulate why your production is worth seeing.

Because the play has never been produced, audiences will have no preconceived notions about it, which gives the marketing director an enormous amount of power over how the play is first presented to potential audiences. Their task is to identify what about your production will appeal to audiences, what types of audiences should be pursued in their advertising efforts, and how the piece fits into the overarching mission and style of the institution. A director should begin a dialogue with the marketing director immediately so you can participate in developing a vision for how the piece should be shared with the public. Do not assume their understanding of the play will match your ideas about tone, style, or even story. It is a new play, so the context you can offer will be especially valuable: make certain you and the marketing office are in alignment.

When I directed my first Broadway production, our marketing director asked me: "what is the event of this show?" This was a promotional question, not a dramaturgical one. They wanted to know where I thought they should focus their attention as they created a story about the play and production to sell to the public. In the commercial arena, the "event" can be a famous title, a famous actor, or a famous writer. With a new play, the event is often something exciting or notable about the subject matter of the play. Challenge yourself to identify the "event" of your production: what is the primary reason why someone should buy a ticket to see it? Share your answer with the marketing director. It will provide them with one clear idea on which to build an entire advertising campaign.

The Blurb

A blurb is a synopsis of the play that doubles as a promotional tool. It is often included in a season announcement along with the other productions a theater will produce in the coming year, so it is possible a blurb will be shared with the public months, or even a year, before anyone sees the play. In the case of a new work, it is possible the script will still be in progress when it is time for the marketing office to write the blurb. This is another reason why speaking with a marketing team early is valuable: the release of the blurb will mark the very first time the public will hear anything about this play, and so accurate and evocative language will have an enormous effect on its reception. When meeting with the marketing director, articulate not only what is on the page, but what rewrites and changes you expect. Help them understand what is written, but also what you anticipate will be there, and how it will look and play in production.

Blurbs are not summaries, they are a tool meant to generate interest, excitement, and intrigue. The goal is to make a potential audience member want to buy a ticket. A blurb need not include every detail, nor does it need to explain the entirety of the plot. So long as the tone of the play is honored—that an audience will arrive at the theater with correct expectations—you can feel confident the text has served its purpose.

Artwork

The production's promotional artwork is also created by the marketing office. Occasionally, a writer or director will have approval over the artwork, but that privilege must be guaranteed in your contract.

Ask to meet with marketing to discuss the artwork. Sometimes they will want to brainstorm with the director, and sometimes they won't, but always request a conversation. If you do meet with them, speak in emotional terms. The feeling of the world of the play, what you hope the audience experiences, and how you anticipate your production will look. Share some of the research you and your design team have responded to and are using as inspiration and explain what it is about the images that resonate with you. Like the blurb, a production's artwork is a piece of advertising. Writers and directors may lament that an image doesn't explain what the play is about, or doesn't feature a specific moment or object from the piece. Because it is the world premiere, nods to anything specific will have no effect on an audience: a hand holding a skull is a reasonable image for Hamlet, but new plays do not have instantly recognizable iconography. A marketing office must capture a feeling with the artwork that is enticing and intriguing.

Research the institution's existing aesthetic and style, and find examples of artwork they have used for past projects that you connect with. Explain to the marketing office why you respond to it: this will provide them with a concrete example. Articulate also what you do not want to see: anything that would spoil the story or would convey the wrong message should be expressed immediately. Do not assume everyone will understand what is and is not to be kept secret from the audience. Marketing offices want the artists to be pleased with the art and language that represent the show, but they also need to honor the overall look and tone of the institution. Because the play is new, any guidance you can provide early will help them advertise the show in a way that balances the organization's needs with your vision for the production.

Press

The press office pursues publicity opportunities for the production and oversees any interaction between a reporter, critic, news or cultural outlet and the creative team. They invite critics and non-reviewing press to early performances, they craft and pitch feature ideas about the play and the artists, they pursue interviews, all in an effort to promote the production. A press office will begin their process with a brainstorming session: what is potentially interesting about the show, who is involved and how might they participate, what angles might appeal to different news outlets. A director can be very useful in these early conversations: you can speak to who in the cast might give an interesting interview, who can speak about the design of the show, and who can articulate the themes and ideas of the play. You can guide a press office toward ideas they cannot imagine, and help develop them into a pitch to journalists. Like your conversations with the marketing office, you are guiding the press representative toward a way of thinking about the play that will honor your work. They want to get as much positive attention as possible: meeting with them to share your perspective will help them understand angles that are both positive in general and specific to your vision.

Production Meetings

Representatives of every department responsible for creating and maintaining the physical production share and discuss plans, budgets, logistics, and schedules a few times over the course of the process. These gatherings are production meetings. It is not a design meeting, it is exclusively practical and pragmatic: what are we making, how is it to be made, and who is doing what?

Directors are the leaders of the creative department, but there are multiple departments and therefore many leaders involved with the production, each with separate responsibilities, challenges, and needs. What these other department heads see when they read a script will be different from you, and so this meeting, led by the production manager, is a chance to share these perspectives. The goal of these meetings is to clarify each department's schedule, activities, and needs: how are they to be met, how they may conflict with or complement each other, what problems they anticipate, and how their department expects to be prepared for tech.

As the leader of the creative team, your job is to advocate for your priorities, share expected challenges, contextualize and explain elements of the script and design that may not be explicit, and to listen to and learn from other departments. This will be your first meeting with all the other leaders who are responsible for realizing the physical production: their unique perspectives will offer you valuable information about how the entire project will unfold.

Preparing for the Meeting

Set the pace of your design process in relationship with these production meeting. If all the department heads meet when you and your designers are still brainstorming, you cannot know what to advocate for or what your priorities will be. If you meet too late, flexibility becomes more difficult for everyone. Your responsibility in the meeting is to report on your progress and to explain any obstacles or challenges. In advance of the meeting, prepare to share the following:

- List the physical elements you need for the rehearsal process.
  Examples include furniture, costume pieces, doors, speakers for music, wigs, props, or any other item an actor may need to practice with.

- Articulate your priorities for tech rehearsal.
  If there are any complicated sequences—violence, for example, or special effects—that you anticipate will take a significant amount of time, you must be certain everything necessary to tech it properly will be ready and that everyone who needs to participate in its rehearsal will be present.

- Make explicit those design elements you consider essential.
  Cuts are a natural part of any process. Make certain the team is aware of which elements are most important to you. Articulating your priorities will help other departments determine their own worklists: make sure your preferences are known and understood.

- Bring attention to potential problems and challenges so all departments can prepare accordingly.
  Only the director can explain moments in the text that might be complicated, or bigger (or smaller) than they may appear. A simple stage direction can, in your production, mean an elaborately staged sequence. And a writer's graphic description of a fight may be only two or three pieces of choreography. Articulating to the group how you imagine these moments will offer every department context and will help them prepare.

- Alert the group to upcoming changes in the script.
  If you know of a rewrite that has not yet been incorporated, or of a scene that may be changed or cut, tell the group. Like you, they will be making their own list of priorities, and they need your guidance to know whether a scene/ moment/design element may be cut.

At the Meeting

In addition to the production manager, the other attendees will be the head of the deck (or backstage) crew, a representative from the scene shop, the head of the lighting, sound, wardrobe, and props departments, stage management, general management, and each of your designers. The production manager will ask each department to give an update on their progress and on the work ahead. Everyone will look at the calendar and any drawings or models the designers can provide.

    A director who can listen closely during these meetings will be able to visualize the road map of the entire process unfolding in front of them. Technical considerations that may seem irrelevant to your work can be great teachers. For example, imagine the group looking at the set designer's drawings, and the head of wardrobe asks "Where will the quick change area be?" They look at the available space backstage while the crew head explains where props and scenery need to be stored. It is concluded that all scenery must go off stage right, and all quick changes must happen stage left. This decision will not appear on any blueprint, and may not be spoken of again until tech. While this may not seem very interesting to a director, a huge creative decision has just been made: all scenery will have to travel in one direction in transition, and the actors in another. How does that impact the flow of people and objects you and your designers had envisioned? How does that complicate or simplify the rhythm and timing of getting from scene to scene? Can you stage each transition with this configuration in mind?

    These conversations, which on their surface are purely technical, will have great impact on your work. This is why a director must attend production meetings: both to express their point of view and to listen carefully to the problems and solutions that will change both the process and the product.

The Calendar

The rehearsal calendar is the metronome that sets the tempo of your process. How slowly or quickly you stage, how long you are able to stay at the table for discussion, how you and stage management plan your tech rehearsals, what is and is not achievable during previews: all of those considerations and more will be determined by the amount of days you have, and the hours within them. Time is a tool: how carefully you plan and how thoughtfully you use it will influence every aspect of your work.

    An institution will build the production calendar based on precedent, the contract, and the scheduling needs of the entire organization. It will be created without your input, and so it will be your responsibility to ask questions and to understand what is being offered. Two people can look at the same calendar and see different things: ask for clarifications and then advocate for what you need.

- How many days are you in the rehearsal room?
- How long are the rehearsal days: 10 a.m.–6 p.m.?
- Can rehearsal hours be adjusted to be longer or shorter?
- What is the span of day for tech?
- Are actors onstage for every day of tech that is on the schedule? *(Sometimes a schedule may read "tech," but could mean "dry tech," which does not include actors)*
- Do all departments anticipate being ready to start with all the design elements on the first day of tech?
- If not, what will not be ready?
- When does production expect them to be ready?
- Will the cast be in full costume in tech?
- What are the tech hours in which actors can work onstage? *(A tech schedule can reflect the total hours in a day, which may not be the same as the number of hours the cast can be onstage)*
- What time is the cast called on tech days?
- What time are the expected onstage? *(the cast will need time to get into costume, wigs, body microphones. Build that time in the schedule)*

Count how many preview performances you get before opening, confirm which previews include an afternoon rehearsal.

- What are the available rehearsal hours during previews?
- Can the cast be onstage during all of those hours?
- Will the crew need to set up and strike during that window? *(Schedules may say rehearsal is from 1 p.m. to 5 p.m., for example, but if the crew is called to start their work at 1 p.m., you cannot begin onstage until 1:30. Then you must finish at 4:30 to give them time to strike. That's a loss of one hour: a lifetime in preview rehearsal time.)*
- When is the "freeze date"? *(the last day of rehearsal)*
- Will you have the entire crew available to you until the freeze date?

- Will your designers be with you until that date?

Do not assume because rehearsals are on the schedule everyone will be available until the freeze date: seek absolute clarity on who will be present, especially your designers and crew.

If you have thoughts, suggestions, or proposed changes to the calendar, a production meeting will be the time to express them. First, because all the people who could support or object to a change will be present, and second, because the deeper every department gets into their process, the more difficult it will be to make adjustments. Your designers and the crew will need every minute for their work, so a director cannot assume other departments can be flexible if schedule changes are proposed later.

Budgets

Money is an emotional subject, and that is true in life and in theater. How it is prioritized and distributed are considerations that will have a direct impact on every aspect of your production.

A director must be able to look at a budget and weave that information into how they approach their work. They must realize their vision with the material realities of the production, not against them. While a director may not know the exact numbers, they must be aware of the rough size of the budget. Like life, there is a finite amount of money and eventually it will run out. Your task is to advocate for what you want before that moment arrives. Ask yourself first what you *must* have, then what you *want*, then what you would *like*. This list can include sets, costumes, effects ... anything that needs to be built, rented, or purchased. It will all be paid for from the same budget, so one ranked list will be appropriate.

Be mindful not to assume that there is funding allocated for everything that appears in the text. Just because a writer has specified in the stage directions that there should be a live band onstage, for example, does not mean the organization has created space in the budget for that gesture. When advocating for your priorities, be comprehensive: elements that may appear obvious to you can be overlooked by someone else, or assumptions can be made that (A) the gesture is not a priority or (B) a less expensive alternative can be found. A cheaper version may be possible, and necessary, but you must know in advance if you are being asked to find an alternative. Conversely, if you have ideas or desires that are not explicit in the text, you must express them as early as possible.

Predicting what is and isn't necessary is far more difficult for a new play. Inevitable changes will surprise you and your team: the element you swore would be the most important may get cut in tech, a new climatic moment is discovered in rehearsal that requires additional scenery. The director's balancing act is to advocate for what you know will be necessary, regardless of cuts or changes, while making sure that your requests do not push the production to its financial limit. The flexibility you must maintain in your creative work will mean leaving room in your budget to accommodate it. Think of your budget as a creative boundary: understand where it is and know when you are getting close to the line so that you don't cross it before you are certain you have everything you need.

PART FOUR

REHEARSAL

In this part we will step through the rehearsal process. How to prepare and how to begin, the value and purpose of table work, getting on your feet, the period of trial and error and the creation of a rough draft, different types of actors, note-giving techniques, run throughs, rewrites, and the presence of the writer in the process.

Rehearsals are a period of time in which the cast, the director, stage management, and those collaborators directly involved with the creation of the performance (dialects, violence, intimacy, etc.) work together in a shared space to create and set the staging, commit the text to memory, and build a map of each character's emotional trajectory in a way that can be reliably repeated.

One way to understand the importance of a rehearsal process is to imagine a production without one. The cast would learn their lines on their own, the director would create staging in their imagination, and all the pieces could be assembled in tech. What that scenario is missing are these critical elements of a process:

- Ensemble building
- Experimentation (trial and error)
- The creation of the emotional and physical logic of the world (rules)
- Time for reflection

The creation of any work of art-by-committee requires time to share, to debate, to ponder, to learn from one another, and to make mistakes. An actor needs time to understand their character not as a separate being or as an internal creative exercise, but as a part of a group of artists, as a participant in the world of the play, and in relationship with the other characters. A director also needs time to learn from the cast, to listen to the text aloud while watching performances take shape, and to be free to not know the answer. It is not a director's job to arrive at rehearsals with all the solutions and wait for the actors to get it "right." A director's official duties—creating and adhering to a schedule, building the staging, making decisions, and leading the room—do not make them any less of a collaborator or artist: you must give yourself time to react and respond, to experiment, to change your mind, and to remain open and flexible. The director's task is to watch closely, as though they are the audience. The value of a director's contribution to a rehearsal process lies not in how well you speak but in how well you listen.

Reading A Play (for rehearsal)

The engine of any story is anticipation. As an audience watches a play, they ask themselves what will happen next. We are not always conscious of what questions we are asking ourselves, but we know *when* we are asking because we are paying attention. We also know when we are *not* because we can feel our minds wander: we become bored, we get lost or confused, and we become conscious of time. We are either struggling to follow what is happening, or we are no longer interested in finding out. We become passive and disengaged.

A story is successful when an audience is curious. When they are curious, they become active participants. The questions a director asks themselves in rehearsal are exactly the questions an audience will ask when they watch the play. These questions are very simple. "What happens next?" is the most basic, the building block of anticipation. A story begins: "Who is that?" "Do they know each other?" "Where are they?" Then the audience's questions become a bit more complex: "Why did she say that?" "Why did he respond that way?" And then "Is he telling the truth?" "Will she stay with him?" And so on. These are "good" questions: they keep an audience curious, attentive, and engaged. The more gradually complex the questions become, the more satisfying the story.

There are also "bad" questions, and a director must be able to identify the difference. To ask "What is going on?" not out of curiosity but out of confusion will lead to an audience to disengage. Gaps in logic, implausible jumps in character action or behavior, scenes without dramatic tension, inexplicable tonal shifts: if a director senses any of these in rehearsal, they can trust an audience will have the same experience later. If something is confusing on the page, those "bad" questions will be passed on to the director to address. If the director cannot

REHEARSAL

solve the problem, it will be passed on to the actors. If they cannot, the confusion is passed on to the audience. They will try to find answers for a time, but will eventually give up.

In rehearsals, actors are experimenting with their roles and approximating how they will play them in performance. What a director is doing is playing the role of the audience, pretending they are watching for the first time. It's a manufactured spontaneity with the purpose of gathering information: as the audience surrogate, you are asking yourself what you notice and how you react. You are also separating the "good" questions from the "bad" to find clarity and to promote curiosity, which leads to anticipation and dramatic tension.

As you read the play in preparation for rehearsal, ask as many questions as possible. Begin with the most basic:

- Where (time, place, setting)
- Who (characters, relationships, histories)
- What (plot, backstory, given circumstances, action, event)

These questions concern the *objective truths* of the play.

The second set of questions are:

- Why (motivation)
- How (action and behavior)

These are *subjective interpretations*. Questions concerning *why* or *how* are the root of all acting choices. Why a character does or says something, why an actor chooses to play a moment as they do, why this action elicits this reaction, and so forth through the entire process. These questions and your answers will reveal your and the company's taste, point of view about the play, and creative interpretation.

Identifying and understanding the difference between objective truth (the fact) and subjective observations (the interpretation) is how a director can cultivate curiosity and avoid confusion. If a company has a clear grasp of who, where, and what happens, scene by scene, moment by moment, they will have a solid foundation on which to build their performances. If the company does not know or cannot agree on the given circumstance, everyone will make their own choices, and the production will become unclear and unfocused. The company's choices will seem arbitrary, the story will become difficult to follow, and the production will become confused.

As you reread the play, ask simple questions and separate them into categories of who/what/where (objective) and of why/how (subjective). The fate of plays, especially new plays, is often decided not by the subjective creative choices of the group but by the strength of the production's objective clarity. If an audience cannot understand what is happening, nothing else matters. This is why you must seek this clarity before rehearsals begin: if a company does not have a strong grasp of the basics, an audience cannot hope to. You want your art to be judged on your taste and your vision, and not by whether or not your production makes sense.

11
THE FIRST REHEARSAL

The first day is an amalgam of adrenaline, excitement, and anxiety. The cast is fully assembled, everyone is finally able to match a name with a face, and the timer set for the first performance begins to tick.

The tone that is established on this day will carry through the process. The emotional temperature of a rehearsal environment is not set arbitrarily: the group creates it together. An effective rehearsal room is positive, supportive, focused, and open. It is a balance between serious and playful, rigorous and relaxed. A director does not need to articulate any of this to the cast, they must embody it. Ask yourself what energy is most appropriate for the play and the kind of atmosphere you want, then lead a company there by example.

The "Meet and Greet"

Introductions of the cast, crew, design, and administrative teams are often called "meet and greets." They are brief gatherings where everyone working on the project can meet their fellow collaborators, including some they may not see again for weeks, if ever. It is a rare and special moment when groups as disparate as marketing, wardrobe, and the cast can be in a space together. Meet and greets can be particularly powerful because it encourages everyone to appreciate just how many people it takes, and how many different tasks need to be performed, to bring a new play into existence.

The stage manager will call the rehearsal to order, and everyone will introduce themselves and share their job title or description. The artistic director may say a few encouraging words about the play and the artists, and the director may be asked to as well. A productive meet and greet speech should be optimistic, complimentary, and brief. This is your first moment to address the entire company as the creative leader of the project: a moment to set the tone and energy you want reflected back to you, to express gratitude for the opportunity to collaborate with present company, and to thank all the collaborators who have worked so hard to get the production to this point in the process. A director may also say a few words about the play: why you love it, why you are excited to share it with audiences, why it speaks to you personally.

Introductions are followed by design presentations, during which the design team will share their work with the company. This step is primarily for the set and costume designers, as their work is easiest to share and will have the most immediate impact on the cast's understanding of the production. While you have been working with your design team, the cast has been mulling over the script with no sense of how it will be brought to life visually: they have been imagining how it—and they—will look. The sharing of the design is a momentous occasion: it is the first time the cast will see the physical production, and it is the first moment when one group of artists shares their work with another.

The set designer will show a model if they have made one, drawings of the space if they have not. They will explain the set's look and style, inspirations for and reasons behind specific choices, and how it may transform over the course of the play. This is a good moment for you and the set designer to speak briefly about transitions (if there are any) with the company. Actors need to understand how the play will travel from scene to scene and the ways in which they will participate in that flow. The earlier they can begin to visualize how the scenes connect to make up the whole, the more time they will have to contemplate their physical journey.

The costume designer will share research in the form of photography collages and/or sketches. Each character will be represented, often with a few different looks if the character changes over the course of the play. This presentation will be closely followed by the cast: the designer's choices not only determine what the cast will wear and how they will look, they will also convey significant decisions about the character's identities: how they choose to dress, to present themselves to the world, what kind of care they take of themselves, and what it all says about their character.

The actors will be reconciling what they imagined the design to be with what it is, which can be a thrilling and occasionally complicated process. Be mindful of their reactions, and note if any actors seem confused or troubled. You'll want to address those feelings during tablework.

The First Read

After introductions and design presentations, the cast will sit down together and read the play. Ask them to read straight through, holding on to any questions until later. This will give you, the writer, and the cast a chance to get out of your imaginations and into the room. It will allow you to hear everyone's first untouched instincts and to hear the play with the company who will bring it to life for the first time.

Actors have confessed to me that they were so nervous at the first read that they were convinced they would be fired immediately after. The director would hear them, decide they'd made a terrible mistake, and move on to someone

THE FIRST REHEARSAL

else. While not every actor feels this way, it is a reminder that the first read can provoke anxiety. Relieve any pressure by articulating the goal of the reading: simply to hear it aloud, without trying to make the play "do" anything, and without any pressure to perform. Just words in the space so everyone can hear the same text at the same time to use as a point of departure. Discourage too many listeners. The producer or AD may want to attend, as will your designers, but the smaller the audience, the less the cast will feel obligated to "perform." Respectfully dismiss anyone from the meet and greet who does not need to hear the first read, and begin.

Set your notes and questions aside. Listen as though you've never heard the play before. This is your one opportunity to hear your production cast without any discussion or experimentation. Pay attention to their natural instincts about their character. Be mindful of how they use rhythm, pace, energy, humor, and emotion to share their perspective on the role. Postpone any judgment: simply listen. The cast is teaching you so much about who they are as artists: their taste, their imagination, their understanding of the world of the play, and of what they see when they look at the page. If you've met with them in advance of the first day, they are also teaching you how they received and processed your thoughts and questions.

Note your reactions:

- What sounded like you'd always imagined?
- What sounded very different and how?
- What new questions arise from hearing this company?

Add those questions to your list. The closer you pay attention to their instincts, impulses, and choices, the stronger position you'll be in to start a collaboration. What you learn from the first read will teach you what you want to discuss and what questions you would like to propose during the next step: tablework.

After the reading ends, finish the day by sharing a few overarching thoughts about the play. Think of this as moment to plant seeds that will grow and flourish over the course of rehearsals. Some possible prompts could be:

- Share with the company what excites you about the play
- Describe your experience of reading it for the first time
- Tell them what you are curious to learn during a rehearsal process
- Share questions you have about the text
- Articulate what you hope to share with an audience
- Bring their attention to the challenges you expect to face

The timing of this sharing is deliberate: if you were to articulate any of this before the first read, an actor may feel as though they're being given notes or instructions, or are being coerced toward a specific way of playing the text. This moment, at the end of the first day, is an invitation for the cast to join you in the space you have been preparing for them so that you can move forward together. You shouldn't feel compelled or pressured to explain the play or to tell them exactly how the production will be: doing so takes away some of the actors' artistic license: they become a little less artists and a little more your employees. This invitation is part of your setting a tone, guiding the group toward your vision so that they can join you, and giving them a sense of a shared goal. With some clear, well-chosen words of encouragement and inspiration, the cast will leave the first day excited and ready to begin.

Meeting with the Writer

After the cast has broken for the day, speak privately with the writer about their perspective on the first read. Learn what excited them, troubled them, and perplexed them. In doing so, you are looking for three pieces of information:

- If they were inspired to do rewrites
- If so, when they expect to do them
- How their response to the read through was the same as and different from yours

An example would be if you were excited by an actor's read but the writer felt they were far from the character as they imagined it (this can happen even with an actor who went through a long audition process and everyone agreed was the strongest choice). Whether you agree with the writer or not, ask questions to better understand exactly what troubled them, and why, and what they hope to hear instead. It is not your job to solve or "fix" what an actor is doing, but you must go into the rehearsal process understanding what a writer is hearing and why there is a gap between what you both experienced. The first read is far too early to consider rewrites to accommodate an actor who isn't "doing it" like the writer imagined, but understanding the writer's perspective now will allow you to begin rehearsals with their point of view in mind.

If the writer is planning on rewrites, they must agree to share them with you first for your thoughts. What you are reviewing is the changes themselves and how they might fit into upcoming rehearsal plans. Tablework, as we will see, is a delicate process in which the framework for the entire process is constructed. Incorporating changes during tablework can transform an early

THE FIRST REHEARSAL 121

rehearsal process into a workshop—pure experimentation—when you need the company's attention focused on working toward the production. On the other hand, if a rewrite is necessary or helpful, why spend tablework discussing a part of the text you know will change? There is no general rule about rewrites early in rehearsals: if they can be incorporated into the text quickly and cleanly without the tablework process centering on script changes, insert them immediately. If they cannot, incorporate them later.

Take some time at the end of the first day to write down any additional thoughts and observations. You have received an avalanche of creative stimuli and information in the course of just a few hours and can expect more to come: give yourself time to connect with your own reactions, questions, and concerns so they do not get swept up in the many opinions that can overtake you in the coming days. Ask yourself what you heard, what you learned, what you're curious about, and what you suspect will need more attention around the table.

12
TABLEWORK

Tablework is the step in the rehearsal process when the company reads, discusses, debates, and arrives at a shared understanding of the text before staging begins. The goals of table work are:

- To create an informal rehearsal worklist in the form of questions
- To separate those elements of the text that are objective fact from subjective interpretation
- To develop an agreed-upon logic of the world ("rules")
- To observe how your collaborators think and communicate

Tablework is a necessary step in a new play process as staging should begin only after the company has a shared understanding of the text. Confusion and conflict most often present themselves in rehearsal rooms when artists disagree about the core meaning of a scene, moment, or piece of text. Neither can be avoided—conflict is an inevitable part of the creative process—but the greater the collective understanding of a text can be at the outset of a process, the more productive it will be. Additionally, the stronger a company's agreement is regarding the logic of the world, the further they can push their choices. An actor who is unsure about the world of the play and their character's place in it will make conservative, safe, fearful choices. An actor who has clarity and a shared understanding with their scene partners will make brave and daring ones.

There are two simultaneous processes unfolding during tablework. The first is developing a shared understanding of the text and the second is beginning to build an ensemble. Tablework will allow you to assess the group dynamics of the company: how well they listen and collaborate, how they problem solve, how successfully they share. This information will help you shape your approach to the company as a whole, and to each actor's individual process. You are learning to speak everyone's proverbial language while inventing a shared vocabulary that will be effective for the entire group.

Customarily, tables are set up in a square, creating a democratic environment. There is no "head" of the table: everyone is an equal collaborator, and this is a dynamic you should encourage. While you are the guide, no one knows more than anyone else during tablework: you are a team of investigators, working together to seek clarity and information. Cultivating an atmosphere of equals will empower your actors to ask any questions they may have and be brave enough to articulate what they do not yet understand. The courage to not know something in front of the group is the key to every successful process, and the building of that confidence begins with decidedly democratic tablework.

Tablework is not an extension of the workshop process. All of your questions, opinions, observations, and subjects for debate are not to be answered or "solved" around the table, they are to generate a worklist for when you get on your feet. Because tablework can resemble a workshop, the patterns are easy to fall into: a question about a line of text leads to a thought about how it could be written/phrased/constructed differently, and suddenly you're overseeing a discussion about what the playwright could change. A writer is welcome to consider anything they hear around the table, but under no obligation to rewrite. A director must bring the group's attention back to the task: the creation of a worklist based on questions. Focusing on what "works" and doesn't on the page will bring you back to a workshop mentality, which will devour valuable time.

Beginning Tablework

Working in chronological order from the beginning, ask the cast to read a scene or section of the play. Starting and stopping—a few pages at most—ask the cast to articulate the basic information:

- Where does the scene take place?
- Who is there?
- What has happened before the scene begins?
- What is each character's relationship to one another?
- What information does each character enter the scene with?
- What do they arrive wanting and from whom?
- Do they get it or not?

Some of these questions may seem obvious, and they should be: they will offer clarity about the facts of the scene (who, what, and where) while prompting conversations about more complex considerations (why and how).

Always begin each discussion with a question. "How much time has passed between scenes, and what has happened since we last saw these characters?" "Why would they say something like that to their mother?" "Do you think he's picking a fight with her? If he isn't, what is he doing?"

Encourage the cast to talk about their character and also about the world of the play. Call attention to what characters say about themselves and what they say about each other. Ask the actors if their character is telling the truth, or thinks that they are. People lie all the time, but actors often take everything a character says as true. Challenge that notion: characters can—and should—be just as manipulative, deceitful, confused, contradictory, and uncertain as real people, so remind the cast to think critically. Remind them also that well-written characters change: an observation about a character's thought or behavior that feels very right at the beginning of the play may feel less so by the second scene.

- Clarify what each character knows and when they know it.
- Mark moments when a character is hearing information for the first time and how that changes the speaker, the listener, and perhaps the plot.
- Ask the cast what is new or different in each scene.
- Ask what changes and when: for each character individually and for the story.

Write down what the cast observes, especially in those moments when they seem confused. Their observations, interests, and questions will be the foundation on which you will approach scene work.

Be aware that inviting the cast to speak so openly can create power imbalances. Make sure everyone feels heard, listened to, and valued equally. Your promotion of a democratic atmosphere will increase the quality of discussion, and will also serve as a teaching opportunity: bullying will not be tolerated, nor will know-it-alls, nor will one actor asserting their opinion or will over another. You are not running a dictatorship, and your openness around the table should not be taken as an invitation for anyone else to become a dictator, either.

Rules

One can think of a rehearsal process as a game that unfolds over a series of weeks. The company plays by making as many different choices as possible before rehearsals end. The flaw in this game, however, is that it would take an infinite amount of time to try every choice, and there would be no way to know how or when to eliminate some and elevate others. Like all games, a rehearsal process needs rules and boundaries so everyone involved can make choices with confidence. Rehearsals can and should be fun, but the language of "play" does not imply everything is fair game. A rehearsal process must have parameters in order to be safe, clear, and productive.

I once directed a play that, on the page, was unruly and wild. Non-linear with bursts of non-sequiturs: songs, dances, characters that materialized and disappeared without explanation or context. My idea was to begin our rehearsal process by letting the cast improvise their way through the play. There would be no rules to this unrehearsed run-through: any thought, idea, or impulse an actor had could and should be tried. About twenty minutes into this experiment, we had completely ground to a halt. No one in the cast had any idea what they or anyone else was doing, let alone why. It was nonsense, it taught us nothing about the play, and worst of all, it was potentially unsafe for the company. What we *did* learn is that if everything is fair game, there is no way to find a direction forward as a group. Instead of making choices, deciding which had potential and building on them, everyone's efforts diffused like smoke: because there were no boundaries, everything just came and went without significance. Even if rules are made to be broken, there must first be rules to break or else there is only anarchy, which may sound intriguing until you try to conduct a rehearsal that way.

The first set of rules can be assumed:

- We will speak the text as written
- We will attempt to understand and consider all stage directions (even if we do not use them)
- Everyone will play the role(s) they have been assigned
- Everyone will honor everyone else's process

The next are the play's objective truths or given circumstances:

- Where is the play set?
- When is the play set?
- What time of year?
- What time of day?

And so on. The company will agree that these are rules: they are not debatable.

These may seem obvious, but you should still propose them to let everyone agree or disagree with them. Rules will become more difficult to set as you shift your attention from objective facts to subjective choices. This is where the group must agree to and set boundaries, a process the director will encourage and oversee. We have all witnessed an acting choice that was confusing, or so far removed from the world of the play that we become conscious of the actor and their choice and disconnected from the story. That is a basic example of a choice stepping out of bounds. Subjective choices will exist at the edges of this game. They involve emotion, action, and behavior. Subjective choices are open to creative interpretation but still require boundaries or else the performances, and production, will become illegible to an audience. Creating these boundaries begins with a close reading of the text.

- Start with the words: what exactly is the character saying? Pay attention to phrasing, punctuation, and other clues.
- Move on to action: what must the character do in order to honor what is on the page?
- Consider their behavior: how do they perform the action?
- Think about stakes: how do the characters respond to the words and behavior of others? What do these reactions teach us about their emotional trajectories?

If you are clear about the words and the corresponding actions, the actor will have a sense of healthy boundaries about the character's behavior. Their choices are no longer infinite but informed and influenced by the text. Seeking a basic understanding now will deepen their work when the actors get on their feet.

I once directed a play that ended with two lovers reconciling after a catastrophic argument. One actor was so overcome with emotion in rehearsal that they continued to weep even after their relationship was restored. They explained that in spite of the text, their response felt honest and appropriate. On one hand, the actor was experiencing a very real and valid emotion. On the other, the text was clear that immediately after the relationship is repaired, the couple laughs and kisses. While emotion and behavior are open to interpretation, the text taught us that the actor's subjective choice (in this case, tears) crossed a boundary of behavior. An acting choice was rewriting the scene, so we needed to find another way to play that moment that felt true to the actor while honoring the story as written.

Setting up rules will give you a clear way to evaluate choices in rehearsal. If an idea is in alignment with the text, we know it is "in bounds." If an idea is so removed from the word or action on the page that it is difficult to understand or to play, it may be "out of bounds." What you are creating is a rubric in which to evaluate choices. The boundaries you set should be considered fixed until you discover a need to change them. This changing of the rules is especially common with a new play, as the text is in a state of flux. What is and isn't in bounds should be changed based on the needs of the play, not on any one individual's taste. If there is a moment, an action, an emotion, or a behavior you discover in rehearsal that feels honest, accurate, or appropriate, then it must be brought to the writer and discussed as a potential change. You and the company have uncovered a potential story discrepancy that should be addressed.

Beware of genres and stylistic -isms, which can feel like rules but are not the same. Words like surrealism, naturalism, expressionism are academic terms that may set boundaries that could limit your choices and may not be relevant to this play. You are making a new and singular work of art: decide for yourselves what is and is not in bounds. All rules should come from the play itself.

As you work through the text around the table, you are setting not only the rules of how the text could be performed, but also of the production itself. For example, what is the logic of transitions? Will the actors break character in front of the audience? Will they carry props and rearrange furniture? Who are they when they move this furniture: do they remain in character or behave as some neutral figure? In this production, you may say, the actors will (or will not) break character between scenes. That is another type of rule to discuss and consider.

The paradox of setting rules is that they are freeing, not restricting. A chaotic, disorganized room—a space where progress is undefined and choices feel arbitrary—will create a tense, guarded process full of frustration and conflict. A room with clear rules, even those in flux, can be playful, rigorous, and quite literally boundary-pushing. The pleasure of rules is having something to push up against.

A Note on Rule Breaking

Rules, of course, are made to be broken. But when? And how? And by whom? A significant departure from the rules of the world can be thrilling. It is the stuff of great drama. A director must approach the breaking of rules not as good or bad, but as intentional or unintentional. A surprising, shocking choice can be an exciting coup de theatre, but a creative team must have control over these choices and make clear-eyed decisions of when, how, and why a rule should be broken: one broken accidentally or without thoughtful intention can feel sloppy, unfocused, or confusing.

The irony of rule breaking is that it is the strength and clarity of the existing rules that make their breaking so powerful. Porous, ill-defined boundaries are easy to break through: it is not very dramatic when they collapse. Solid boundaries, busted open, can be cathartic.

Learning about the Actor's Process

As you pose questions to be considered and set up the rules of your game around the table, listen to how the actors communicate: how they speak about the text, their characters, and the world of the play. This information is as valuable as anything else you will receive during tablework. You are learning about their creative process: about how they work with a director and with a text. You are observing an artist's mind at work, learning what matters to them, and understanding what they see on the page.

A director must be able to speak everyone's creative language to build the most successful collaborative partnerships: tablework is your opportunity to understand an actor's approach to their work. Some actors will be steeped in Method or another style of training. Others work visually and will want to understand how a scene will look before they can inhabit their character. Some actors thrive around the table, as discussion and intellectual stimulation are how they find their way into a role, while others need to work physically and will have little to contribute until they are on their feet and in their bodies. The more clearly you can identify their individual processes–what they see and feel, how they think, what they understand, and how they understand it–the stronger your collaboration will be.

Building an Ensemble

No actor's process happens in a vacuum. In addition to learning about each actor's mind and approach, you are learning about them within the context of a group. A series of relationships are being established around the table, and a director must both guide and observe that process. A cast will agree and disagree: what matters is what you notice and how it can inform how you communicate. You are taking the group's emotional, creative, and professional temperature. Maybe some actors love the play and others doubt its quality. Maybe some are afraid to ask questions or to appear unintelligent in front of the group. Maybe one doesn't like another actor's choices, opinions, or points of view. Maybe some don't like directors!

A company is usually on good behavior with one another during the first few days of rehearsal, but discussions about the text can reveal more than they might realize. Take mental notes of company dynamics. You cannot preempt or avoid conflict if two artists do not like each other, but you can certainly avoid pouring gas on a fire, and you can also be prepared if you need to act as a mediator. All you need to do is pay attention: everything you need to know about these burgeoning relationships will be on display around the table.

Guiding a group toward an ensemble is different from making friends, or from making certain everyone loves one another. A director is responsible for cultivating an atmosphere of respect, of creative freedom, and of professionalism. Two actors may not like each other, but they must work together with a spirit of generosity. A director can lead by example during tablework to make this clear. If an actor gives another actor a suggestion, a director should intervene and clarify that suggestions are not notes or instructions: they can be listened to or disregarded. If an actor tells another how to play a moment, a director must explain that this process will not include actors giving direction to each other. If an actor demands that a line should be changed or rewritten, a director must remind the group that any rewrites are the writer's decision to make.

What you are doing is setting up another set of rules about how this ensemble will work together. Everyone is entitled to an opinion, but an opinion that transforms into an instruction or demand from another artist is out of bounds. A director can express this, but the strongest and clearest way to articulate it is through example.

Running Tablework and Moving Forward

Sometimes a topic will come up that is so compelling that everyone will want to share their thoughts. Suddenly, you find you've spent hours in discussion without having read a word. The subject may be pertinent to the play, but even something relevant or interesting may not be useful. A director's task is to keep tablework focused on generating the best questions to address on your feet: discussion is critical to understanding the world of the play, but if it veers away from an active effort to understand the text, there is a limit to its usefulness. If the company starts making associations that are not relevant to the text, guide them back to questions about the play. If an actor likes to tell stories that do not seem directly related to the text, bring the room's focus to the scene under discussion. When you feel a topic has exhausted itself, ask the company to read the next section aloud.

Disagreements will occur during tablework. This group of artists, who may not know each other, have been working privately in preparation for the rehearsal process and are now asked as a group to share their thoughts. Differing opinions are inevitable, and those differences may feel stressful or threatening to an actor. Steer the conversation away from the notion that one opinion needs to "win" or to be "right." Everyone will have thoughts, questions, and observations, and none of them can be deemed better or smarter or more correct than another until you are on your feet. Remind the cast that conflicting points of view is an encouraging sign: it means there are many different ways to try a scene, a moment, or a line. Like all questions that come up around the table, a disagreement should simply go on your list of questions.

There will be actors who want to hold the floor, who will try to take control of the conversation, who want to be the first to share a thought or opinion, or who refuse to move onto the next section. The solution to this scenario is a paradox: you must assert your control over the room so that it can be democratic. One way to do this is to ask questions of those actors who haven't had as much opportunity to speak. After reading a passage, ask a question of an actor who has shown themselves to be less willing to chime in and begin with their point of view. Another is to remind the cast that we are not trying to solve or to answer any questions, simply to present them now for later investigation. That way of working can feel threatening to an actor who is uncomfortable with the unknown, so reiterating that open-ended questions are not a sign that we cannot find the answer but are simply preparing for a next step may be helpful.

The Role of the Writer during Tablework

Established work is given the benefit of the doubt. A company doing Shakespeare may struggle with a section of the text, but they understand the responsibility of finding a solution is theirs alone. Obviously, since that playwright is not available for rewrites, that is immediately clear. A play that has never been done before, however, may be approached in a very different way: the writer is present, and there is an understanding that changes can and will happen. A company may become less inclined to give a challenging section the benefit of the doubt and may simply ask that the writer change or "fix" it. Furthermore, the writer may feel pressured to make changes, even when there has been no request to do so. Because a script must be unpacked, analyzed, and investigated during tablework, a writer may feel as though every line of text and every word is being doubted or met with skepticism instead of with healthy curiosity. An actor *should* say things like "I don't get this part" or "why would I say that?" around the table, but a writer may take that as a criticism of their work.

A director must set rules during tablework about how the writer and the cast will interact throughout the process.

- Encourage the company to lead with the benefit of the doubt, as they would with an established play.
- Make clear that even though the writer is present, it is not their responsibility to make changes based on these discussions.
- Help the writer understand that questions are necessary for tablework, and that curiosity is not criticism.

As tablework unfolds, encourage your writer to listen:

- Notice what the cast is curious about or confused by
- Note which sections are more difficult to understand
- Keep track of unexpected thoughts or ideas

Remind the writer that they are not responsible for explaining their work. Like everyone else in the room, the writer should be focusing on questions, not on providing answers. A writer may want to make changes based on what they learn around the table, but they should refrain until they can see the work on its feet. They should always feel welcome to offer their point of view, but explanations at this stage may not be useful: they will tell an actor what to think or how to behave, and may shut down healthy exploration.

That said, there is no need to waste time dwelling on objective questions while the author is sitting right there: if you don't know where a scene is set, just ask them. Even after the development stage, there may still be elements that are clear to the writer but are not on the page. Actors, because they see the world from their character's perspective, may catch details you and the writer have overlooked. An objective question posed by an actor could sound like: "It doesn't say in the text that my character is in this scene, and I don't have any lines, but later on I seem to know everything that happened: am I there or not?" That is a question a writer can, and should, address. It is the subjective questions, why and how, motivation and behavior, that a writer should allow the cast to wonder about, to wrestle with, and to experiment with on their feet.

This dynamic you create between the writer and the cast will carry through the entire process. A cast should be heard, their opinion valued, their concerns/questions/struggles validated. A writer must be empowered to make changes when they feel it serves their vision, and to refrain when they don't. A company that is taught, often through the silence of the director, that a writer will make any change they want will have little incentive to stop. If a writer begins to feel like the actor's employee, that the interrogation of the script has transformed into an interrogation of their skill, they will get defensive and may refuse to make changes, or to view any note—valid or not—as a criticism. Even worse, they may become insecure and doubt what they've written, leading them to try to address through rewrites every question an actor poses. If rules are not established during tablework, a writer may become either entirely inflexible or a servant to the cast's whims. Both scenarios can be avoided if you shield the writer either from the responsibility of defending their work or from endless changes for the company's approval. Disagreements will arise—a writer may insist their point is clear on the page, whereas an actor may argue it is not in the text and therefore impossible to play—but those disagreements cannot be addressed until the moment is staged and everyone can observe it together.

Ending Tablework

Tablework is about building curiosity and enthusiasm for the next steps: too many hours of discussion can lead to a loss of momentum. If a cast becomes bored, they may begin to seek out problems on the page that do not exist. On the other hand, rushing through tablework can lead to confusion. If the cast is still struggling with objective questions, you are not ready to get on your feet. If tablework has become overrun with tangential conversations, unfocused attention, and unhelpful dissections of the text, move on.

You'll also know when to end tablework based on your rehearsal calendar. If you have four weeks in the rehearsal room, for example, and you are on pace to spend a week around the table, ask yourself if that feels appropriate. Each play and process is different, but always err on the side of getting on your feet quickly.

There will always be more questions to ask and subjects to discuss: if you feel confident you have enough questions percolating to get on your feet, begin.

If you feel you are spending too much time around the table, ask yourself why:

- Is this cast particularly cerebral?
- Do they seem reluctant to get on their feet?
- Do they prefer the safety of discussion?
- Is the play especially confusing?
- Does it need more development than you had thought?

Actors are naturally intuitive and may be teaching you something about the play without articulating it: the reasons for a slow pace may be deeper than simply time management.

End tablework with another reading of the play. This is a way to return to the text with fresh eyes, deeper insight, and excitement about everything you and the company want to try. You've spent days pulling the play apart, brainstorming ideas, asking questions, and learning about your collaborators' minds and processes. A reading can bring a company's attention back from the analytic to the creative, which is where you want them as you pivot to staging.

13
BUILDING A ROUGH DRAFT

Getting on Your Feet

The portion of the rehearsal process that we could call "staging" is actually a multi-step process involving different tactics and approaches, each stage culminating in a run-through of the current "draft" of the piece. It is not one straight line from tablework to tech, it is a series of mini-processes, each with their own goals and challenges.

Your first "pass" through the play will be the creation of a rough draft: a complete staging the actors can walk through, and that you and the writer can watch in its entirety. This is a period of trial and error—of strong and wrong—similar to the workshop process, but instead of generating data for contemplation (and perhaps rewrites), the rehearsal rough draft is a time for you and the actors to begin to understand for yourselves how the play behaves in three dimensions.

Rough drafts of any creative project are messy: that is natural, inevitable, and by design. Building them by committee is particularly exposing, vulnerable making, frustrating, and illuminating: you and the company are pushing off from the safety of the table and into the unexplored waters of the physical production. Your goal is to make a complete thing, a staged draft, and in doing so, collecting information about how the world feels and moves, and how each piece fits into the whole.

The First Time the Play Falls Apart

An older actor once told me that when he is struggling to figure out how to play a moment, he asks himself: "Now, if I were a human being, how would I do this?"

Everyone is a genius around the table. The ideas flow, the questions are intriguing, and everyone can feel comfortable, clever, insightful, and inspired. And then something happens. You get up on your feet, and suddenly no one remembers how to sit normally on a chair, things like doors and phones feel like foreign objects, and words feel leaden and confusing to both the speaker and listener.

The play will fall apart three times during your process. This is the first, but the cause will be the same each time: the previous step—in this instance, tablework—gave everyone (director included) confidence that you had "figured it out." Tablework created the sense that everyone had an unimpeachable understanding of text: all that needed to happen was some trial and error to address your questions and the production would be ready. This feeling is dashed the instant you get on your feet. Your fantasy version of the process evaporates and suddenly everyone is learning how to walk and talk again as though for the first time.

The only way to proceed is to embrace this feeling. You're learning how the play works on its feet, you're learning to cast off preconceived notions and fantasies of how it was going to look and sound, and you're discovering the logic of how the world works in practice. This step is not a sign of a problem: a director must remind the cast that this just another part of the work, disorienting though it may feel. This moment is temporary, and eventually the company will become accustomed to the space, to the text, and to their characters. Instill in them the bravery necessary to not know what to do, or how to be.

The Confidence of "I Don't Know"

We often talk about good choices as a sign of talent or wisdom. One wants to make a smart choice, the perfect choice, a brilliant choice. We congratulate actors on their interesting choices, we admire the bravery of idiosyncratic choices. Conversely, we worry about bad choices, wrong choices, dumb choices. Choices are exposing: they are displays of our tastes, and therefore of ourselves. The long road to find what feels like a right choice for any artist travels through many, many failed attempts: there is no other way to get there.

The creation of a rough draft is a period of time in which you are working primarily with what doesn't feel right. You are making choices that do not feel good, and in so doing, learning what might feel better. The difficult truth of this process is that the worse a choice feels, the more information it will provide. A director's task is to create a space in which actors feel safe in this very exposing, vulnerable-making space of "not-knowing." They need to cultivate an environment in which actors can feel supported enough that they can fail in front of you and their fellow cast members without feeling judged. Many artists work in mediums that allow them to make mistakes privately. Actors have no such luxury: their rough draft happens in front of their collaborators. How long can a group of actors stay in such a delicate psychic space? A director must keep a space safe for mistakes for as long as possible. The longer you can keep the room in an exploratory mindset, the more information you can gather, and the quality of your eventual choices will be that much stronger.

There can be pressure in any collaborative setting to find the quickest answer. That way of approaching your work is seductive: it is a scary thing to live in a place of ambiguity, of not-knowing. To exist in a space of intelligence and solution-based decision-making creates the illusion of safety and comfort, but in reality it is restrictive, unimaginative, fearful, and potentially competitive. The best ideas are not plucked out of thin air by a genius, they are discovered through this process of trial and error, and the strongest position an artist can take during this work is to say "I don't know."

That may not be the first phrase that comes to mind when we think of confidence, but it is in a rehearsal room. A director must be very comfortable saying I don't know, and encouraging your collaborators to say the same. "I don't know" is liberating. It is not an admission of ignorance but a way to organize time. What you are saying is "I don't know *yet.*" It is a delay, a postponement of judgment, a close relative of the "yes, and" of improvisational logic. A rough draft is constructed by making a choice, and then another, and then another, while taking your time, listening, considering, and observing. Not-knowing relieves pressure, creates freedom, and stretches time.

We try multiple choices not only because we are working by process of elimination, but also because we are learning by comparing one to another. If you were to commit to your first choice, then you and the company would know that you are operating from a place of fear: that first choice might seem safe or right "enough" to avoid the messiness of mistakes, and no risk would be necessary. Trying a moment a second way, then a fourth, sixth, and so on only strengthens your ability to identify what has potential and why. The more choices, the more options, and even if the first choice turns out to have been the best one all along, a group can only know that based on how it compares with their other attempts.

Every rehearsal room should have a multiplicity of opinions, personalities, and points of view: disagreements should generate more ideas, not shut them down. A director who says "Let's try it both ways" or "Is there another version we haven't thought of?" or "That's an interesting choice, let's keep experimenting" is putting themselves in the most optimal creative position and is encouraging their collaborators to proceed with the same mentality. You are teaching the cast that this is how the room will operate, and how experiments will be conducted. Not-knowing is not a void that needs to be filled, it is not a knowledge deficit. It is a powerful and necessary way to explore, and it is the director who must cultivate, support, and defend it.

How to Prepare

Rehearsal preparations require balancing what a director plans to do and to accomplish with an understanding that experimentation can be unpredictable.

A director can think of their rehearsal plans as a structure on which to build: too rigid and it will be inflexible, too loose and it will not be supportive.

Before you look at a scene on its feet for the first time, review all of your notes going back to your initial responses. Sounds, ideas, and images, the discussions from your design meetings, your reading and workshop notes: even if they feel outdated or no longer useful, remind yourself of the creative journey that led up to this moment. Have that information fresh in your mind as you watch the scene take shape. Review the basics—who, what, and where—and revisit your and the actor's questions from around the table.

A director can control what happens in a rehearsal room, but they cannot dictate how productive any given day will be. All they can do is arrived prepared, knowing what they want to work on and why, and ready to embrace the natural twists and turns of an artistic process. The more prepared you are with ideas and questions, the more flexible you can be. The less prepared, the harder it will be to improvise.

At this point in your process, you have absorbed many opinions, considerations, desires, and points of view. This preparation time is personal. Ask yourself:

- What do I want to work on?
- What do I want to see?
- What do I want to know more about?
- Where do my curiosities lie?

Everyone's needs and wants should be considered, but these questions are about your taste, and your creative inquiry.

Running a Rough Draft Rehearsal

Begin each rehearsal by rereading the section you will be working on, script in hand so that there is no pressure to be memorized. Use this time to reiterate the objective truths (who, what, and where) and to remind the group of the central questions you posed to each other around the table. Ask the cast if they have any new thoughts or questions about the scene, and offer up any of your own. This time allows you and the cast to bring your attention back to this scene, to remember what you had discussed, and to get the mind focused as the cast begins the process of inhabiting their roles.

Then get up on your feet. The longer you discuss, the more difficult it may be to take the leap. Set aside intellectualization, which can lead to fear or judgment, and try something to see how you feel about it. The first experiment can be the most difficult: do not delay, simply jump in.

BUILDING A ROUGH DRAFT

Keep blocking as simple as possible: very little instruction, no micromanagement. Determine where everyone should be when the scene begins, and allow the cast to step through the opening moments on their own. You may have an idea of how the scene could look, but do not force the cast into recreating it. Their discoveries will teach you, and each other, more than any predetermined blocking pattern. As you watch and evaluate the different versions, make suggestions that pertain to behavior and motivation, not technical considerations about where they are standing, when they move, etc. An actor will stand up from their seat if the energy of the moment demands it, they'll cross toward or away from a scene partner if how they are feeling dictates it. Encouraging the actors to connect with how they're feeling is the strongest and most effective way to stage a scene: concerns of stage picture should wait until much later in your process: understanding the space through how it feels for the cast is the ideal way to build a first pass.

Often, you and the cast may find yourselves stuck. The cast is still trying to understand the physical logic of the space, they will be holding and reading from their script so their focus will be split and the natural flow of staging may grind to a halt. When this happens, make a quick choice to try something different. Ask the cast to sit on the floor, rearrange some furniture, ask actors to switch positions with one another. Turn the entire scene around so the cast is playing with their back to you. The goal is to keep the exploration loose. Fixating on a staging problem or trying to make a choice work can drain creative energy and momentum, can derail a rehearsal day, and can set a critical tone. Staging should not be an obstacle to trial and error.

This way of working is helpful for the director, too. Suggesting a change that pushes you away from your preconceived notions of how a scene might look will loosen you up both to what it is and what could be. If you are still struggling, however, move on and return to that scene another day. You and the company may need more time for contemplation, or you may have discovered a textual problem that needs support from the writer.

In these early staging days, do not push yourself to refine or perfect anything. Your goal is to find some choices that feel authentic and that have potential. If you feel you have that and a rough staging to support it, you have enough to move on.

Losing (and regaining) the Music of the Text

The biggest casualty of building a rough draft is the text's rhythm, pace, and momentum. The slowness that comes from stepping through the play for the first time, the constant starting and stopping, the acclimation to the physical space, and the holding of scripts mean honoring the natural cadence of the text is impossible. While the final read-through around the table may have felt energetically appropriate, the building of a rough draft does away with anything resembling the pace and shape of what the writer intended. This is inevitable, but there are some by-products of this that a director should be aware of.

The first is that this slower pace will invite the addition of a lot of extra blocking, props, and behavioral business. An actor may feel strongly their character would make a drink, fiddle with their phone, change their shoes, or smoke a cigarette. The impulse to create business is part of the exploration process, but it is also a signal that the actor is feeling a need to fill a gap in the play's natural rhythm. The actor understands instinctively, if not intellectually, that the timing is off, that the scene is slow, and that they need to compensate. Their feeling is correct, but adding unnecessary props or stage business is only a temporary solution. Once the company has command over their lines and the physical shape of the production continues to develop, the pace will naturally quicken and there will not be a need for extraneous objects or behaviors.

The Writer while Building the Rough Draft

Not everyone can work on the play at the same time. A cast needs the space to wrestle with, to be frustrated by, and to question the text. During the building of the rough draft, the writer must let the cast challenge and be challenged by the text. Because the cast needs this time to ponder, doubt, and struggle, there should not be any rewrites. An actor should be able to say "I don't know" without being offered an explanation or new text. The first days an actor is on their feet will elicit many different feelings: this step is necessary, and new writing will not make it happen faster. Quite the opposite: rewrites during this part of rehearsals will just prolong the period of trial and error.

If the writer is in the room during experimentation, actors may feel more pressure to "get it right" or to perform in some way they imagine the writer wants. That feeling can limit a company's bravery and increase their vulnerability. Watching intentional mistakes and the inability to capture the music of the text can discourage a writer. During a workshop, that energy was easier to witness because that time did not end with an audience. In rehearsal, everyone is aware that the clock is ticking, especially a writer watching the creation of the very first draft. Their impulse may be to "fix" a scene in order to avoid a natural part of the process, which will lead to tension between the writer and the company.

Ask the writer to spend a few days out of the rehearsal room once tablework ends. They will learn very little about their play during this stage. The writer will receive more reliable and useful information if they take a step back and return to the room to see a full stumble-through of the rough draft. If they can watch a run, you can discuss a shared experience and then talk about rewrites and changes. It is better to look at the entire piece on its feet—even in this rough state—than to ask the writer to watch trial and error. It creates an unfair situation for both the writer and the company. A director must provide the cast with room to work on their own, and they must provide the writer with the best way to see and understand what progress has been made, what seems to have potential, and what remains a struggle.

Measuring the Success of Rough Draft Rehearsals

If this part of the process is trial and error, if you embrace "I don't know," how is progress to be made, and how can anyone tell? While this work is exploratory, it must build toward the next steps and cannot continue indefinitely.

Sometimes you'll find a choice that feels wonderful—exciting and full of potential—but that does not seem to fit with what makes sense for the character or the scene. Do not throw it away yet: there are clues in that discovery, either about the text or about the rules you have created. It may mean you need to rethink something about the play or the character. If the results of an experiment feel good, even or especially if they do not fit with the word/action/behavior, keep it and continue to ask why.

Progress simply means you are either moving toward or away from your goals. Some rehearsals you will feel adrift or stuck, and that information is its own reward. In your reflection time, ask yourself why your questions and experiments are not moving you forward. From there you can generate new worklists and, similar to making a drastic staging change, you can bring in ideas that may shake you and the cast loose.

You and the company are looking for a version of the scene that has potential. One that makes sense, that addresses some questions, and that feels repeatable. Don't overrehearse or overthink it. If you've found a way to play the scene that feels worth doing again, that is enough. The simplest way to evaluate the success of a rehearsal is to ask if you could run the section all the way through from beginning to end. If the answer is yes, you are ready to see it within the context of a stumble-through. For this part of the process, that is all success you need.

Democratic Rehearsal Rooms

A director could very easily assert themselves as the authority on the play. The lone artist who knows all the answers. They could teach the company what the play is about, how they should perform it, and what is a right and wrong choice. The success of that process would be measured by how well the cast pleases the director, the resident expert on the play.

What I'm describing is not fiction, or even that uncommon, but there are flaws in that way of working that helps us understand the value of a democratic approach. A goal of any rehearsal process is to cultivate the actors' ownership of their performance. A performance cannot be captured and frozen, so an actor is building something that is strong enough to be consistent, and malleable enough to be repeatable under different circumstances. An actor must have confidence in their work and in their understanding and interpretation of their role. A dictatorial process will rob an actor of these things. They will have no ownership of their performance because it will be based on the actor's ability to please a director or to follow their instructions. The end result is not a collaborative work of art.

Dictatorships are rooted in fear. Fear of not being listened to, fear of being challenged, fear of not being right, and fear of not being in control. A frightened director is scared to admit they do not know, that they may not have the best or right answer, or that someone else's idea might be superior. There is an egolessness to working in a democratic way: the most promising ideas should be followed, regardless of who led the group there. A democratic process is not only the most ethical way to work and the most fun, it also promises the best possible version of the production.

14
PREPARING AND ORGANIZING A REHEARSAL DAY

Planning a Rehearsal Day

Build your daily schedule by evaluating your short- and long-term goals. Begin with what you want to accomplish the next day. Be mindful of how quickly or slowly you are working through the play. If the script is 100 pages long and you are working through ten pages a day, are you comfortable waiting a week and a half to see a stumble-through? Do you want to see a run sooner than that? How many pages will you need to stage every day to do a stumble-through when you prefer? Thinking in this way will help you understand the daily pace you need to set.

The first few days of staging rehearsal will teach you a lot about tempo. You can expect them to be generally slower in that you're all building a vocabulary and fumbling your way through. Even accounting for the tentativeness of the first days, you will be able to sense how you and the cast are moving through the text, how challenging your questions are proving to be, and how much trial and error is necessary. A text has a way of setting a natural rhythm and it will be your task to either slow down or speed up the flow of the work.

Meeting with Your Stage Manager

Each rehearsal day should end with a meeting between you and stage management. Together, you will plan the next day's schedule and compare notes about what you observed during the day you've just completed. Discuss what seems to be working well, what needs more attention, and how the cast is doing, individually and as a group. You and stage management are both watching rehearsal unfold, but what you notice will be different: share what you see and ask them to do the same.

When planning each rehearsal day, here are a few questions you and your stage manager should consider:

Pages per day: Not all scenes and moments are created equally, so to schedule a day based only on the page numbers is impractical. Break the play up into scenes (or sections) and consider the emotional and physical complexity of each part: you may have a sense of the degree of difficulty from your time around the table. For the first few days, err on fewer pages as you learn how the play feels to stage without rushing. Once you have a sense of how much you can accomplish in a day, you can increase the amount of daily work.

How to order the worklist: the first days on your feet will teach you about how the company works, including the most productive parts of your day. Some groups begin with a burst of energy, some struggle to focus until later in the day, some are unpredictable and depend on the nature and emotional quality of the scene. When planning a day, use that information to determine how you want to order your worklist. Is violence or intimacy how you want to begin the day? Is staging a physically demanding scene at the end of the day going to be productive? It is ideal to work in sequential order, as it will help the actors develop their psychological and emotional arcs, but there will be times when working out of order will yield the best results.

Staggering calls: Being respectful of actors' time is another consideration that may change the order in which you work. Staggering calls means your stage manager will ask actors to come only when working on their scenes so you are not keeping the cast waiting. To the degree that you are able, arrange the day so an actor does not have huge gaps in between when they are being used in the room. There are multiple scheduling considerations that go into each day, but staggering calls should be a priority for the morale, rest, and focus of the company. It is a sign of respect for the cast's time and is always appreciated.

Outside commitments: Staging is the primary, but far from the only, consideration during a rehearsal day. When planning with your stage manager, ask if there are actor conflicts, if there are costume fittings (which happen during rehearsal hours), if there are press commitments like interviews or photo shoots, if an actor wants time to work privately on their dialect. Nothing can derail a productive day faster than a conflicting need you didn't know about and were not prepared to accommodate.

Violence, intimacy, and privacy: Moments of violence and intimacy must be scheduled further in advance because you cannot assume those collaborators are always free. You must also plan ahead because the scheduling of rehearsals that involve violence and intimacy must be carefully orchestrated. You must make certain all the cast members involved with these moments are available (no conflicts), and you must keep the space intimate on those days. Artists or staff not involved directly with these scenes need to be kept out of the rehearsal

PREPARING AND ORGANIZING A REHEARSAL DAY 143

room. If you cannot work with the actors necessary or with the fight or intimacy director, you must postpone. Do not attempt a rough draft on your own and do not insert an actor into a moment of intimacy or violence after it has been staged.

Integrating new pages: If the writer has new pages to distribute or changes to make, begin the day with them. You should always be present when an actor is given new pages, so do not send or allow the writer or stage management to send changes to the cast in advance. Beginning the day with new pages will allow time for questions and will give the company time to read, reflect, and ponder. You want that work happening only in rehearsal, when you are available to them to discuss.

After the schedule has been set, review the stage manager's rehearsal notes. Throughout the day, they have been writing down observations, questions, and concerns, very often about the design or physical aspects of the production. Props that were discussed, costume ideas, blocking discoveries that might influence the set. Many of the ideas that come up during a rehearsal day, especially in the early stages, are the result of improvisation or brainstorming. A stage manager will ask if you really wanted this or that prop, if you are actually adding an actor to this scene, if you do think the set needs another door. Sometimes it's true, in which case, that information needs to be shared through the rehearsal report. Sometimes it isn't, and the idea in question was not a legitimate change or request. This information will make its way into a daily rehearsal report (which the entire staff of the production will receive), so reviewing stage management's notes together before the report is distributed is a necessary step to avoid confusion.

Rehearsal Reports

A rehearsal report is a document, written by the stage manager, that summarizes the rehearsal day. It is shared with the designers, theater staff, and everyone involved with the production except for the cast. Its purpose is to give everyone the same information at the same time, to document the events of the rehearsal, and to explain the shifting needs of the production. A rehearsal report will include the basic information of the day: what time it began and ended, what scenes were worked on and for how long, which actors were called and when, who else was in attendance, and if there were conflicts, absences, or lateness. It will also include a short paragraph summarizing the work that was accomplished. Then the report is split up by department (set, lights, sound, costumes, management, production, etc.) and all information relevant to that department will be shared there. A designer or shop manager will look for their department, read those notes, and adjust their worklist accordingly.

A rehearsal report note for a specific department will read:

PROPS

>ADD: One Apple iPhone, the appropriate model for 2014, no case, distressed. It will need to ring.
>CUT: the box of donuts
>CUT: the paper grocery bag for the donuts
>ADD: a cluster of bananas (perishable)
>ADD: a white plastic bag for the bananas

And then elsewhere on the report:

SOUND

>ADD: the sound of a 2014 Apple iPhone, preferably coming from the actual device (see first note under PROPS)

The report will end with the next day's schedule, or that information will be shared with the group separately. Rehearsal reports for a new play have one significant difference: the inclusion of rewrites, script changes, and new pages. This information needs to be shared daily, as it will affect the work of multiple departments. Do not assume small script changes will not impact other collaborators: they will, and in ways you cannot predict. The rehearsal report for a new play doubles as an inventory of script changes.

Read every report, even if you are aware of its contents. You need to have an understanding of what information is going to your team, if there's anything you would like to add or anything you would like to explain to your designers directly. The rehearsal process is a time in which your attention is very much in the room and with the cast: be sure what the report is sharing with your designers is complete, helpful, and clear.

15
ACTORS

While directing a new play in Tokyo, the cast and I (through the help of a translator) would often talk about the differences between American and Japanese rehearsal processes. While there are many, there was one the company found fascinating. In Japanese rehearsal rooms, the director will clap once to signal the scene has begun, like a film director shouting "action." I explained that typically, American directors and actors will finish any discussion, the room will fall silent, a few seconds will pass, and then the actors will begin the scene. What, the Japanese actors asked me, is happening in those few seconds?

There is a reason there are so many theories of and approaches to acting all over the world. No matter how succinctly we describe what it is and how it's done, there will always be something about the art of acting that we understand only instinctively, that exists just beyond the boundaries of intellectual thought. That's what makes acting so satisfying to do and captivating to watch: no matter how elegantly we talk about it, there will always be a piece of it that is magical, primal even, that transcends language. That is why we are drawn to acting as an artform: why so many people are compelled to do it, and why—when it is honest and truthful—there is nothing else like it. Like religion, philosophy, or any other art, every generation will write about it, wrestle with it, make discoveries about it, claim to have "solved" it, but it is that untouchable area of mystery that makes the artform transcendent. What happens during those few moments of silence before the acting begins? Something beyond words.

The writer may have created the story, and you may oversee the creation of the production, but it is the actors who do the telling: they are the bodies in the space with the audience and they are the ones entrusted with sharing the play, performance after performance, while creating the illusion that these events are happening for the very first time. You must respect not only an actor's art, skill, and occupation, but also the transformation they undertake. It is something you—and even they—can understand only to a certain point. The rest is magic.

I didn't have a good answer for my collaborators in Tokyo, and I suspect no one else does, either. But my inability to explain made perfect sense to them: what they were really asking is if Americans had come up with a word for the mystery. I had to confess that we hadn't. The inexpressible part of acting is universal.

The Actor as Artist

Objectively speaking, acting is the art of a human being pretending to be someone else—or some variation of themselves—in order to tell a story to an audience. Acting is the process of creating a truthful set of behaviors in an imagined set of circumstances so an audience can suspend their disbelief and pretend what they are witnessing is, in some way, real. This is true regardless of how naturalistic or stylized a piece is: an actor pretends, and the audience has an intellectual, emotional, and physical experience. Using the text as a blueprint, guide, and rulebook, an actor will create a character—behaviors, mannerisms, relationships, a physical and emotional life and all the complications, complexities, histories, and contradictions that come from being human—that can be repeated in a reliable way. If the writer's process is to imagine fully realized humans and then capture what they picture using dialogue, then the actor's process is the opposite: they begin with only the text and proceed to build from it a complex, multidimensional human being. The director serves as the conductor of this work, aiding and guiding the actors through the process of lifting the language off the page and into three dimensions.

Acting involves an enormous amount of courage. Because it is a play, it will involve conflict, and regardless of the tone of the piece, that conflict may be intense. An actor must convey to the audience that they are actually falling in love, having their heart broken, suffering from cancer, losing a child, becoming a king, winning the lottery, or committing murder, over and over again, night after night. It takes an incredible amount of emotional awareness, maturity, and strength to convince yourself you are injured six nights a week at 10:15 p.m. without it taking a psychological toll. As the director, you must be actively aware of the gravity of this task, and of how taxing and emotionally exhausting it can be.

Actors do not exist to do something a director has told them to: they are not mimics or puppets. An actor isn't supposed to play a moment or build a character exactly as you want them to; they are supposed to take what you offer them and make it their own, thereby improving upon it. They are your collaborators and partners, and their work must be respected, valued, nurtured, and honored through every step of your process together.

Acting in New Work

The key difference between acting in new work and an established play is the changes that will be made to the script, and therefore to the character. If everything we know about a character comes from the text, even the smallest rewrite means the character has changed. A director must remember this during the process: every word, pause, and piece of punctuation conveys meaning and influences the character's behavior, so rewrites both great and small will have a significant effect on an actor's process. Even changes an actor has asked for will require time and effort to integrate into a performance. A rewrite for one character will influence how another character sees/hears/understands/experiences them, so any change for one character will impact the others: a rewrite is never self-contained.

You and the writer cannot know if a moment is successful without the full commitment of the cast. Marking through a scene or playing it without complete emotional commitment will not teach you or the writer if rewrites or changes are necessary. Therefore, the actor must play each moment as fully realized as possible, even while knowing it may not last in its current form; furthermore, the moment may change as a direct result of the way the actor is playing it. This is a paradox for any actor working on a new play: they must commit fully to the play as written, and also understand that their doing so may lead to changes. An actor in an established play can work on every moment with the confidence that the text they are speaking in rehearsal will be identical throughout the process: what they read aloud on the first day will be the same at the final performance. An actor in a new play must assume the text is subject to change and must proceed with full commitment anyway. This balancing act is often the most mentally and emotionally challenging part of rehearsing new work.

Actors know this when they begin a new play process, but no one can anticipate how much change will happen, and when, and how those changes will effect the building of their roles. The director must provide the cast with time to wrestle with, doubt, absorb, integrate, and understand rewrites, while respecting that the writer will have their own needs and desires. Both parties need time, space, and support to do their work and to adjust to changes.

Rough Drafts in Front of Others

A person visiting a sculptor's studio, when seeing a half-carved block of marble, would never say "that doesn't look like a person at all!" The visitor understands that they are looking at an art object in process and that judging it at such an early stage would be ridiculous. When watching actors in rehearsal, though, a visitor could say "that doesn't look believable at all!" and be taken seriously. That is because actors are creating humans, and since we *are* humans, we all consider ourselves experts on the subject. We think we can identify in an instant what looks "right" and what doesn't because that is part of our natural conditioning. We move through the world interacting with other people: judging and scrutinizing them, trying to understand their body language, mood, and behavior.

Like a sculptor in their studio, the actor in rehearsal is building something from scratch. They are creating a fully realized human with themselves as the tool, and need the same grace and understanding an observer would offer an artist working in any other medium. Because actors are wrestling with human behavior, something we are programmed to recognize constantly, we can feel an impulse to comment on their process prematurely. A director must be aware of this dynamic when observing rehearsals: an actor in process must be treated with the same patience as a sculptor who has just begun to cut into stone.

The Director–Actor Pact

The actor–director relationship is based on a very simple a pact: the actor will agree to stand up in front of an audience, speak words they did not choose, and pretend to be someone else. They will wear clothes that are not theirs, have emotions that do not belong to them, and behave in ways that are sometimes ridiculous, vulnerable, or potentially embarrassing. They will open themselves up to a room full of strangers, exposing themselves emotionally. And they will do all of this without the ability to see for themselves how they appear. The director will agree to watch this performance and report back to the actor what they see in the most honest and useful way possible.

An actor is putting an enormous amount of trust in the director, and the only way for this relationship to succeed is if the director tells the truth, and if the actor believes them. The actor takes a creative leap, and the director must catch them. If the actor does not trust the director, they will not jump.

An actor, by making a choice in rehearsal, is implicitly asking the director to watch and report on their experience watching it. A director is the actor's mirror. If the actor believes what the director is telling them and respects their taste, the pact will strengthen and the actor will make braver choices. If the actor does not believe the director, or the actor does not trust the director's taste, then they will make only those choices that feel the safest. We have all seen productions in which each actor seemed as though they were in a different play. Usually this is not because of a lack of skill or talent, but because the actors did not trust the director. The pact broke, and the actors made their own choices without the benefit of a reliable mirror. Where there is trust, an actor will become more daring in their choices. And the more daring a cast becomes, the more exciting their choices will be, and the more cohesive they will become as a company.

Trust is built through time and honesty. Actors deal in truth: you cannot deceive them. The more you tell the cast exactly what you are seeing, the more they will believe you. There will be disagreements—a choice an actor feels excited about is confusing to you, or you love a choice they did not like doing—but so long as the actor trusts you, they will remain open to risk or to parting ways with safe choices. Conversely, if you trust the actor, you're more likely to give a choice they love the benefit of the doubt, even if you can't yet see its merit.

Listening to the actors, understanding their point of view, and believing them when they tell you how it feels inside a role breeds trust. Proving to the cast that you are watching them closely, that their every choice is being thoughtfully and seriously considered, that you have great respect for their work, and that you have an understanding of how exposing their process can be will create an artistic bond between the director and actor. Your role as the audience is only as successful as how much the cast believes and trusts you.

Communicating with Actors

All the creative genius in the world cannot help a director who is unable to articulate what they are seeing. What you say to an actor, how you say it, and when you decide to share must be a director's primary consideration.

After you watch a scene, approach the actors and begin your conversation with "the what." Articulate what you saw without judgment or editorializing: simply state what you noticed. That approach leaves the door open to a dialogue. Ask the actors what they noticed and how they felt, and compare notes. From there you can agree on what you learned, and can make decisions about what you might want to try differently.

How you choose to share an observation will determine its success and potency. If you are unclear or confusing, you can trigger frustration or miscommunication. Based on your observations during tablework you already have a sense of how each actor thinks, and you will be able to anticipate how they might receive your thoughts. You shouldn't self-edit, trying to guess how to phrase each observation for maximum effect, but you should know which actors thrive on debate, which are more cerebral, which prefer less talking and more trial and error, and so on.

Another approach is to lead with questions. After the cast has run a scene, ask "How did that feel?" Letting the actors speak first can empower them by prioritizing their experience. It can also release any fear of judgment. If an actor knows that at the end of each run they will immediately receive notes, they will naturally try to get it "right" to avoid criticism. Beginning with questions can sometimes make actors uncomfortable, however: they just want to know what the director saw. You do not need to guess which is more useful: try a few approaches, and let the actors teach you which is most productive.

Now that you have shared the "what" and found the best way to offer an observation, discuss adjustments. While the variables are infinite, there are only three options: run the scene again without any changes, run it again in a completely different way, or save some choices while incorporating new ones. How you deliver this information will directly affect the success of the next attempt.

If you want to try the same choices again, clarify them: "What is intriguing to me about this version is ..."

If you want to incorporate new ideas: "Let's stay with this choice a little longer and try adding/subtracting/changing ..."

If you want to start over: "Let's set this version aside for a while and try something different."

When you choose to share an observation is often the most important decision of all. The right note at the wrong time can do more lasting damage than no note at all. This will be true throughout your process, including and especially during the creation of the rough draft. You may observe a choice that you don't like or does not make sense. Ask yourself if that needs to be addressed immediately, or if the observation can wait. Often, letting an actor discover for themselves what doesn't feel right will give them more agency. If a director takes away, diminishes, or insults an idea while it is still taking shape, the actor may feel scrutinized and may make fewer brave choices. Letting a choice you don't like or understand survive for some time is often an opportunity for you to learn. Why do you feel so strongly opposed to this choice? What exactly is confusing you? Allowing yourself to sit with those questions may reveal far more useful information than what would come from a quick note. Giving yourself time to reflect will also allow you to be clearer and more concise when you do share your observations.

When you decide to communicate with an actor should also be influenced by the atmosphere of the room. If an actor is struggling, if the rehearsal that day is tense, if emotions are running high, ask yourself if your thought will be well received in this moment. Your goal is always to be understood, so be mindful of how the circumstances of any given day can influence your ability to be heard.

Common Actor Challenges and Solutions

Every actor has a singular approach to their work. They may have been trained in a specific style or as part of a program that adheres to a certain philosophy. They may not have any training, but have natural talent and have learned by doing. Regardless of their background, they will bring to every process their own points of view, ways of working, past experiences (positive and negative), and artistic techniques. And while there can be no predictable "type" of actor, there are some common behaviors and challenges a director may encounter: below are some observations on how to understand and address them.

New Plays and the Method

Method acting is a blanket term we use for the different schools of acting that derive from Stanislavsky. The basic idea is that an actor should dive deeply into the emotional and psychological life of both themselves and their character with the goal of fully inhabiting the role. This work is usually best suited for plays that could be described as emotional realism and/or naturalism.

Challenge: Because this way of approaching a role is deeply internal, a method actor may make decisions about the character that are not fully supported by the text. Most actors who use the method understand that their process is their own, and that their fellow cast members are not obligated to change how they work to accommodate the method actor's process. There are occasions, however, when an actor's method work will pull them from the agreed-upon rules of the world. When this happens, a director may find themselves navigating an argument about something that does not exist in the text.

I once worked with an actor who created an elaborate backstory for her character. Focusing mostly on her imagined mother (who was never mentioned in the text), the actor privately constructed a deep and painful history of emotional neglect. As we began working on our feet, the actor would get very upset at certain behaviors from other cast members. The choices were confusing, but we felt as a group we should honor her creative process. Finally, after a particularly intense outburst, I asked the actor if she was feeling comfortable. She explained that the other characters onstage were behaving "exactly like my mother," so while her performance did not relate to the circumstances as written or to the rules of the world, she felt her reactions were valid because of her character's backstory.

That was an extreme scenario, but a more common one would be to hear an actor say: "My character wouldn't say that." If it appears in the script, then the character says it, but that statement often reveals a gap between the logic of the world as the writer imagines it and the individual actor's understanding of their role. This is a particularly complex situation with new plays, as the writer is not only in the room, they are also still in the process of creating the role. No one can claim to be an expert on the character: it remains a work in progress. Statements like "I can't say that" can spiral into conflict between the writer and actor: as the actor spends more time with the character, they may feel as though they understand the role better than its creator.

Solution: An actor has every right to create the story that best serves their creation of the role. But when that work overshadows the objective truths of the play, generates subjective choices that do not fit within the rules of the world, or the actor imposes their personal decisions on the rest of the cast, it must be addressed.

A director must meet one-on-one with the actor to discuss the choices that have been made, the backstory that has been constructed, or any other work that has pulled the actor away from the text. Using the script to support your points, articulate why their choices may make sense for the character as an individual, but how they are out of bounds regarding the rules of the world. Be specific: cite exact words and actions in the text that support your argument. This work may be frustrating (it can be difficult to push against an obstacle that did not exist until the actor created it), but be patient: method work is deeply personal and emotional. Casually disregarding or dismissing a choice may be taken very personally.

Ask the actor to articulate not only the choices they have made, but how they arrived at them. Often, you can find a moment in their journey where they veered from the text into their own story. Working from that moment can help an actor see that they didn't do anything "wrong," and then you can encourage them to find an emotional logic and backstory that suits both their process and the text. These moments can feel alarming—the refusal to read a line, for example, can create a lot of conflict and confusion that is difficult to untangle—but it is an opportunity to see inside an actor's process, which can be useful to you both.

Text Over-Analysis

Challenge: Actors will continue to wrestle with the text throughout the process. Questions, doubts, and confusions cannot all be resolved neatly around the table. In fact, the more time an actor spends working on a rough draft, the more confused they may become. This is a by-product of the awkwardness of early staging and the loss of the music and momentum of the text. An actor may feel the play doesn't feel or sound "right," and if they do not feel comfortable, they may increasingly scrutinize or blame the text. This is common: judgment typically means the actors are struggling with the text, and perhaps doubting the language until they can feel it working.

You may encounter an actor whose dissection of the text exceeds these typical struggles. They may come into rehearsal with skepticism about their character, someone else's, the plot, or the story. They may fixate on gaps, jumps, or holes in logic. This way of thinking can lead to a belief that the play doesn't work. The actor may doubt the play's quality or the writer's skill. The challenge of this behavior is that it is unlikely to stop on its own: like a tenacious detective, if they are looking for a problem, they will find one. Most often, this behavior reveals a crisis of confidence: either in themselves, in you, or in the play. The actor is nervous and lacks trust, and that feeling is playing out as relentless scrutiny. You find this pattern emerge most often during the rough draft phase: some actors do not like the feeling of not-knowing, and will take it out on the play.

Solution: Because the source of this negative energy is often not the text, defending the play will rarely bring an end to this pattern. Explain that their concerns have been heard, that you will watch the play unfold with their feedback and observations in mind, and that the best way forward is by continuing to experiment and, only if the writer feels it necessary, to make changes accordingly. Discussions about what the actor doesn't feel works on the page are not a useful way to proceed: only getting up and trying will answer any doubts, including those of logic, character, and story. Because the root of this situation is a crisis of confidence, find ways to highlight successes in the room as proof of progress. A director should not try to convince an actor a play is good or worth doing, but they can show it works through the typical trial and error of a rehearsal. The one scenario you must avoid is to ask the writer to make changes to appease the actor. Not only does that betray the democratic nature and the rules of the process, it will be seen as confirmation by the director that the actor's doubts are correct.

Shadow Directors

Challenge: "I don't know" is a wonderful tool for an egalitarian process, but for a certain type of actor, it can feel like an invitation to assert themselves over a process. They may feel they *do* know, that they aren't interested in mistakes or failure or trial and error. An actor—especially one that does not like to look foolish or vulnerable—may feel that not-knowing is a waste of time, an indicator of weakness or indecisiveness, and that they must step in to fill a void. These actors may try to take control of a rehearsal process, undercutting you and the atmosphere you have created.

If an actor feels emboldened to tell other actors, or you, or the writer, what to do, that must be stopped immediately. The longer that energy exists in the room, the more difficult it will be to change. Besides the obviously destructive nature of that behavior, other actors may come to believe that competition is the only way to advocate for their ideas or to be heard. The group dynamic will become greedy and combative: everything you had been trying to avoid.

Solution: You must make explicit that a collaborative approach is how the process is going to unfold, and it is the director's responsibility to decide what type of rehearsal process will best serve the play. Explain that not-knowing is a deliberate choice that must be adhered to, and that a dedication to the spirit of trial and error is both intentional and necessary. This is a moment in which you must assume control for the good of all, and for the health of the process. While you are cultivating a shared creative space, there are situations in which you must be the unequivocal leader. You have been entrusted with the responsibility of running the room, and the cultivation of a space for exploration is conscious and thoughtful, not the result of weakness or ignorance.

Attention Imbalance

Challenge: Actors will expect or demand different types and amounts of attention from their director. Some seek praise and assurance, some prefer to be left alone, and some desire conversation, debate, or even conflict. A director must decide how they want to share their attention: these expectations or demands are yours to meet or not. Occasionally, you will work with an actor who demands a disproportionate amount of your attention. It can be difficult to identify this pattern, as it usually grows into a challenge slowly over time, and isn't as immediately obvious as the behavior of, say, a shadow director. The challenge is that you need to be available to the entire company, and you need space to watch, reflect, and do your own work. If you are constantly in conversation with one actor, you risk becoming an acting coach, promoting an imbalance of attention, and stealing focus away from your own process.

Solution: Make a special effort to create space for the other actors. This could come in the form of asking them questions first, it could be in letting the room know you are interested in exploring something about a specific character (not the one played by the actor in question), it could be that you tell the actor in question that you need to try a few different choices before you're ready to discuss anything further. No matter the approach, what you're doing is shifting focus away from the one actor and onto the group without shutting that actor down. Silencing the actor or drawing attention to their neediness may provide you with a short-term solution, but you are introducing a punitive energy into the space and that will cause a different type of damage to the rehearsal atmosphere. Finding ways to open up communication to the entire group without reprimanding this actor will be more beneficial than trying to change anyone's rehearsal behavior.

Playing Favorites

Challenge: You will connect with some actors more easily than with others. It's possible you already know and love some members of the company, and others you'll be meeting for the first time and will immediately gravitate towards. There will be actors that you share a similar creative sensibility with. They will have ideas and make choices that may feel as though they have read your mind, as though their instincts are in perfect alignment with yours.

Actors like these can make a director feel very comfortable. That comfort can lead to favoritism, which can manifest in many ways: how you respond to their ideas, how much and what kind of attention you pay them, if and how you prioritize their suggestions, how much time you spend with them during breaks. Actors are intuitive: they do not miss anything. If you feel more at ease with one actor over another, they will all notice, and that dynamic can breed competition and jealousy; furthermore, you may find yourself less rigorous when watching the "favored" actor's work. You trust they will find a solution so you give them less feedback, and then later in the process their work may feel under-explored or under-rehearsed compared with those actors for whom the process was more thorough. This is because you didn't encourage your "favorite" to keep experimenting, to dig deeper, to challenge themselves. Your feelings clouded your goals and made you less rigorous, and their performances—which seemed so inspired early in the process—may not be as deep, complex, or refined.

Solution: Regardless of which actors you know, have worked with before, or have a natural creative ease with, you must be equally focused, attentive, and professional with them all. No one gets preferential treatment, as both the rehearsal room dynamic and the performances themselves can be negatively impacted.

The Yeah Yeah Yeahs

Challenge: You may encounter an actor who purposely avoids the director: the opposite of the attention seeker. They may not be interested in your observations, notes, or suggestions, and they may have no interest in the actor–director pact because they feel there is nothing you can tell them that they don't already know. I once worked with an actor who, when I would approach them with a thought, would say "yeah yeah yeah" in an effort to shut me up.

Solution: This can be incredibly frustrating, especially for a director who has taken great care to develop an atmosphere of communication and openness. One solution is to stop trying to engage the actor in discussion and only offer suggestions. Instead of sharing and comparing thoughts on an experiment, simply tell the actor what you would like to try next. Trying to engage in conversation with an actor like this can be tempting, but it rarely leads to progress. Anything you need to express to an actor can be conveyed in what you ask them to try. Concentrate your attention on experimentation and let the work speak for itself. If they refuse, challenge them. Explain that you will want to see the scene many times in many ways, including the current suggestion. What you're doing here is setting a boundary: you are cultivating a free space, but not one in which anyone is free to dismiss anyone else, including the director. "Let's do this next" is the strongest and most productive way to assert yourself.

Age Differential (older actors)

Challenge: Working with older actors is enormously rewarding. Actors with decades of experience love to tell stories of their successes, disasters, dramas, victories, famous collaborators, and the various highs and lows of a life in the theater. They are a wealth of knowledge and wisdom, the kind only achievable through experience, and they are able to see a process through the eyes of someone who has been through it thousands of times, but who can still experience the thrills, challenges, and triumphs as though it's all brand new.

Some older actors are less likely to listen to the thoughts and ideas of a director, particularly a younger one. They can be dismissive, or they can assume their experience gives them license to direct other actors or to dictate how the room should be run. This is further complicated by the fact that very often the older actor is right. They do have more experience with new plays than anyone in the room, they can have insights quicker than yours or most of your collaborators, and yet, they are still part of an ensemble and need to honor the dynamics of the group. Your challenge is to respect them while demanding respect in return.

Solution: It is best to appeal to their wisdom: their experience has taught them that even the best actor can cause the production to suffer if they make their own choices or try to direct from inside the play. They know that not trusting the director will lead to an unfocused production. An older actor may struggle to trust a younger director, but if you approach them with a combination of respect for their long history and with gentle reminders of how important a healthy ensemble is, they will use their natural leadership to help bring the company together.

Note: remember that an older actor may need more time to memorize lines. That may impact when you integrate rewrites, and how many are possible. If the writer wants to change a scene but an actor needs days [or longer] to memorize the text, it is the director who must figure out a path forward that honors the writer's desires and the reality of the actor's process (this is true of actors of any age, of course). This is something to consider as far back as the casting process: if the play features an older actor, the writer must be prepared to respect how quickly they learn lines and for their process to be a determining factor of how, when, and how many rewrites can happen.

Age Differential (young actors)

Challenge: A young actor can be eager, enthusiastic, and fearless. They can work tirelessly, they can be more open to feedback, and they may commit to any idea fully. It can be a pleasure and a joy to be in a room with younger actors, especially in the early, generative phase of a process.

What you should be mindful of is that many young actors have more experience in school than in a rehearsal process. Many of their previous directors may also have been their teachers, and they may have far more history with established works than with a new play. This process—the rewrites and changes—may be new to them.

Remember that they may come into the room steeped in their academic training and are accustomed to being part of a process with other actors who are training in the same way. That every actor in your room will have their own process and their own way of working, and may not be interested in discussing it, may be a shock to a younger actor. They may also struggle to understand a director's way of communication, as they may be more accustomed to the language of academia.

Solution: Set clear expectations about your role and what you expect your relationship to be. This conversation can happen during your pre-rehearsal meeting. A young actor may not know a director is not an acting teacher, or may not understand the difference until the process begins. If you can name the ways in which this process may be different from their experiences at school, they can begin to understand faster. Articulate what elements of their creative process you will be discussing with them, and what you will leave them to discover on their own. Help them understand that every actor comes from a different training background—some formal and academic, others through experience—and that this variety is a virtue and not a hindrance. Guide them through the changes that will happen during a new play process. Above all, offer them positive encouragement. They are doing something, or many things, for the first time in your rehearsal room. They may have no sense of how they're doing without a teacher in the room, so while you should not assume that role, you should take any opportunity to support them and acknowledge when they're on the right track.

Communication Boundaries

I was once a part of a process that became so overwhelmed by rewrites that rehearsals began to feel like a workshop. The cast could not construct a role or chart an emotional path because every day new pages would arrive that would undercut their efforts.

Late one night, two of the actors called me. They had been discussing the process at a bar and asked to meet with me. One of the actors was an old friend; the other was the lead actor with whom I'd had a difficult working relationship. Because I didn't want to ignore my friend, and felt this was perhaps an opportunity to win the favor of the lead actor, I agreed to meet. At the bar, they listed all of their complaints about the rehearsal process: how unproductive it was and how nervous they were to be in front of an audience. At the rate rewrites were being distributed, they feared they would never be ready to perform. Then they told me they had talked through the play, solved the dramaturgical problems on their own, and wanted me to share their proposed rewrite with the writer.

I made a number of mistakes in this scenario. The first was that I let the writer dictate the shape of the entire process. I did not protect the time the actors and I needed in order to prepare for performances, and did not advocate for the cast when I could see them suffocating under the weight of daily rewrites. The second mistake was that I met with collaborators in a social situation and not during rehearsal time. This gave them preferential treatment and taught the cast I was willing to discuss the text in the absence of the writer. The third mistake was that I thought because one actor was a friend this meeting would be productive, and that because the other actor and I were not working together well, meeting in an informal space would provide us with a chance to repair our relationship. The fourth was that I made myself available to colleagues at a moment's notice and was not protective of my time. The fifth was that by meeting with them, I was teaching them that accepting notes from one artist about another's work was acceptable behavior.

A director must set and uphold clear boundaries about how and when information is shared. All discussion with the cast must happen in rehearsal, notes will only be given or received in a professional space, and informal, side conversations will not be tolerated. If you are friendly with members of the cast, set a rule that when you are not in rehearsal, you will not discuss the work. Even a roommate or romantic partner. Not only does this avoid hurt feelings, distrust, and unfair power dynamics, it will give you the necessary time and space away from the room to reflect on your thoughts and feelings. A director who is always available to the cast is also a director without time for their own creative process.

Actors will meet on their own to debate, discuss, and vent about the play, about the process, about the writer, and about you. This is healthy and natural. A director once told me, when he declined going out for a drink with the cast: "they need some time alone to hate me." That may be an exaggeration (sometimes), but it's useful to remember that actors need time to socialize, and the director's presence will set a different tone. Setting and maintaining communication boundaries will allow everyone to understand when the play should and should not be discussed and will set your collaborators at ease: they can feel confident there are no conversations happening in their absence.

16
THE STUMBLE-THROUGH AND THE NEXT DRAFT

When a carpenter builds a piece of furniture, they must first connect all the pieces they have created without glue, nails, or any other permanent connectors. They take this step for two reasons: to make certain all the pieces are accounted for, and to see if and how they fit together. If two or more pieces do not, the carpenter must dismantle the entire object and make necessary adjustments. They repeat this step until all the pieces cohere properly, and only then everything is affixed. A carpenter cannot get too detailed or over-confident with one section until they are certain the entire thing works as a complete object. They must develop every piece at roughly the same rate, none too far ahead or too far behind. Otherwise, they will have to break what they have made in order to make changes.

Doing a stumble-through of your rough draft is the same act as a carpenter laying out each piece of their furniture. Stepping through the entire play will allow you to see everything you have made so far without committing to any definitive choices that would be difficult to undo. You can observe what you have accomplished and see how all the different pieces fit together. Suddenly, you can begin to understand the work you've done within the *context* of the whole. This is a fundamental shift of the rehearsal process: once you have put the entire play on its feet, you can see how each part affects the story.

It is called a "stumble-through" to frame expectations appropriately. It is a chance for the cast to perform the entire play from beginning to end without stopping. Since the cast is not ready to perform anywhere near the play's proper pace, to call it a "run" is to set unrealistic goals. A cast is not ready to run and should not try: they *should* stumble, learning about what they have made and teaching you what to do next.

The Timing of a Stumble-Through

It's natural to feel resistance to stumbling through the entire play. Shouldn't you go back and clean up what you've done, especially the experiments you ran during those early days? You've learned so much about the play since then, you may tell yourself, and you can't stand to watch something so unfinished.

Until you see each section in the context of the whole, you cannot make informed choices about what to change, or how, or why. A stumble-through is your chance to observe what you've made, in its current state, before you begin another pass of detailed work. The cast's job is to step through the play to begin to understand their overarching emotional journeys. They should note what feels good, what does not, and when. Your next work-through of the play must include the information you and the cast gather from this stumble-through, which is why going backwards to "fix" or "clean up" the rough draft will simply postpone this necessary step. You cannot shift to more detailed work without understanding how each piece fits together, and that information can only be gathered from a stumble-through.

This step is advisable for any process, but it is a necessity with a new play. When rehearsing an established work, the entire team can proceed with the knowledge that the play can be successful: the question is whether or not this production will be. With a new play, one cannot assume. There is no guarantee it will work until it can be heard *and* observed.

Preparing the Company

The stumble will be the cast's first attempt to tell the complete story. Until now, they have been able to stop and ask questions. Now they have the chance to experience it without interruption, experiments or adjustments, and without the director's voice as a guide. It is their first step toward claiming ownership of the production.

A cast may feel vulnerable before you begin. A stumble can feel exposing, even embarrassing. Remind them that they are not trying to "do" the play, they are simply stepping through the results of your experimentations. A stumble through is a diagnostic, not a performance. Assure them there will be parts they will forget, that were left as place holders, that some moments will feel wrong, and that all of it is welcome information. Also remind them some of the work may feel fantastic or surprising: there is no way to predict what may happen in advance. The goal is to learn about what you have and what you want to do next, so as long as you are gathering that information, the stumble-through can be considered a success. Be transparent with the company about this so they can approach this exercise with a shared sense of curiosity and with appropriate expectations.

Because the rough draft is so far from a version you can "run," you should not invite anyone who has not already been in the room. Even one spectator—a designer or a theater staff member, for example—can make a cast feel the need to "perform" and undercut the educational tone you are trying to set. Ask your stage manager to make it explicit on the daily schedule that the stumble is not an open event and that no one is invited. Assure the cast, who may be nervous regardless of how you've framed it, that this will be private. The only exception is the playwright.

The Return of the Writer

You may feel this moment is premature for the writer to rejoin the process, and you would be correct. The actors are still finding their footing, the play lacks any semblance of rhythm and pace, dramatic tension and stakes are absent, there continue to be more questions in the room than answers, and yet a writer must take all of this in. They must reenter the process a bit too early so they can contribute to the work before any of the pieces become too attached to one another. If the writer rejoins too late in a process, the cast may feel more confident and clear in their choices, and may be less adept at incorporating rewrites and changes. The timing of reintegration is important: a bit too early is exactly right.

A writer must understand where you and the cast are in your process. Explain to them in advance where you are in terms of staging, pace, and discovery. You don't need to disclaim or apologize for anything they are about to see, but offering them context before will avoid unnecessary confusion. You will know in advance which sections will be clearer than others: there is no need to keep that information from the writer.

Watching the Stumble-Through

Until now, there have been two elements for the director to observe in the rehearsal room: the text and the artists. The stumble-through is the introduction of a third: the physical production. At readings and workshops, in auditions and around the table, a three-dimensional production existed only in your imagination. Now, there is something to watch, to react to, and to learn from.

It has been some time since you've heard the entire play straight through, so the stumble will allow you to reacquaint yourself with the play as one complete art object. Assume the role of the audience: listen, observe, and remain aware of the questions you are asking yourself. Notice when you are confused, rapt, bored, or attentive. Focus on staying present and seeing the rough draft in its current form. It can be very easy to become preoccupied with what you remembered from your experiments, with what you thought you would see versus what you are seeing, with what was forgotten or changed. Lingering in your thoughts will prevent you from seeing clearly what is playing out in front of you, and that gap will inhibit the stumble's usefulness.

Pay close attention to moments of confusion: that is a sure sign there is something in the sequence of events that is not yet working. From this point in the process onward, nothing happens in a vacuum. No choice or idea is independent from the whole. The source of confusion may be a writing, performance, or directorial issue, but that can be determined later. Mark those moments when you feel lost as an audience member: they will help you determine your worklist for the next pass through the play.

Meeting with the Cast Post-Stumble

Most stumble-throughs elicit a combination of emotions from the company: elation that they made it through the play, surprise that they were able to, and trepidation about the amount of work that lies ahead. Your conversation with them immediately after should bring their attention to very broad observations. Share your experience of watching the piece, help them understand the audience's perspective. This is a major moment in the actor–director pact: it is the first time you will reflect back to them how it felt to watch it. Avoid specifics: share with them the general sensation of watching the play, those areas that seem to be heading in a positive direction, and those that will need more experimentation. Share what you learned about the story: about its shape and about where you want to focus your attention in the coming rehearsal days. A director should be both honest and encouraging. A stumble-through is a marker for how much work has been accomplished and how much still lies ahead: highlight the accomplishment of getting to this point, regardless of how rough the current draft may be.

Meeting with the Writer

I have worked with writers who wept after a stumble-through because they were so moved to watch their play come to life. I once worked with a writer who leaned over to me and whispered "that was f*cking unwatchable." How a writer will respond cannot be predicted. The most common reaction, though, will be their lamenting the play's loss of momentum. It can be difficult for a writer, who always has a clear sense of the music of their text, to hear the right words but not the right timing. Moments may lack humor or power, the story may lack tension and release, a climactic moment may not feel any different

THE STUMBLE-THROUGH AND THE NEXT DRAFT

from the rest of the story. There is no way to avoid these problems in a rough draft: remind the writer that this is part of the process.

The writer is your first collaborator to see your rough draft, so their perspective is invaluable. Encourage them to articulate their experience of watching. Ask what they learned, how they felt, what troubled them, and what confused them. Ask if they noticed any gaps in logic, implausible leaps in character behavior, repetitive sections, ideas, or moments, and anything that felt out of order. You are seeking understanding about their overall experience as well as their understanding of the moment-to-moment sequence of events. Observations about the cast's emotional clarity or intensity, about their ability to play humor or tension are not yet useful as a stumble-through cannot accurately capture those elements. What you need to know is if the writer thinks that everything necessary for the story is present and in the correct order.

A stumble-through will give the writer a clear picture of where you are in process, but it is not always a reliable barometer of what parts of the play do and do not need immediate text changes. Avoid advocating for rewrites based only on what the writer saw in the stumble. They may want to revise in order to fix the pace, or to punch up the drama or humor: all of those rewrites would be premature. The only rewrites to consider at this stage are ones that fill plot or character holes, or a reordering of scenes or moments for narrative clarity.

This meeting is also an opportunity for you to share any questions or struggles from the building of the rough draft. You will have inevitably encountered moments that were confusing or unclear, moments the actors struggled to play, sections that remained opaque to you and the company in spite of your experiments. Now is the moment to put these challenges and concerns on the writer's radar so they can either provide their perspective, offer suggestions, or begin to contemplate rewrites. As you begin to create the next draft of the play, they should be present in the room: they should come into the space knowing what questions you have and what struggles you're facing so they can participate in the finding of a solution. Share these thoughts only after the stumble, not before: they should watch for their own experience and not look for your thoughts or suggestions.

If the stumble-through was particularly challenging for the actors, it's possible a writer may feel in this meeting that they are being blamed for any difficulties. Bring their attention to the text. If you suspect there may be a beat missing in a scene, for example, and the writer disagrees, do not debate them: look at the text together and ask them to help you see how these moments fit together. That is not a challenge, simply a search for clarity. Often, by looking at the text together, you will either find something you had missed, or the writer will see where a step is missing. You want the writer to understand your questions and concerns and vice versa so you can both begin rehearsals for the next draft with a shared point of view and focus on what sections may need attention in the form of rewrites. You are creating a list of moments, thoughts, and ideas you want to pay close attention to during the creation of the next draft.

The Next Draft

There will come a point in your process when not-knowing will begin to feel unproductive. A group of artists can only experiment together for so long before fatigue sets in. This is especially true for a process with an endpoint: actors are always aware of how much time they have before they step in front of an audience. You may feel this shift occurring naturally, and it will often present itself around or immediately after the stumble-through. A cast will become less enthusiastic about educational failures and more interested in what does work and in recapturing the play's shape and rhythm. You may feel the same. What you and the company will soon realize is that, by having lingered in that space of not-knowing, the most promising choices and clearest decisions will reveal themselves faster and with greater confidence.

There is another reason we embrace not-knowing until after the stumble-through. The word "decide" comes from the Latin "decidere" meaning "to cut off." The -cide is the same root as homicide, regicide, patricide. To make a decision is to kill off other choices. It is two simultaneous actions: declaring what something *is*, and declaring what it *is not*. This is why you have sustained an atmosphere of experimentation for so long: making decisions too soon will prematurely limit your options.

You can think of your rehearsal process as unfolding in two parts: pre-stumble (tablework and experimentation) and post-stumble (decisions and run-throughs). This is a psychic shift for the company that you must explain and encourage. Questions, confusions, and challenges will remain, but the process of trial and error will accelerate and begin to focus on more specific moments. As stronger choices becomes easier to identify, a consensus can often be quickly reached. You now have the gift of context: because of the stumble through, you can understand each moment within the scene, the character's overarching trajectory, and the play. You can work with a clearer understanding of where you've been, how you got here, and where you need to go. If you have spent enough time experimenting, the choices that feel good now can be trusted. Keep them and move on: you will try them the next time you run-through the play, observing how they work in context.

As the process becomes less experimental, you can bring your attention to how each moment fits with the next. You will work sequentially: each gesture, line, and movement influencing the next and then the next and so on, understanding each moment's impact in context. You are inching each piece closer together,

THE STUMBLE-THROUGH AND THE NEXT DRAFT

cutting, pasting, and orchestrating. Like a carpenter attaching the pieces together after making certain they fit, you can begin making decisions and firm, confident choices. This work is how the momentum, pace, energy, and music return to the play.

Post-Stumble Rehearsals

The rehearsal days after the stumble tend to have a quicker rhythm. You're all more familiar with the text, you have shaken off the initial discomfort of getting on your feet, you are more comfortable with each other as a group, and you now have the confidence that comes from knowing you can step through the entire piece. Even in its roughest form, you now have a production that exists, and a draft on which to build the next. You have created a shared language, a collective way of working, and that will make all the upcoming changes, adjustments, and refinements easier.

Plan to work large sections at a time, sequentially whenever possible. This will allow you to see the narrative shape forming, which will, in turn, inform your adjustments. Working this way will also give the cast a sense of the flow of the play, which is where they should be concentrating more of their attention. This is the moment to encourage them to think about timing and rhythm. The company will be eager to run sections at-pace: they need to know how it feels to play extended sections at the right tempo and energy. Some emotional qualities are almost impossible to capture when the pace does not support it: by paying attention to timing, other improvements will naturally follow. This work will allow you to give more specific notes, and will also give the writer a chance to experience the music of the text.

Your work on this draft may teach you that some early experiments no longer make sense. This is part of your editing process. Unnecessary business, extraneous staging, or bits of irrelevant behavior are pieces of scaffolding that are no longer necessary to hold up a scene, moment, or performance. As you and the company slide the pieces together and attach them, you must cut those elements that no longer serve the momentum.

While this work is happening, you must make time during rehearsals for costume fittings or possibly interviews or press commitments. Props designers and production staff may be dropping off new items based on what they're reading in the rehearsal reports. You may schedule more frequent visits from fight, intimacy, violence, or dialect directors and consultants. In short, your intimate space is starting to open up organically and necessarily, and while that can be exciting, it will create a shift in rehearsal room energy. Maintain focus in spite of visitors and schedule juggling. The needs of the production should not interfere with your and the company's work.

Begin work on each section by reviewing your thoughts from the stumble-through, sharing your observations and asking the actors for theirs, then telling them what you are curious to see and to try differently. If there are rewrites (to be discussed in the next chapter), now would be the moment to incorporate them. Couch your observations in relation to the rough draft. "Before, we were playing a moment this way. During the stumble, I noticed this moment did not seem to fit with the rest of the scene. Now, I'd like for us to try these new ideas." Run the section with these adjustments and evaluate how they work, then give new adjustments and run it again. Do not give the cast more to consider than you think they can process. Your goal is to prepare for the next run-through: you do not need to cover every thought or idea. Let spontaneous discoveries inform your adjustments: your stumble-through notes may become increasingly outdated as the cast gets more comfortable and confident.

Questions and moments of confusion will remain: work to get them smaller and more manageable in size. Keep track of what and where they are, and continue to try different experiments to address them. Think of all of your options: can you find clarity through performance? Through direction? Through new text? Try different solutions, one at a time to avoid confusion, and then let them be until you can see them in a run. A director's impulse can be to keep working on a scene that doesn't make sense, but this rarely yields results. Better to try a few attempts and then stand back and see it in context before frustration or exhaustion takes hold.

Giving Actor Notes

As your work becomes more specific and decisive, the way you communicate with actors will change. During the creation of the rough draft, you were primarily asking questions and offering suggestions ("What if we tried this?"). As the work becomes more detailed, you will be giving the company notes.

The word "note" comes from the Latin "notare," which means to notice. It can be useful to think of notes as observations as opposed to judgments, corrections, or criticisms. As an actor becomes more emotionally aligned with the role, it can be increasingly difficult for them to differentiate between a note about the character and a criticism of the actor. Notes can very easily be taken personally, so a director must be thoughtful about how they phrase feedback. Approaching notes as "this is what I saw" is upholding the actor–director pact: you performed, I watched, and now I am reporting back on what I noticed. By framing notes this way, you are reflecting on your experience, which is a subtle but important distinction from a comment on the actor's performance. This can relieve tension and alleviate frustration. You are simply two artists discussing a choice and brainstorming how it can be changed or improved. If the director begins with judgment, the actor is put in a defensive position where they either have to agree or resist. It is the choice between "This is what I noticed" and "This is what you need to do." An actor will hear the difference and respond accordingly.

Because an actor must think both in terms of their moment-to-moment work and their overarching emotional trajectory, there is no such thing as a small note. As your work becomes more focused and detail-oriented, an actor will be thinking surgically: a small note about the delivery of a line or the changing of a gesture may impact far more than just the moment under discussion. Remain aware of how the actor is feeling about their work in general. A director who continues to give notes to an actor who is clearly struggling is ignoring a larger problem. Ask yourself if this is the most productive time to offer feedback. When you give a note remains the most important consideration for its efficacy.

Avoid giving the same note over and over again. It will frustrate both you and the actor and it will not solve what is not working. The repetition will either make you both defensive or will damage the actor's confidence. Consider why you feel compelled to give the note, and why the actor is either resistant or unable to take it. You both need to take a step back and have a deeper discussion. Explain why you feel the note is important, and ask the actor to explain their reticence. Very often, the actor is struggling with something larger and more significant than just the moment in question: the struggle is simply revealing itself there. Make time for the actor to explain any confusions or frustrations they may be wrestling with. If conversation is not yielding results, be patient. Let the moment continue to play as-is: another (better) note, or the root of the actor's struggle, will reveal itself. This tension can also be a sign that the writer needs to help with a revision. Sometimes an actor can be resistant for personal reasons, but often they are reacting to something that doesn't work in the text, whether they can articulate what that is or not. Repeated notes cannot fix that: only discussion, consideration, and time.

Never pick on an actor. Directors can occasionally feel one actor is not keeping pace with the rest of the company. Their choices aren't as strong, they do not seem to fit into the world of the play or into the ensemble, or they do not seem to understand (or care about) your notes. The result can be the constant noting of the actor, which is a manifestation of your frustration. If you feel you are doing this, take a step back and try to understand the cause. Is it the actor themselves, their performance, or your inability to communicate successfully with them? This pause for consideration will alleviate some tension: the actor will have time to work without fear of constant judgment, and the rest of the cast will also enjoy a release from unhelpful energy. Actors, even those that do not get along, are very protective of one another. If they see the director picking on one actor, their impulse is almost always to defend them. Focusing unhelpful energy on one actor threatens to spoil your relationship with the entire company.

Pausing for reflection will give you time to identify the root of your frustration, and then you can consider how best to address it. That could be a one-on-one conversation with the actor, an adjustment to how you communicate with them, or an admission to yourself that maybe the actor is somehow not of the world of your production. How you resolve a discovery like that will depend on the circumstances, but it begins with understanding the root cause of constant notes.

Difficult Notes

The stumble-through may reveal deeper problems with the play. They can relate to the text, to your vision, or to a performance. Something you may realize is that an actor is approaching their character in a way that does not fit with the rest of the cast or with the world of the play. It usually has little to do with skill or talent and everything to do with alignment and cohesion. If you feel an actor's choices and the creation of their role is veering away from the rest of the production, it must be brought to their attention immediately. The longer you wait, the more difficult a redirection can be.

No actor wants to hear that their character needs to be rethought, that the choices they have been making are not effective, or that drastic changes are necessary. It can shake an actor's confidence. On the other hand, if the actor has been on the wrong track, it's very likely they have felt it, so while there may be a moment of shock, anger, or frustration when you introduce the conversation, the actor will almost certainly feel a sense of relief as the new path reveals itself. The first step is to determine how you got to this point. It could be that ideas during tablework created an unhelpful understanding of the role, it could be that your experiments were useful for one actor at another's expense, it could be that you and the actor have not been communicating well and it was not until the stumble-through that you learned this.

If an actor's performance is out of sync with the rest of the company, you will almost always learn this during the stumble. An actor rarely drifts from the world of the play later in the process. While most actor notes should be shared in front of the company so everyone can be aware of potential changes, conversations with an actor about larger issues like these are best held privately. An actor may express frustration, embarrassment, or confusion, and you should give them the opportunity to experience those feelings away from the rest of the cast. Any discussion of significant changes to an actor's approach should happen in the rehearsal room (preferably with stage management in the room so they can listen) before or after a rehearsal day.

- Be honest: they need to understand the gravity of your observation and the size of the task ahead.
- Consider solutions in advance: telling an actor they are on the wrong path requires the sharing of positive ideas about what to change and how you might go about it.
- Relieve them of blame: situations like this happen, especially with a new play and a new role. Remind them that this is not about talent or skill, it is sometimes just part of the process.
- Leave yourself open to questions: you cannot know how an actor will feel about more difficult notes. Let them express how they are feeling and remain open to their thoughts and perspective.
- Develop a plan: you and the actor should agree on which proposed solutions seem appropriate and achievable, and then incorporate them into your rehearsal plans for the coming days. The sooner you can work with large readjustments, the better.

Actor Ownership

Why does a director have to be so thoughtful when giving notes? Can't they just tell the actor what to do? What is wrong with giving instructions?

Remember that two central goals of a rehearsal process are for the cast to feel a sense of ownership of their performance, and for them to feel confident they can repeat it in a safe and reliable way. In front of a camera, an actor needs to hit the emotional notes correctly only once: the technology preserves it forever. A stage actor, however, needs to create a path they can walk over and over, following roughly the same emotional trajectory each time. This is their responsibility to the story: if a character needs to fall in love, for example, they need to calibrate their performance to achieve the appropriate emotional conditions to do so. Because a stage actor must deliver their performance to the audience directly, they must feel absolute agency over their own work. This is why giving actors time and space to discover for themselves what works is preferable to a director telling them. Eventually, the director will leave, and the actor must walk the path without your outside perspective. The rehearsal process is when an actor builds an emotional and physical track that they can move through over and over. This work requires practice and the building of stamina. Your task is to empower and encourage.

17
REHEARSAL ROOM CHALLENGES

By now the rehearsal room has a reliable and predictable internal logic. You understand each actor's process, you know how you work as a group and as individuals, you have observed which actors get along and which do not, you have seen how the company handles and resolves conflict (or doesn't), and everyone has revealed themselves to the group, intentionally or not. A director once told me that there are no secrets in a rehearsal room. Everyone sees everything, and the openness and vulnerability necessary to create a work of art will show everyone at their best and most complicated. In short, you have identified the group dynamics that are specific to this company. Some will be encouraging, while others will present challenges. A director must be able to identify the difference between a passing obstacle and signs of something more significant. This is also true about the work the company is generating in post-stumble rehearsals. The first task is to notice the issue, the second is to locate the source, and the last is to find a resolution. As they say in medicine: treat the cause, not the symptom.

"Pushing" or Overplaying

"Overacting" is the playing of a moment, a scene, or even an entire role in a way that is so over-illustrative that the actor breaks with the reality of the circumstances and begins telegraphing emotion, story, or behavior. It is breaking the rules of the world by acting in a manner that is incongruous with the rest of the company. We call this "pushing" because the actor is forcing an emotion instead of allowing it to happen naturally. The cause is almost always an actor's crisis of confidence. They may doubt the text, their scene partner, the rules of the world, their own ability, or the director. The actor does not believe a performance in alignment with the rest of the company is enough, so they are filling this confidence gap by pushing to make the moment, line, scene more "dramatic." This behavior can make an actor feel more confident in a superficial way, which is how it can become a pattern. Giving an actor who is pushing a note like "tone it down" or "pull back" will just exacerbate the problem, so a different approach is necessary.

An actor may not consciously understand they are feeling insecure, so to be told they are pushing may come as a surprise to them. Do not initiate this conversation with the assumption that an actor will be able to articulate what is causing the problem, or even to admit or acknowledge there is a problem to address. Pushing can sometimes feel great: it can be fun to be over-dramatic. A director should bring the issue up to the actor during rehearsal hours, but one-on-one: they should not feel put on the spot or forced to defend their acting choices in front of the group. It's possible the actor just needs some reassurance from you, but if pushing has presented itself as a pattern, this conversation is necessary to determine that.

Even if the actor refuses to believe they have been overplaying, they will usually agree that something has felt "off" in their work. Once you and the actor agree, the conversation can pivot to questions of cause and solution.

Begin by explaining what you are seeing: that the actor is not playing the reality of the circumstances. Articulate that their performance seems to be focusing too heavily on generating an emotion than on playing the scene with their partners. Give them specific examples, then ask if these observations make sense to them. Providing them with some specifics and then giving them the space to explain their experience from inside will often reveal the source of their discomfort. An actor who does not trust is a fearful one, so this conversation may make them defensive. The actor should not be made to feel reprimanded or judged: while you need to articulate what you are seeing in rehearsal, this should be framed as an opportunity for the actor to speak openly and honestly about how they are feeling and the ways in which they might be struggling.

Encourage the actor to focus less on "doing" and more on listening to their scene partners. Ask them to take in what they are hearing and challenge them to respond as truthfully as possible. If pushing is the act of self-generating drama, then the actor must release themselves from the burden of trying to create something on their own. If the actor likes the feeling that simply listening and responding gives them—they usually do—the doubt will begin to loosen, and so will the overplaying.

Occasionally, an actor will push because they may believe if they aren't struggling they aren't "doing enough." If their work feels comfortable, an actor might think, if they are not feeling a lot of tension, then they aren't making exciting or worthwhile art. Remind them that playing a scene without pushing does not imply an artistic shortcoming: to have found a way to play a moment/scene/role that feels good may mean they have found a place in which the character sits comfortably in the body. Assure them this is not a problem but something to embrace: it means they are trusting the text and circumstances, as well as their scene partners, to support them.

"Marking" or Underplaying

The opposite issue is an actor withholding so much emotion or expression that the reality of the circumstances is undetectable. We will call this "marking," as the actor appears to be stepping through, but not fully inhabiting, the physical and emotional life of the character. It can be difficult for a director to distinguish between an actor who is playing their role too small to be detected (this is often true for actors more familiar with being in front of a camera) and one who is making a choice not to fill their performance with the necessary energy. The root cause, however, is often the same: fear. To open up, to commit fully, to let difficult or messy emotions flow forth can feel exposing, vulnerable-making, and frightening. If an actor continues to mark, it usually means they are blocked, and very often the block is because they are scared.

Before you approach an actor about interrupting a pattern of "marking" a role, you must determine whether this is just part of the actor's creative process. Some actors play to their given circumstances, in this case a rehearsal room, and so encouraging them to open up may feel dishonest or inauthentic. There is no large audience, they might argue, there is only you! Also, an actor may not commit fully until they can feel the music and momentum of the piece. Pace generates tension, which generates emotion: an actor may not fill a moment emotionally if it does not feel honest, so many actors will mark during the trial and error period and into the stumble-through.

Marking becomes a challenge when you enter the more decisive part of the process. You, the writer, and the other actors cannot make informed choices if an actor refuses or is unable to rise to the emotional circumstances of the play. If you feel confident this how the actor has chosen to play a moment (conscious or not), then you should speak with them as you would with an actor who is pushing. Articulate the pattern you are noticing and invite the actor to talk about any concerns or trepidations. They may also be surprised to have this conversation. Because the actor is most likely feeling fearful, avoid blame or implications of failure: the last thing a nervous actor needs to hear is that they aren't "doing it right" or that they are holding up the rest of the cast. That is very likely part of what they are afraid of.

The solution to an actor marking is encouragement and empowerment. Often, they are listening to their scene partner and are making smart, emotionally grounded choices, they just aren't filling them completely. While encouraging the actor to listen and respond to their scene partner is useful advice, the fear is internal, so what the actor needs most is a confidence boost. Find a moment in the play that actor has a pattern of marking (something relatively low stakes to start with) and gently challenge them to play the moment in full. The chances are good that, by playing the scene at a larger scale, they will get to experience what that feels like: usually it feels great. To inhabit a moment completely and have a positive experience doing so can provide a huge confidence boost, and that success can be applicable to other moments in the play. Through this experience, a fearful actor can feel a performance level that is aligned with the emotional circumstances. Nervousness will begin to recede as successes in the rehearsal room begin to accumulate.

The alternative is that, by encouraging them to fill the role, the actor will resist. This behavior can present itself as a fight, tears, passive aggression, or any other form of conflict. While these situations are never pleasant, they usually reveal some truths about why the actor is fearful and what is at the root of their behavior. An explosion of emotion can be difficult to navigate, but the chances are high you will learn what the actor is afraid of, and you can then begin to untangle those feelings.

Getting Off-Book

Most actors are eager to memorize, particularly after the stumble-through, as they can feel the pages in their hand slowing them down and disconnecting them from their scene partners. Holding a script or constantly calling for line can feel like a weight or a burden.

Often, setting a date for the cast to be fully memorized isn't necessary, as actors tend to crave the confidence of knowing their lines. With a new play, though, actors may be less likely to commit a text to memory, as they (correctly) suspect changes are coming. If you sense memorization is not a priority, set a deadline for when you want the company off-book. As always, you and the writer need to hear the lines verbatim in order to know what changes to consider. Setting a deadline before the stumble-through is usually premature, but by the time you start your next draft, the cast should be able to perform without pages and rarely call for lines.

Paraphrasing

It can be easy to grow frustrated or to jump to conclusions if an actor does not know their lines or continues to paraphrase. If an actor struggles with their lines or paraphrases even after giving them line notes, there is more significant problem than a simple lack of preparedness. An actor who cannot remember their lines is almost always confused about the line's meaning. This misunderstanding has affected their ability to learn and retain their lines, and that problem will not resolve itself on its own. Usually it is the opposite: unaddressed paraphrasing will become more frustrating for both you and the actor.

Begin always with the benefit of the doubt. An actor calling for line, an actor paraphrasing to the point where the text is unrecognizable, an actor not giving the correct cues to their scene partners: all of these can be disruptive, but do not assume the actor is not fully committed. Sometimes they may think they understand a line even though they have memorized it incorrectly. Not only does this mistake change the meaning of the one line, it can affect the next one and the next, until an entire sequence of the play has taken on a different meaning in the actor's mind, stemming from one memorization error. Actors are problem-solvers: if a line doesn't make perfect sense to them, they will erect an entire logic around it to make it work. If the line was learned incorrectly, that logic structure could be based on something very wrong. In this case, a line note will not help because an entire sequence of flawed logic needs to be untangled.

Look at the text together with the actor. The longer you're on your feet, the more time has passed since you've sat down with the pages together. The best case scenario is that the actor will realize that they have misremembered the line and they will be relieved to learn the line as written makes more sense (and then all the logic they had built was not necessary). What's more likely is that you and the actor will have to debate the meaning of the line, and your task will not be to "win" this argument, but to help the actor see that it is their understanding of the line that is leading them to speaking it incorrectly. The forgotten or paraphrased line is the result of a misunderstanding, so the more succinct you can be in identifying what is being misunderstood, the easier it will be to resolve the problem.

If an actor can never remember a line, there is something about the character's thought process that the actor is not grasping, or outright rejecting. Sometimes an actor is embarrassed to admit they don't understand a line or moment, so they make up meanings that may not exist on the page. Addressing this early is critical to the actor's comfort and success. The longer they rehearse with the wrong or forgotten lines, the more the pattern is reinforced, and further they commit to the wrong words. The repetition of incorrect lines makes their undoing harder with every run: it is not something to simply "clean up" later.

On a few occasions, I have worked with actors who had difficulty reading or memorizing but did not want to share that information. If you suspect an actor may need more support in their memorization, offer it to them: no questions asked, no discussion necessary. You do not need to pry (there is a reason the actor did not mention it), simply offer them additional support and let them know whatever is most useful to them (someone to run lines with outside of rehearsal, for example), you will make sure they have it.

Stage Business and Behavior

Many actors love stage business: extra pieces of blocking, comedic bits, pantomime, additional props, or added choreography that does not appear in the script. These gestures can be creative, inventive, and hugely fun to experiment with, but too much business will upstage the text and interrupt the dramatic action. A funny or fascinating bit of stage action—typically something discovered during the period of trial and error—can distract focus from the text, the actor, or the story.

When you shift your attention to shape, momentum, and pace, stage business from the previous draft can often transform into an obstacle. If making decisions means the killing off what doesn't work, that will include extraneous business. Often, it will naturally fall away: "It was fun while it lasted, but now it's in the way." A challenge can present itself when an actor is using stage business as a crutch, something to hide behind. The root of this behavior is anxiety. It can be exposing for an actor to stand onstage without a prop to ground them. It can be uncomfortable to stand still and serve as an active listener during a long monologue. If some stage business is interfering with the rhythm or comprehension of a moment, it must go, but be prepared for an actor to resist, either because they love it, feel they need it, or they don't know what to do without it.

In this situation, discussion may not serve you. An actor can and will happily justify why the object or blocking is necessary, but the task is not for you or anyone to be convinced, it is to honor the natural flow of the text. If the piece of business is an interruption, it doesn't matter how funny or inspired it is: it's in the way. The solution is to ask the actor to try the scene without the business. They may resist, but running the scene without it will almost always feel immediately better (even if there is some sadness around the loss of a beloved prop or action). The new version will be faster, cleaner, clearer. The play is tightening up naturally, and "extra" moments will feel more and more unnecessary. As much as an actor might love something they've invented, they will love the feeling of moving at pace far more. The solution is in the proof, not in the discussion.

Added "Vocal Notes"

If a violinist added a few notes or rests to a piece of Mozart, we would agree they are rewriting his music. An actor adding small words and sounds like "um, uh, like" is doing the same thing. An actor will make many creative choices and decisions, but they should approach the text with the same rigor as the musician. While an actor may feel these additions make a line of dialogue sound more "natural," they are adding notes to the proverbial score, changing the shape, rhythm, and sometimes meaning of a line of text.

Sometimes these additions come from actors struggling to remember their lines, searching for the right word, or trying to recall the most recent rewrite. As we do in life, "um" is a stalling tactic, a way to hold the listeners' attention while searching for the next word. But sometimes these words or sounds become ingrained in the actor's memory. Rarely will an actor consciously decide inserting "uhh" into this line of dialogue will be a massive improvement. They are usually not aware they are doing it. Often it happens because they understand the rhythm of the line intuitively, so they add a sound as a placeholder while they remember the rest of the text. Added sounds early in the process can actually be encouraging: it means the actor knows how the line should sound when the play is operating at full speed. The problem is when the vocal notes become memorized. This is the linguistic equivalent of stage business: as the play begins to pick up speed, these sounds slow down the text. One sound may not matter very much, but the accumulation can be very disruptive to logic, story, and flow.

Ask the actor to listen to themselves and mark when they've added extra beats to their lines. Once they become aware of it, they can begin to eliminate them. It may be difficult for an actor to do at first, especially if they have learned and rehearsed the text with them, but remind them that everything they need to convey should and can happen *on* the words. Unlike a conversation about why some lines are being paraphrased, this adjustment should not require any discussion. As the play begins to gather speed and lift off, eliminating these sounds will make both the work of the actor speaking and of the audience listening smoother.

There are moments, however, when the addition of an "uh" or a "like" is potentially appropriate for the character or the moment, and this should be discussed with the writer. Even the smallest changes affect meaning, intent, and motivation, and so a writer must have the final word on any additions.

Miscast Actor

In the rehearsing and rewriting of a play, it can become clear that an actor has been miscast. Luckily, this is very rare, but it does happen, and when it does, it is the director who must find a solution. The miscasting of an actor in a new play is usually no one's fault: the role as you and the writer imagined it can drift once you start working in three dimensions. The actor was perfect for the idea of the character, but for whatever reason, they are less so in practice. Because actors are almost supernaturally aware, they may know before you that they are no longer fit for the role. It may become clear in the notes they're receiving, in the rewrites they're given, or in the way you or the writer speak about the character. In short: the role that they were given is not the role that currently exists. The ground has shifted under their feet, almost always through no fault of their own, but that leaves the director with difficult decisions.

You have two choices: proceed with the actor you have or replace them. If you decide to proceed, you must be very honest with the actor. This is easier than it sounds: because an actor almost always knows the truth, they will be relieved to name what they've been feeling. Explain your experience of the drift: how it happened and where you see the role now. Encourage the actor to articulate their experience and ask them how it feels. The goal of this conversation is to sense if the actor is up to and enthusiastic about the challenge of this rare circumstance. If the actor remains open and invested, then you can proceed with confidence that, even if the actor is no longer an ideal match with the character, they are going to bring positive energy to the role and to the process.

If the actor is resistant, if they do not like the direction the role has taken, or if they do not feel confident they can play it as it's currently written, then you need to have a frank conversation about whether or not they should proceed with the production. This can be a devastating situation for all involved, but an actor who has lost faith in their ability to play a role, or who has become convinced it is a bad part for them, is almost never an actor you can inspire to rejoin the company. Assure the actor that this has nothing to do with their talent or their work: this is an uncommon and unfortunate difficulty of working on a new play that is coming to life for the first time.

Before you consider parting ways with the actor, remember that a play in flux will continue to change. It has not reached its final form. A writer should not feel obligated to rewrite their play to accommodate an actor, but you and they can focus on the actor's strengths, and because it is likely the play will continue to grow, the actor may be even better suited for some future version of the character. The conclusion that an actor is miscast, and a conversation with them about it, should only happen after you and the writer are certain the drift is too far to overlook. Never speak to an actor about their "rightness" for a role during the rehearsal process unless it is clear beyond the shadow of a doubt that a threshold has been crossed. Any suggestion of doubt too soon can shatter an actor's confidence and destroy the actor–director pact beyond repair.

Conflict Resolution

Conflict in the rehearsal room is inevitable: the variable is how a director chooses to handle it. You are overseeing a group of people working together in close proximity for an extended period of time. You are making a work of art in collaboration that requires a multitude of opinions and near-constant emotional availability. Conflict is completely natural. It is a sign the group is present and being honest about their thoughts, feelings, and experience.

There are many sources of conflict during a rehearsal process: ego or personality clashes, fear, anxiety, insecurity, competitiveness, artistic differences, a loss of faith in, trust of, or enthusiasm for the play, the production, or their collaborators. Particularly with a new play, an artist may think or say "This isn't what I thought it was going to be" or "This isn't what I signed up for." Every process will have emotional highs and lows, moments of euphoria and moments of doubt or even despair. Stretches of discontent and frustration are not an indicator of conflict, and it is not a director's job to make sure a process is always happy or content: a productive, generous, and professional space is all that is required. But a director must be able to identify the difference between the natural emotional ebb and flow of a process and a problem that needs your attention.

Conflict emerges from tension, resentment, repression, distrust, and constant negative behavior. It presents itself as a collision between artists (maybe you are one of them) that transcends common disagreement. Almost all conflicts in the rehearsal room (and in life) start small, so pay attention to these moments, especially if the negative energy does not seem to pass. Not every incident of friction needs a conversation, but a true conflict will almost never dissipate on its own.

It can be a natural impulse to avoid conflict. If it is ignored too long, however, it can cause irreparable damage. Since there are no secrets in a rehearsal room, if there is a drop of tension between two actors, the entire room will know. If a director is frustrated with an actor, everyone will sense it instantly. This is why identifying and naming conflict is critical: it can easily metastasize into a larger problem if left ignored.

A director's role when conflict presents itself is:

- To identify and name the conflict
- To take the initiative to address it
- To guide the artists to a resolution

Begin by making sure all relevant parties are present (do not hold private conversations as it will breed distrust), and name it: you have noticed tension and it is interfering with the work. Do not lay blame or force anyone to defend themselves: you are creating an opportunity to speak openly and honestly, and to clear the air.

Keep these conversations on topic. This is a creative space and always a professional one. No personal attacks, no judgment on anyone else's work or taste. Lead the group toward the root problem: everything else is superfluous. Make sure everyone is given the chance to speak and be heard and that everyone has listened with an open mind. Very often, simply naming a conflict will give your collaborators a sense of relief. Because everyone can feel its presence, being able to discuss it openly can ease a significant amount of tension. Resolution can take many forms, but the basic goal is to return the room and the process to one of generosity and openness. Everyone does not need to be friends, but they do need to work together in the spirit of collaboration.

REHEARSAL ROOM CHALLENGES

You are the artistic leader of the project, but you are not the cast's employer. If there is a conflict that is not creative—a collaborator mistreating or being inappropriate with another, for example—that must be shared immediately with the producing organization. Directors often feel as though they can fix anything, or believe that because it is their rehearsal room, it is their problem and their responsibility to solve it. If there is behavior that is an employment issue, you must alert the appropriate parties. You risk being liable yourself.

Remember that although you must negotiate the complicated emotions of a rehearsal room, you are not a therapist. You cannot solve the complex issues of a collaborator and you should not try. Bring any issues that cause you alarm to the appropriate party of the producing organization to seek either their guidance or leadership. Creative conflicts fall under a director's jurisdiction. Interpersonal, professional, or behavioral ones must be handled by the producing organization.

18
REWRITES

When confronted with something new, we can struggle to see it objectively. We might reject it because we don't recognize or understand it, embrace it because its newness is seductive, exciting, or refreshing, or judge it by comparing it with what was there before. If the new object feels familiar, we tend to like it better. If it feels radically different, we may embrace it too hastily or resist it. A director must understand this dynamic as rewrites are incorporated into the rehearsal process. Changes to the text are an emotional experience as much as they are a technical one. Learning new lines can be a struggle, but that is nothing compared with asking an actor to reimagine and rearrange the internal life of their character. The text is the actor's foundation, so any change will feel as though the ground is shifting under their feet.

There are more obvious struggles: no actor wants to lose lines, to have their role get smaller, or to feel as though they weren't performing the line "right." Getting new pages can be thrilling, confusing, frustrating, or relieving. You cannot anticipate how you or an actor will react to any change, but you can be aware that any rewrite is going to elicit an emotional response.

The period of rehearsal after the stumble-through is the ideal moment for any big changes. Soon you and the company will be doing runs, so now, when the rough draft gives way to a more detailed one, you must insert the writer's most significant rewrites. A "significant" change would be a brand new scene, a full rewrite of an existing one, a reordering of events, or a new plot point that changes the story. Inserting big changes now will allow the actors to integrate them just as their work becomes more specific. This is why reintroducing the writer to the process a little too early is the perfect time.

Planning Rewrite Rehearsals

The conversations you had with the writer after the stumble-through should have given you a sense of what changes you can expect. Some writers are more organized than others, but no matter how they work, you must know what rewrites to anticipate so they can be worked into your rehearsal schedule. A writer arriving to rehearsal with new pages you were not expecting and had not planned to work will lead to a logistical headache and to unproductive days.

Review the potential rewrites you and the writer discussed. Begin with major revisions: big cuts, new scenes, rearrangements, reorderings, and anything you agreed on based on the stumble-through. Then make a list of what the writer may want to change, or is curious to observe in rehearsal. If there is a moment that does not seem emotionally clear, for example, the writer may want to wait to make changes until you, they, and the cast can work on the scene all together. The stumble-through is helpful for a writer in that they can see and understand so much of what you and the company have made, but it will also generate questions about pace, story, stakes, and tension. If the writer is suggesting a rewrite for a section that you feel needs further exploration, ask the writer to wait until you can see the scene in rehearsal together. Only you will know the difference between which elements need changes and which are not yet ready for text revision. This list of potential changes will shift as you work—ideas will fall away, new ones will be added—but it can be a useful document to keep track of and to remember your and the writer's initial impulses immediately after the stumble-through.

While rehearsing in sequential order is ideal, exceptions must be made for large text changes. Because this window of time is about adjustments and decisions within the context of the whole, the cast must be made aware of any big changes that will have a profound effect on the plot. The sooner a cast can be made aware, the faster they can absorb this new idea and let that information influence their moment to moment work. There is no point in making detailed adjustments if a big rewrite will upend them later.

Receiving New Pages

The writer should share all rewrites with you before anyone else. Receiving changes from the writer at the same time as the cast puts you at a disadvantage: you will be forced to form an opinion instantly and publicly. It wastes time and undercuts your ability to manage the flow of a rehearsal day. An actor should never be given a rewrite without your being present and without your approval. If changes are given directly to the actors, it can derail a rehearsal, even an entire process, and you will not be able to stop it.

Read the changes and remember that their newness will influence your judgment: pay attention to your reaction but do not rush to conclusions. Remain open to the rewrite and try to understand what the writer is addressing with the change.

- Is this change an improvement?
- Does it fix a problem?
- Can the problem be fixed another way (performance, staging, etc.)?
- What new questions does this change elicit?

The rewrites do not have to be perfect: questions can remain. If you feel they have strong potential to address a need or to fix a problem, that is enough to bring them into rehearsal. Work with your stage manager to schedule time to incorporate the new text. Devote extra time for rewrites, even smaller ones, as the cast needs time to process what the change means for their character.

If you feel the change is not successful, however, share your reasons with the writer and try to reach a consensus. Do not bring rewrites you do not agree are improvements into rehearsal. The writer should be able to experiment with new ideas and to hear changes aloud, but too much trial and error with text will confuse the company. Endless new pages for the sake of experimentation will frustrate a cast that is beginning to grow more confident and clear: it will feel to them as though you are reverting to a workshop process just as they are making decisions about their roles. Balance the writer's desire to try new things with the cast's need to continue building their performances.

If you feel you are receiving new pages that change little, be judicious about whether or not to bring into rehearsal. You don't have the time and the actors do not have the emotional and psychic bandwidth to try new versions of the same scenes day after day. There will be occasions when you will be given a rewrite that you can't judge without seeing it. If that is the case, begin the day with hearing it aloud, stage it, and then let that version exist overnight so you, the writer, and the cast can ponder. Time is usually the best teacher in these situations.

Under-rewriting

Some writers will begin a process confident that their play is finished. They feel no changes or rewrites are necessary: if there is a problem or question, the director and actors will resolve it. It can be challenging to have a writer present who wants you to work as though the play is established. You and the company may have legitimate questions, concerns, or suggestions that the writer will not address. Rarely is this way of working a surprise: a writer will almost always reveal their willingness (or not) to rewrite during the development process. While it can be frustrating to see potential changes go unexplored, the clarity of your circumstances—a writer who claims to be "finished"—will allow you and the cast to proceed knowing who carries the responsibility of making something work. The writer may provide observations and give notes, but the text is set, and any problems, obstacles, or challenges within it will be solved through direction and performance.

While a director cannot force a writer to revise their work, make certain they are confident in their decision not to make changes and that they aren't avoiding rewrites out of fear. Sometimes a writer is scared the play is not sturdy enough to revise, that it will all fall apart if they begin to experiment with the text. Writers can also worry there isn't enough time for rewrites, or that they aren't capable of making the necessary improvements. If you suspect the writer has any of these thoughts or feelings, act as a guide for them. Assure the writer that the play is strong enough to withstand rewrites, that they owe it to their work to make it the best it can possibly be, and that you and the cast support their willingness to make changes. Your confidence can be contagious: if a writer trusts there is time, that improvements are possible, and that the play will not unravel, they are more likely to continue their work.

Over-rewriting

A more common situation may be an over-abundance of rewrites. This is often a sign of a crisis of confidence. The writer may feel the play is not good enough, that it isn't clear, that it doesn't make sense, that what the writer wants to convey will not be understood, or that this *one change* will make all the difference. They may also feel the rough draft's lack of rhythm is a flaw in the writing. If the playwright continues to revise and to send you new pages and ideas, your challenge will be how to manage the flow and to decide if or how to integrate them into the process successfully. Evaluate the revisions with an open mind, but slow the process down so you are not bringing in new material every day. Give both you and the writer time to consider these changes. Ask the writer where the idea came from, about how the current version feels insufficient or ineffective, and what precisely they hope to achieve. Often, you will find they are worried by what they feel is not on the page or not yet present in the actor's performance, and so your task will be to show—through your work with the cast—that the moment is working effectively. This is another opportunity for confidence-building: a director should show a writer how successful the text already is, and how direction and performance will naturally improve a rough draft simply by repetition, practice, decision-making, detailed work, and an increase in pace, momentum, and dramatic tension.

Another over-writing scenario is when a writer is so open and generous that they eagerly accept any suggestion. For example, if an actor questions the meaning or doubts the quality of a line, a writer may immediately offer to change it. This way of working can appear generous, but it can lead to a situation in which the writer is no longer collaborating with but working for the group: when this dynamic is set, the writer's creative point of view will get lost. With your support, a writer needs to reserve the right to not make a change, to let something an actor (or the director) finds confusing remain as is, and to stand behind what they wrote, even if some of their collaborators struggle with it.

Rehearsing Rewrites

After you have approved them, all rewrites must go to stage management. It is their responsibility to keep an official and up-to-date version of the script. If any changes skip stage management and go directly to the cast, you must assume they are not being recorded.

The distribution of rewrites needs to happen at the top of the day. Ask the actors to read the changes aloud, and before any discussion, ask them to read it again. No judgment, no analysis, just the words. The cast will also have reactions to the rewrite's newness, so your task is to let the text simply exist before it is scrutinized. Before you discuss, put it on its feet and run the scene or section. You and the writer must see it before you make any decisions. Do not yet worry about the logistical concerns (if the rewrite introduces a new prop, if it eliminates a piece of staging you had grown attached to, if you know an actor will hate being asked to do something new in this section): focus on the text itself. Before you open the room up to questions, ask yourself how you feel about it, and why you may feel that way. Ask the cast to step through it again, then give yourself time to contemplate how you feel before determining the next steps.

What you do next will be your decision, so do not rush yourself or succumb to outside pressure. If you think the rewrite has potential, tell the writer and company and ask for their thoughts. If an actor is resistant, ask them to articulate why, but remind them that you must keep experimenting. Continue to work on the new pages so you can grow accustomed to this new version. It is only when the older version recedes and the cast becomes more confident that you and the writer can effectively evaluate the change. If, after seeing the rewrite a few times, you feel it is unsuccessful, discuss privately with the writer. Try to reach a consensus, even if it takes up rehearsal time: a cast will get confused if you bring in pages without deciding whether or not they will remain. You should be able to end the rehearsal by telling the cast the rewrite will stay or that you will revert back to the previous version. A state of limbo for a rewrite will make it impossible for an actor to continue working on their role. If you are undecided, tell the cast to keep working from the older draft. That will give you and the writer more time to contemplate. It is likely the moment does require a rewrite, just not the current one. Try to address the change the following day: the cast will be eager to know if they need to learn something new, and the less time they spend wondering what changes are in store, the better it will be for their process.

Now that the writer is an active participant in the room, an actor may think "Fantastic! Now I can tell the writer what hasn't been working for me." A writer may think "Now I can just tell the actors how I want them to do it." While incorporating rewrites, a director must establish clear rules of engagement between the writer and actor: the former needs time to see their rewrites on their feet, and the latter needs time to metabolize new pages. Neither the writer nor the actors should tell each other what to do. That is their pact: the words on the page belong to the writer, the performance to the actor. Both are welcome and encouraged to ask questions, voice concerns, seek clarity, disagree, but both have a right to resist notes. If a writer has a thought on how a moment can be played, they should share that information with you. If an actor feels a line must be rewritten, that should be shared with you as well. If the writer or an actor exerts too much control over the other, one will lose their creative agency. The writer needs to feel as though their story is being told and the actors need to feel as though they have creative ownership of their role.

19
RUN-THROUGHS

Imagine a painter working on an enormous canvas. As the painting nears completion, they must do very meticulous work, just a few brush strokes at a time. After a few changes, the painter must step back to evaluate their progress. Two things are happening in that moment: they are looking at the painting from the perspective of the eventual viewer, and they are observing how their most recent changes affect the whole. A run-through is the same act: it is a director's chance to step back from their work to see how everything fits together. They can judge the effectiveness of recent changes, and they can experience the work as an audience member. What a director also learns from watching a run is what should go on subsequent worklists. The list is then implemented in rehearsal, the director steps back to watch a run again, and the cycle continues.

Run-throughs give the company an opportunity to experience the complete physical and psychological journey of their characters. It's called a "run" because the actors are feeling confident enough that they no longer need to stumble or walk through the story. A run is an opportunity for an actor to synthesize notes, rewrites, changes, and ideas: it is a chance for them to practice. At a certain point, discussion will not be as useful as putting all the pieces together so the actor can understand what works for them, what does not yet make sense or feel right, what questions remain, and what moments may feel incongruous. In the same way the director needs to step back to see the whole, so an actor needs to experience the entire story to learn what is and isn't working.

A run will provide the writer with a chance to hear their play at the rhythm they've imagined, at-pace for the first time since it was read around the table. Because they can hear what they wrote while watching the action, they can make more informed decisions about what they may want to change, what they feel is working effectively, and what suggestions they may have to offer. Rewrites that are born out of run-throughs should be efforts to improve, clean, or clarify. Fully present and engaged with the actors, a writer can see where problems or confusions remain, where jumps in plot or emotional logic happen, or where text changes can support or elevate what is already there. Very often the best and most exciting rewrites happen during this phase, as the writer is responding to a clearer, more complete three dimensional version of their play.

For stage management, a run is a chance to understand the production as a piece of moving machinery: they can record the running time of each section, note potential needs for any transitions, and predict technical and logistical challenges. Stage management will watch a run with a mind toward the incorporation of design elements and crew in tech. They will make observations such as where and when a costume change should happen and how much time they will have to complete it. They can prepare for a complicated sequence of cues. They can note a complex transition and can begin to map out how it might happen. In short, they are watching the traffic patterns of bodies moving through space—their entrances, exits, and everything in between—as well as creating a flow chart of what must happen backstage.

When to Run

Because a run is about practice, evaluating changes, and creating a new worklist, you want to run frequently enough so that the entire piece stays fresh in everyone's mind and that detailed work and rewrites can be seen in context quickly. You should plan to run about a week after the stumble-through. Less time and you may not get all of your worklist done, more time and you risk losing sight of the whole. Returning to runs fairly often keeps the entire play in the forefront of everyone's mind: you do not want to work on only a few sections and let others languish, as they can be forgotten and will require more attention later. As soon as you feel you have made so many changes that you need to see them in context, schedule a run.

Run-throughs can have magical properties: sections that baffled you and the cast during rehearsal may suddenly become clear, a line that was always confusing to you can make sense in context, or a question you had been struggling with finds an answer; conversely, moments you felt confident about may strike you as confusing. The unpredictability of these discoveries is the case for incorporating runs into your process too soon rather than too late. Do not let perfect be the enemy of good. There will always be more items on your worklist, but postponing runs can lead to unhelpful detailed work that will inevitably get cut or changed later.

Run the play in the rehearsal room enough times so that the cast feels clear and confident going into tech. You and the writer want to feel as though you have exhausted all of the ideas you can try without an audience there to watch. It is time to stop running when you feel collectively like there is nothing new to learn. Do not run the play so many times that the cast becomes either bored or fatigued. Repetition for the sake of "drilling" the play will simply tire out a company and potentially lead to habits that are difficult to break. You want the company's energy, excitement, and morale to peak just before you enter the space.

Setting Up a Run

Let the company know a few days before you're planning a run-through. They may want to run lines, review notes, or otherwise mentally prepare. The first runs should be closed to visitors: the cast should not feel pressured to perform for anyone who hasn't already spent time in the room. It is an unnecessary pressure and will teach you and the cast little.

On the day of a run, set up the event with some rules. Ask that the cast not stop unless necessary. Remind the cast that the goal of the run is not perfection, but to learn what is and isn't working. It is an opportunity to observe the current version: to test recent changes and to generate a list of what needs attention before the next run. This reminder is to set the appropriate tone and to encourage the cast to think in the same way. They should be evaluating the work from within as you are from without. Ask them to run at pace as best they can. Allowing everyone to experience the play at its intended rhythm will teach the room more than restarting in an effort to get every word, gesture, and movement just right.

Have someone on-book (following along with the latest draft of the script). Accuracy is important: during a run, an actor may revert to an older version of a scene, add a line that was cut or drop a line that has been added. Since the goal is to keep moving, encourage the cast to call for line and to continue, even if there is confusion. Any text questions can be addressed after the run.

Once you've set the rules, give the room over to stage management, who will call places. Empower your stage manager to oversee run-throughs. The cast should get used to their being in charge as you get closer to tech rehearsals.

Watching a Run-Through

Everyone has had the experience of writing down something important, placing the note in a prominent place, and then promptly forgetting it exists. This is human nature: we are more likely to overlook something we see all the time as opposed to something new or different that will catch our attention. At this point in a rehearsal process, a director can become so overwhelmed by juggling the needs of the company, new pages and notes from the writer, scheduling logistics, and preparations for tech that significant elements of the play can go ignored. Questions go unasked, and obvious problems can exist right in front of you that you may not notice. A run-through is a time to step back and see the play as it is. It is an opportunity to engage with the thing you have made, as it is right here and now. You can allow yourself to be present: no one is going to ask you a question, no one will need anything from you, you do not need to give feedback or adjustments. All you need to do is remain aware, notice what you see, and pay attention to how you feel.

Ask questions as if you were seeing the play for the first time. It is very easy to fall into the trap of asking yourself: "What do I need to fix?" "Why is he doing it like that?" "Why won't this moment work?" It is also easy to concentrate on how you imagined a scene would look or what you wish it would be: thoughts that can bring your attention away from the action. There will be time to sort out what you felt worked, what didn't, and what to do about it later. Spending a run scribbling notes about blocking or pacing, letting yourself become frustrated by an actor's performance, or succumbing to despair that one part of the play continues to confound you will pull your focus away from what is actually happening. You will have a skewed perspective on what you saw and your subsequent worklist will reflect your distracted thoughts and not your focused observations.

As you watch, take in what's happening in each scene. Ask yourself the simplest of questions:

- Do I understand where I am and what is happening?
- Do I know who is everyone and do I understand their relationships?
- What does everyone seem to want?
- Do they get it?
- How, or why not?
- When do I feel myself paying attention?
- When do I feel my mind wandering?

These questions can seem basic after so many weeks of detailed work, which is why you need to reconnect with them. These are the questions the audience will be asking and will determine how they will engage with your production. They will teach you where there are still gaps in the story, in emotional and behavioral logic, and in the given circumstances. Returning to objective questions is the strongest way to bring your attention to those elements you are most likely to overlook, and they will provide you with the clearest worklist for subsequent rehearsals. Soon your attention will be overwhelmed with the incorporation of the design and with technical challenges. This is a time to reconnect with the basics of the story and an opportunity to make certain that the who, the what, and the where are lucid and well-articulated. A run is an opportunity to be reminded of what is right in front of you.

Post-Run Notes

If you were able to stay present, immediately after a run you should have more feelings than specific notes. Try to stay in that mindset. Your goal is to transform those feelings into ideas, and then into a worklist. Meeting with the cast to talk through specific notes and adjustments may not be time well spent.

Actors are also learning a great deal for themselves from repetition and practice, from their internal processes, and from each other. What they need from you most is your singular perspective. What did the play look like from outside of it? What affected you and what confused you? Begin by sharing your overall impressions and experience. This is what the cast cannot know or sense on their own. Keep this conversation short: share observations, avoid detailed analysis. If you find yourself engaging with an actor too long about any one moment, thought, or idea, that is a sign to pause the conversation and put the moment on your worklist. Share some thoughts on what you might want to work on in the days ahead, and ask the company if they have any sections they want to rehearse before the next run.

A director must uphold the actor–director pact in these moments. Your impulse might be to put a positive spin on the run-through even if it was confusing or frustrating. Remember: everyone knows everything in a rehearsal room. If the run was a disaster, you must acknowledge it. If you lie, the cast will know, and while you might think you are boosting morale, you are actually undermining your relationship with the cast in a moment when they need your honest perspective most.

A successful run-through is one in which you are given a lot to consider and to put onto your worklist. They are about gathering information. It can be stressful for you or the company to experience a rough run-through, but so long as you are learning, you should feel encouraged by your progress.

Making a Worklist (the daily top ten)

There is an old story about the out-of-town tryout for *Fiddler on the Roof*. The original structure of that show was a musical revue of short stories, and it was said to have been an irredeemable disaster. There were rumors circulating among the company that the producers were going to shut the show down immediately to save time, money, and face. The director, Jerome Robbins, gathered the entire team onstage: cast, musicians, dressers, crew, truck drivers, understudies, everyone. He sat them down and said (to paraphrase):

> This show doesn't work. It's bad. You know it and I know it. So this is what we're going to do. This afternoon, we're going to fix ten things. And then tonight we're going to perform the show and it won't be good. And then tomorrow afternoon we're going to fix more ten things and tomorrow night when we do the show it still won't be good. And then we'll fix ten things the next day, and ten the next, and ten the next, and by the end of the week we will have fixed sixty things. And by the end of next week, we will have fixed one hundred and twenty things. And then we'll know what we've got.

You cannot "fix" a show that doesn't work. What you can do is identify a handful of problems you want to address and begin there. And then you will address a few more, and then a few more after that. This process—intentional and deliberate—is how directors turn struggling shows around, or make good productions great. Ten things, every day. It is the art of setting an achievable daily goal for the entire group that favors clear, realistic expectations over panic. This way of working favors process. It breeds a mindset of patience, bravery, thoughtfulness, and care in a moment when it could be easy for a group to rush or to make impulsive decisions. Approaching your work in this manner organizes time in such a way that suddenly two weeks, which can feel like not nearly enough time to fix a disastrous show, will transform into a structured period of 120 improvements.

Create a daily worklist of ten items to rehearse between run-throughs. They should not be the ten most difficult or the ten most urgent challenges. They should be a combination of acting notes, blocking notes, rewrites, small adjustments, and larger issues. If you begin with the ten most difficult fixes, you will get only a few done, triggering further panic. If everything is a priority, that means nothing is, so vary your list to make it achievable. You will not see the results of this way of working immediately, but you will see it. When you're running low on time and need to maximize every moment of rehearsal, this is the most efficient and productive approach.

Rehearsals between Runs

If runs are a chance to step back and see the whole, the days between are an opportunity to return to detailed work, armed with your list of ten things. Break up your list between what can be addressed via discussion and what needs to be worked on your feet. Continue to keep your verbal notes brief. You are in a period of the process in which doing and seeing outweighs discussion. A helpful verbal note between runs could sound like "Next time we run it, could you try _____ in that moment?" The actors are learning from doing: long notes sessions rarely increase the quality of subsequent run-throughs.

Divide your worklist by department. If a moment is unsuccessful, contemplate which artist may be in the best position to fix it. Ask yourself if the moment is most likely to be improved through performance, direction, or writing. Because not everyone can work at the same time, you must come into rehearsal having made a decision about where the work on this moment will begin. It is far faster to experiment with acting and direction, while a rewrite can take a significant amount of time. Identify the problem and consider the solutions: rehearsals will be far more productive if you begin with a clear sense of where you would like to begin, and who you would like to make the first attempt at addressing a problem.

Actors during this time might feel excited, nervous, or some combination of both. They may be eager to get into the theater, which could make them resistant to notes, or they may be worried they are not ready to leave the room, which could make them want to over-rehearse. While you should be aware of how the cast is feeling, you should not tailor your worklist based on the energy of the room. If there is a big rewrite that you and the writer agree should be given to the cast and rehearsed before tech, you must schedule time to rehearse it right away. If you feel a significant change in a character's trajectory or behavior is necessary, you must work with the actor now. Tech is a time for many new considerations: do not wait until you are in the space to make a change or give a note that can be done in rehearsal.

Actors are resilient. They can do miraculous things, especially when time is short and an audience is fast approaching. If you have confidence in the actor and they have confidence in themselves, you can give them a huge rewrite and in just a few hours they can make it sound as though it has always been there. They can rearrange their synapses quickly and completely, as though the older version never existed. Always be mindful of how many changes you are giving an actor, but if there is a big rewrite you feel certain must go in, trust that the actor will be able to handle it. While the change may be intimidating, your confidence in the quality of the revision will be both encouraging and inspiring.

The rewrites a writer can generate during the period of run-throughs can be incredible: intelligent, illuminating, and profound. Make room on your worklists for rewrites, and begin every day with new pages. Some writers can feel as though the end of rehearsal is their last chance to make changes, and that concern can sometimes result in a flurry of unhelpful rewrites at the last minute. Those changes to the script that do not feel like improvements will confuse actors, take up time, and do little to prepare the company for tech. It will be your job to make the worklist, and that includes deciding which rewrites will go into the script before tech, and which will have to wait. This can be frustrating for a writer, who will want every change to go into the script before tech, but you must use your judgment and prioritize: rewrites are one of many considerations you must evaluate before tech. A revision you suspect may be coming from a place of panic should wait for further consideration.

A Note on Reflection Time

The final weeks and days in the rehearsal room can feel hectic. The energy in the room becomes heightened, nervousness can present itself in all sorts of different behaviors, and the room is opened up to more collaborators and therefore more opinions. Time will seem to change: the days will seem shorter just as you hope to get more accomplished, and the leisurely pace of exploratory work will seem like a distant memory when run-throughs and worklists take up hours of a rehearsal day and every minute seems of great consequence.

You must give yourself private reflection time during this part of your process. The energy may feel very different, but a director must continue to have windows of time to reflect, just as you did when you first read the play so many months or even years before. The evening after a run, or the morning after, give yourself time to look through your notes, to revisit the script, to think about what you saw and how you felt. Let this private time help you decide what you want to work on and in what order. This process cannot be rushed, as your worklist is the architecture of your rehearsal time and will only be as strong as your ability to identify exactly what you want to work on and why.

If a director skips this time, or rushes through it, they risk losing their artistic sensibility. They become facilitators, crossing items off lists in an effort to "fit it all in" or to "get it all done." The frantic nature of final rehearsals can be contagious, and a director's vision can be a casualty. Give yourself time to connect with your responses and build your list from that foundation. Otherwise it is a race you are running without a creative compass to guide you.

Designer Runs

After one or two "closed runs" it will be time to invite more collaborators into the room to see the work. This is an exciting moment: the actors will have a new audience to perform for and the designers can begin to marry their imagined versions of the production with the reality of what you've created in the room. Just days before tech, all of the artists will finally be in the same space together.

The designer runs must be scheduled according to both your and their needs. Most designers will need to be in the theater in days leading up to tech to prepare with the crew. The load-in calendar will affect the designer's schedules, which will, in turn, affect yours. Your stage manager must cross reference everyone's availability so that (A) you can schedule run-throughs when they are free, and (B) you can space out your working days and your runs so you can maximize your working time. Always schedule runs with enough time between to incorporate changes. Running the same version twice will only reinforce a draft that is in flux, and you and the company will learn very little. Knowing when you need to run for the designers will allow you to plan in a way that can be to everyone's benefit.

During a designer run, the lighting designer will bring their blueprints, or light plot, to spread out on a table. They will watch your staging closely and will note if they have lights in their desired locations. The goals of focus, when the designer and the crew position the lights, will be based on what they observe in the room. If you anticipate a drastic change (maybe the restaging of a scene you have planned but have not yet implemented), tell your designers. Changes during tech are inevitable, but every way you can offer context to your designers about what to expect will help everyone's process. Your sound designer may have already given your stage manager cues to play in rehearsal, so they (like you) will be an audience member, taking it in, paying attention to tone and rhythm. Your costume designer, who will be familiar with the company through the fitting process, will be paying attention to entrances, exits, blocking and behavior that may affect clothes, and transitions. Your set designer will observe the staging, transitions, props, and composition of bodies in the space.

Backstage crew members may also watch these runs. Anyone who will participate in transitions, quick changes, prop placement/maintenance, and generally make the production possible may be watching, probably for the only time, as once tech begins they will be at their necessary positions. Giving them a clean, clear run will offer them context for their work backstage.

These artists are thinking through technical considerations as much as they're watching the play. It can be helpful to remind the actors of that: they are not always the most engaged audiences. During the vulnerable time just before the company leaves the rehearsal room, a cast can assign a significant amount of meaning to a crew's reactions, or lack thereof. The rehearsal room has been a sealed, private space, and suddenly there are many new people watching, many of them strangers. The crew will have their own logistical considerations to pay attention to. If they don't have a strong response to the performances, that is not in any way a commentary on the quality of the work.

Artistic Director Notes

The arrival of the artistic director can spark anxiety in the writer, the company, and yourself. They are your employer, and in many ways the last word on the production. Most ADs understand that their presence can be stressful and are generous and complimentary with the cast. Someone in that position has done this many times, and they know they are entering the space during a sensitive moment. Others, however, can be cold with the creative team, which can be intimidating. As always, let the cast know in advance who is coming and when, including the artistic director. Schedule time to meet with them after they watch a run, as they will want to give you feedback.

When it comes to notes, there are generally two types of artistic directors: those who will give one or two overarching observations, and those who will give an enormous amount of detailed ones. An artistic director who watches a run having not been in the room since the meet and greet can be enormously helpful, as they can see your progress with entirely fresh eyes. While your designers will provide new perspectives during a run, they will be watching for specific considerations, but the the artistic director is taking in the entire piece: they do not have to pretend as though they are seeing the piece for the first time, they simply are. Their perspective can also be an enormous asset because they don't have any knowledge of the day-to-day rehearsal room dynamics. They do not watch with any information about interpersonal or creative struggles, so they are coming in with a clean slate. All they can see is the work in progress, and will be able to speak about it accordingly.

Receiving notes from this perspective can be intimidating. An artistic director could say something like "It's great, but it's a comedy and this isn't very funny" or "Everyone is good in it, but you need to give the story some forward momentum." The other kind of artistic director can overwhelm you in the opposite way. They may have pages of notes that are very specific and very prescriptive. Sometimes they are simply an explanation of how the AD would have directed the play. In those instances, they are not commenting on what you created but are trying to get you to direct their version. This conveys a lack of trust or interest in your creative vision.

A few large notes or many little ones can be equally frustrating. A common impulse is to reject both outright: the production is yours, and you will not compromise your vision. In both instances, a director should not do anything yet: they should wait. Continue your work as planned, but keep the producer's notes in mind. As you watch subsequent runs, notice where you may or may not agree. The sweeping notes tend to be most useful because they offer a new perspective, allowing you to watch with fresh eyes. They may wake you up to something right in front of you that had disappeared.

Regardless of whether or not you accept a producer's notes, they will challenge you to consider what you've made. These notes will give you the opportunity to make changes based on the perspective of an outside observer with a vested interest in a successful production, or they will offer you the chance to defend your artistic vision. This is why waiting before you respond to a producer's notes is worthwhile: you want to accept or reject them based on their artistic merit and compatibility with your vision, not because of ego or of fear.

Final Days in the Room

With any play, but particularly a new one, there will remain questions and confusions when the rehearsal period comes to an end. Scenes or moments still do not make sense to everyone, questions remain unanswered, logic problems go unresolved. This can be an unnerving feeling, so you must be honest with the company: there are sections that still need work, there are questions that persist. Continue to put them on your worklist but do not let them take over the entire process. A troublesome section can devour an entire day, so while it should be prioritized, it should not eclipse everything else. Furthermore, working on a section over and over may only reinforce what isn't working, and rattle everyone's nerves. Make a few changes to the scene in question, try it during a run, assess, and put it on your next worklist.

Remind the cast, the writer, and yourself that you still have time. The last rehearsal is not the dress rehearsal, so the plan will be to keep working and to expect the cast to do the same. Very often it is only time that will reveal a solution.

End the last day in the rehearsal room with a run-through. Consider it a punctuation mark at the end of your process. Working through isolated moments just before tech can feel unsatisfying, like ending with an ellipsis when you and the cast want an exclamation point.

Remind the company that this is the draft you will begin tech with, it is not the final draft. There will be changes ahead once the design elements get incorporated. Some of them you can predict, many you cannot. Your goal has always been to create the strongest draft possible to go into the space with, so if you feel you are ready to see your work in collaboration with the design and in the context of the theater, you are ready for the next step.

PART FIVE

THE SPACE

In this section we will step through the tech process: how to prepare, what to expect, how to collaborate with your designers, how to create a rough draft, and how to refine it. We will also look at the role of a director during the dress rehearsal in anticipation of the first audience.

While you and the company were in the rehearsal room, the set was built, costumes were purchased or constructed, lights and speakers were hung, and the theater was prepared for your arrival. Then, suddenly, many artists and their creations are sharing space. Each element is no longer a solitary project: they are now all in conversation with everything around them. Tech is the moment in which all of your collaborators will work under one roof simultaneously, enjoying the excitement and weathering the complications that arise from combining all the disparate elements that will make up the production. Months of conversation and theoretical planning can be observed and experienced at the same time: you and your collaborators are pivoting from the imagined production to its realization.

This stop in the process is, above all, about relationships: the performances in relation to the set, the set in relation to the lights, the lights in relation to the costumes, and so on. A director in tech must identify, understand, and respect the needs and desires of each artist and department, address the natural frictions that will arise, and bring them all together to honor your vision and to achieve aesthetic harmony. You must remain aware of the relationships between each creative element and between the artists themselves. Nothing can be evaluated out of context from this moment forward, every choice and decision will affect the entire group and the entire piece. A director must shift their thinking to take in many different elements in order to prioritize clarity, cohesion, and harmony.

20
PREPARING FOR TECH

Pre-tech Production Meeting

Time takes on a peculiar shape in tech: it is painstakingly slow while passing by far too quickly. You and your team will have time to do your work, but because there are so many departments working simultaneously, there must be a clear plan and schedule in place before you begin. Tech requires every artist, every crew person, and every technician to move together as one, and that synchronicity is only possible if everyone knows what to prepare for and how. Communication among departments is critical to your success. You can only work as quickly as your least organized collaborator: you must decide in advance what you need, what you want, and what information everyone must have so they can understand the goals of each day.

Before you move into the space, ask stage management to schedule a meeting. This is a planning and strategy session in which the director, stage and production management, the designers, and heads of each department will share updates about their progress: which elements on their worklists are finished, which are not, and which are on or behind schedule. It is an opportunity for all departments to list their priorities, challenges, obstacles, and needs. Because everyone is sharing the same space, work can no longer happen on individual schedules: you and the group must now think about the order in which work needs to happen, how much time each task will take to complete, and how to prioritize every department's needs to make the tech process as smooth and productive as possible. Stage and production management should schedule this meeting close enough to tech so that everyone can accurately predict what will and will not be ready, but that leaves enough time to make adjustments in case the information shared at this meeting requires changes to priorities and worklists. The goal of this meeting is to create a calendar that will meet everyone's most urgent needs, to provide the group with clarity about the daily tech goals, and to make everyone aware of each other's progress and remaining obstacles.

In anticipation of this meeting, make a list of what information you want to share with the group. Because the focus will be on the calendar, think about how you would like to work through the play (for example: chronological order, transitions first, to start with a moment of violence, a special effect, or some other potentially complex moment). Working in chronological order is generally best for the design team as they build a visual vocabulary, which is easier to do in order, but if the play has many complicated transitions, consider staging them first to save time later. Discuss your options with stage management in advance of the meeting.

At the meeting, begin by articulating your priorities. Share with the group what you anticipate the challenges will be, what sections of the play you suspect will require the most time and attention, and what design elements you must have ready so that you can work in the predetermined order. Stage and production management will create a tech schedule taking into consideration the order in which you want work. Huge amounts of tech time can be lost by a lack of preparedness, so while it is inevitable that you will face unforeseen obstacles, the more organized your days are, the more you can expect to accomplish no matter what surprises present themselves.

Call attention to any stage business, transition, or staging that may take extra time. Will you be working with open flame? Automated scenery? Blood? Nudity? Firearms? Where do those moments fall in the play? Work with stage management to determine on which tech day you might reach that section. If there are moments of intimacy or violence, you must bring in your fight or intimacy director the first time you see those moments onstage. Make certain all the necessary parties can be there before you work those moments into the schedule. Think through the entire play and flag moments that may take time and the attention of multiple departments to address.

Share information from the rehearsal room that you feel is useful for the group. If an actor is nervous about the amount of costume changes, inform the wardrobe department. If an actor needs help remembering entrances and exits, let the crew know so they can hang cue lights or otherwise offer support. Anything you want the crew to be aware of or to anticipate should be shared at this meeting. While you have spent time with many of the different departments that will be in tech, most of the actors and crew will be meeting each other for the first time. What have you learned about the company during rehearsals that you feel would be helpful for the designers and crew to know? How can you help this group get a head start on continuing a generous and productive working environment?

Dry Tech

"Dry tech" is a meeting between you, your designers, and stage management where you map out lighting, sound, video, or any other cues before you work with the actors onstage. By this group talking through the play in order, you can begin to understand where exactly lights or sound may change, and can begin tech with a rough idea of what will happen when. It will also give stage management the opportunity to write preliminary cues in their calling script. In general, dry tech can give stage management and your designers a head start on building cues, and will give you all a chance to create a vocabulary so you do not have to start from scratch when you get into the space.

Because the days leading up to tech are very busy for your designers, a dry tech period is not always possible. With any time you have available, meet with the most recent draft of the play and talk through the script together. Wherever you think there may be a cue, stop and discuss what it might be. Sound effects, music, lights going on or off, and especially transitions: where the actors will enter and exit from, what props or scenery may need to move, to be placed or struck, who will be responsible for moving them, and what action is necessary backstage to make it possible. You are doing two things: creating a map of movement on which designers can build ideas, and sharing your vision of rhythm and pace. During tech you will have to address questions you could not have anticipated: the clearer and more aligned you can be with stage management and your designers about what you do know and what you do want to see, the freer your attention will be to handle the unforeseen challenges.

Because so many departments have so many tasks to complete in the theater before tech begins, it is rare you can have time onstage in advance. If it is possible, however, use that time with the full crew, your designers, and stage management to look at lights, listen to sound, and run transitions without the cast. This work, particularly for a complex production, can save you and your team an enormous amount of time. It will give you the opportunity to have conversations and make decisions with fewer voices and considerations in the space. The first time you see the set under light, or hear a sound cue from the audience, is a moment that will require your complete attention. These first responses should not be rushed. In the same way that you need time to reflect when reading new pages, so you must give yourself room to observe the look, movement, and sound of the design. The more people in the space, the more potential distractions, so unrushed time to observe and respond before tech can allow you to contemplate how these visual and sonic elements work in conversation with each other. The more you can learn about the emotional and visual logic of the design before the actors arrive, the easier it will be to make decisions later, when there is less time and more people in need of your attention.

If you are unable to dry tech, on or off stage, at the very least map out your transitions with stage management. Decide who is responsible for what, who goes where, and in what order. Leaving the staging and solving of transitions until you are in the space will devour your time and can lead to rushed, impulsive, unconsidered, and potentially dangerous decisions. Transitions need planning and a reliable visual logic. If you can create a map for them in advance, you can give the crew instructions, walk the cast through them, and then build the design around the choreography. While the map is subject to change, and it likely will, you will be giving everyone a clear point of departure. Then you and your team can see it and respond, as opposed to building something using trial and error when there is no time for experimentation.

21
TECH

Tech is a series of longer rehearsal days in which the entire cast, the designers and production teams, backstage crews, and stage managers work together in the space to assemble all the many elements of the production. The last draft from the rehearsal room is restaged on the set with lights, sound, costumes, props: everything that is expected to be a part of the production is integrated into the piece during tech.

For the cast, tech is a time to get acclimated with their costumes, with the set and props, to settle into their dressing rooms and to meet the crews, and to begin understanding the theater space. They have only performed in the rehearsal room until tech, so their understanding of the dimensions, size, and feeling of the set was inspired by blueprints hanging on the rehearsal room wall and tape on the floor. Not only are the actors acclimating to the set in three dimensions, they are learning about the size of the theater itself. Tech is when the company begins to understand how to scale their performances appropriately for the space's size.

The crews will learn and practice their performance tracks and understand their duties before, during, and after each performance. Departments like stage crew, light and sound board operators, props, and wardrobe have their own list of tasks throughout the show that need to be created, learned, and rehearsed. The process of developing, revising, and finalizing each crewperson's responsibilities will happen during this time.

For designers, tech is their moment to see their work in context, to experiment and play. Tech is not simply putting actors in costumes, programming light cues, or rearranging scenery. It is the designer's time to be creative, to understand how their imagined work exists in reality, and to engage in a period of trial and error. Tech is always much faster than a rehearsal process, and yet the artists responsible for the visual and sonic life of the show need the same type of process to explore and investigate, just as you did in your early days of rehearsal.

For stage management, tech is the moment when they take on a more active leadership role. They oversee these rehearsals, running the space, and communicating with all the designers and all departments, on and off stage.

For the director, tech is a time for synthesis. You are observing and reacting to all the elements together, understanding how the story is and is not different in this new context, and asking new questions prompted by a huge amount of new stimuli and information.

The Second Time the Play Falls Apart

A lighting designer once told me that the first day of tech is always deeply humbling. Their planning and strategizing, their plots, notes, cues, and weeks of preparation are all speculative, he said, until the actors are onstage and they can finally start turning on the lights. Unlike other collaborators who can do a significant amount of work before tech, a lighting designer—like many of the artists that join you in tech—has to build their first draft in front of the entire group.

The process of slowing the work down to create another rough draft can be a confusing or frustrating experience for actors: once again, their rhythm is lost, their timing gone. The jokes that landed so well in rehearsal disappear, emotional through-lines are severed, and the music you worked so hard to find in the rehearsal room is gone. You must remind the cast that it will all come back. Better, even, because the upcoming draft will have the design to support and complement them. The draft from your rehearsal room has not fallen apart (as it might feel to some actors), it is opening up again to make space for new collaborators, new suggestions, new ideas, and new points of view. A director must teach the room that everyone is where they need to be for their own process: no one is behind and needs to catch up. This way of working requires a collective bravery to release one's grip on previous versions so another large step forward—one that incorporates new elements and involves the entire group—can be taken.

Tech requires a generous spirit, as so many people are working together, each at a very different starting point. A designer should not feel rushed because they are only beginning their work in the space: they need time, encouragement, and creative freedom as they integrate their work into the whole and you collectively work toward rediscovering the play's natural rhythm.

The Writer in Tech

Some writers want very much to watch tech, others find the process torturous. Since this time is about introducing a new group of collaborators to the process, encouraging the writer to take some time away from the space can be advantageous for their peace of mind. Like the first days on your feet in the rehearsal room, pace and momentum will disappear, and the writer cannot expect to hear their play while the designers begin their work.

Remind the writer that the script must remain unchanged or "locked" during tech. The actors are going to be absorbing a huge amount of new information: processing rewrites is a task they cannot take on. Furthermore, everyone in the space needs to be working from the same draft. Stage management cannot track changes or insert new pages while they're running a tech rehearsal. If everyone has different versions of the script, the building of cues will not match and confusion is inevitable. A writer may argue that it's a waste of time to tech in a line or moment they know is going to change. There is truth to that, but the time spent implementing new pages will eat into valuable time onstage. Your priority must be to give the designers as much time as possible to create a draft of their work. A locked script is the only way the group can move forward in an organized and reliable way. There will be time for text changes after tech is over.

The First Day, Introductions, and the Crew

When you arrive on the first day, introduce yourself to everyone. Every crew person, every designer's assistant or associate, every board operator, every person in the space: learn their names, who they are, and what they do. This is an appropriate and respectful way to begin tech. It is also necessary information. The space will be full of people performing many different tasks: you need to have an understanding of who is doing what. In tech you are a band of equals: a director may have more say in creative decisions than someone who sets the props, but a director is no more crucial to the production's success: if you need proof, try doing a performance without the propsmaster. Everyone contributes equally to the success of the production, and it is part of a director's work to remind everyone of that through their treatment of the entire team. A crew should be empowered to do their best work and eventually to take ownership of it. They are responsible for maintaining the quality and artistic integrity of the production long after a director's work is done: treat them as your peers and trusted allies and you can expect the same respect in return.

Every theater space has a different type of and relationship with their crew. This will have an enormous impact and influence on the tech process and on how the space operates in general, so a director must know who they are working with in advance.

Some spaces are union houses, which means the crew is affiliated with a labor union. They will have rules about breaks, schedules, responsibilities, and assigned tasks. A director being onstage during a break, for example, or handling props is not permitted. Actions and behaviors you may be accustomed to may be off limits, so ask your production manager in advance if you are in a union house and if so, learn what rules are in effect and how they need to be followed.

Many theaters have a house crew, meaning they use the same core group throughout a season. This is particularly true for institutional theaters. In this scenario, your production is one of many they will load-in, tech, run, and load-out in a year, so they may think of artists as guests or visitors in their space. Be mindful of this dynamic and respect their knowledge of and history with the theater.

A third scenario is the hiring of a freelance crew, which is common in smaller spaces and with independent producers. These crews can vary in terms of experience, but it's likely some or all of them have limited experience in this particular space, so they will need additional time to learn about the theater itself.

Tech days begin with work calls. These are scheduled blocks of time in which the crews will be given worklists from production management that reflect the needs and requests of the design team. The crews will then stop their work at a designated time, clean and set-up the space for wherever the creative team wants to begin, and go on their lunch break. A director can arrive whenever they want, but customarily not much earlier than the cast: the work calls mean the space will be busy with activity. The cast's tech day begins with a half-hour call, usually in the early afternoon when the actors will get into costume. Because they are settling into their dressing rooms, meeting the wardrobe crew, and putting everything on for the first time (not only the costume, but wigs, body microphones, make-up, etc.), the first day will take longer than the allotted half hour.

When the cast has arrived to the stage, the stage manager will ask that everyone introduce themselves. This is when you can begin teaching the group that your tech rehearsals will be respectful, generous, and egalitarian. Thank everyone for being there, and for all the hard work they have devoted to getting the space ready for tech. After introductions, stage management will take the cast on a tour of the space. Join them, as this is helpful information for you, too. Your ability to make changes and adjustments is only as strong as your understanding of how the backstage space is arranged.

Building a Rough Draft

After introductions and the tour, the stage manager will call everyone to places. Everyone will take their positions for the top of the show unless you have decided to tech a specific section first.

A sound cue plays, the lights come up, and the actors begin their performances. They experiment with props, settle into their costumes, acclimate themselves to the set and to the scale of the theater. Or, conversely, there is a disagreement about whether the lights or sound should begin first, confusion about how the actors know when to enter, or a prop has gone missing. In short: your fantasy of stepping methodically through the play, effortlessly transitioning the rehearsal draft to the stage, is dashed almost instantly. This is natural. Everyone is learning how to work together, there is no shared vocabulary, and no one is comfortable yet. It is the same sensation you experienced when you got on your feet for the first time. This is why a framework of cues created in advance is useful: at least you have some structure to begin your work. Slowly, and then slightly faster, cues are built. Actors are able to step through longer and longer sequences without stopping, everyone begins to breathe, and the rough draft begins to lurch into existence. You will watch, wandering from designer to designer, sharing what you're seeing and how you're responding, asking them what they see, and together building the visual logic of the production. This process—starting, observing, stopping, discussing, revising, proceeding—is the shape of early tech rehearsals.

Pay close attention to all the new relationships forming. Begin with the cast: observe them in relationship with the space, with one another, with the audience. This is a more sophisticated and complex form of blocking: you are understanding the story of each moment compositionally. An actor standing in front of or behind a chair tells two very different stories: if they are in front of the chair, are they feeling confident? If they are behind, do they have something to hide? And which choice is best for the audience's understanding and visual experience? A director's job is to understand the subtle and important meanings of both and make a decision accordingly.

Tech is another moment to wrestle with conflicting feelings about newness. You are evaluating the ways in which light, sound, costume, video, and scenery are different from what you imagined. How do these new elements interact with the actors' performances? Do they seem elevated and complimented or overshadowed? In what ways are design and performance working in harmony? Challenge yourself to be specific about why some moments/ideas/images are successfully balanced, then apply that information to moments in which the performances recede or get lost in the design.

Notice how each design element relates to each other. Is the light complimenting the set or is there aesthetic friction between them? How does the color palette of the costumes work in relation to the set? Are lights and sound synchronized, and should they be? What story are you telling about the world of the play if they work in tandem? What story are you telling if they are intentionally incongruous? Remain aware of the questions you are asking yourself as you watch: your taste and curiosity are your most useful tools as you begin to understand the visual and tonal logic of the production.

Questions can feel frightening during a tech process, as you may feel you have such little time to address them. Luckily, you are not asking them alone. All of the designers are looking at and responding to the collision of the fantasy version with the reality of what they and you are now witnessing. Everything was perfect and clear in your minds, and now you are presented with a different set of challenges and ideas.

All of this may feel familiar because you are stumbling through the play again: trying experiments, finding a choice with potential, and moving on. As was true in the rehearsal room, your goal in the early stages of tech is to create a rough draft so the actors can experience stepping through the show in the space, the crews can learn what it feels like to complete their tracks, and you and the designers can see how the piece does and does not cohere. During the creation of the rough draft, do not devote too much time to any one moment. You cannot know if the opening cues make sense until you see a rough draft of everything that follows. This is the logic of furniture assembly: do not spend too much attention and energy on one element until you have an understanding of if and how all the pieces fit. Trying to perfect a moment prematurely is the most common trap of tech rehearsals: it can waste time and provide you with very little information.

Every exploratory process involves hitting dead ends. In rehearsal, you could try something drastic to find a new direction, or you could set the moment aside to revisit later. In tech, however, you should avoid drastic changes to shake loose ideas. If you and your designers feel stuck, give the problem time to remain unresolved. Designers are working very quickly in tech: they need opportunities to step back and see their work in context. Unlike rehearsals, trying many different versions of a moment in tech can be enormously time consuming. Significant adjustments will change everyone else's cues and tracks. A "quick" experiment involving a brand new idea can take hours if no one is prepared for it, so while you and the designers should remain open to discoveries and play, let blocked moments or big changes wait until you have a plan. Put them on a worklist to return to later and move on: very often ideas or answers will come through teching another part of the play. There is no need to force a solution when it has not yet revealed itself.

Process Questions

As you create the rough draft, consider the following questions:

– Are you providing your designers with enough time and space to experiment? During the trial and error period of rehearsal, you would encourage the cast to not-know, and you would never tell them a choice was "wrong." Designers need the same support to make their strongest work. You may feel more aware of the time in tech: do not let that anxiety inhibit creative exploration. A designer needs space and freedom.

– Is what you are seeing clear and promising enough for a stumble-through?
If you are excited about how a moment is taking shape, if the actors and crew are clear about what they need to do and where they need to be, and if your designers are encouraged by what they've created, that is enough information to know you can move on. This is especially true for the first few scenes and transitions, in which you and your designers are only just beginning to build a visual vocabulary. It is the director who decides when to move on: take stock of your feelings and of your collaborators'. If everyone feels confident enough to try a moment in context, keep going.

– How is the room's energy and tempo?
Circulate, visit designers' tech tables, and check in frequently with your stage manager. Are there any departments in crisis? Anyone particularly behind, struggling, or stressed? If so, how can that be remedied? You cannot be everywhere at once, and you cannot fix everyone's problems, but you must be aware of how everyone's process is unfolding. Eavesdrop. What people choose to tell the director and what you want to learn are not always the same information. Listen to different departments and how they communicate with each other.

– What are your designers noticing? What do they see? What seems to excite them, and what are their challenges? What experiments seem effective, and what new questions or ideas are they eliciting?

Scheduling Challenges of New Work

When teching Hamlet, everyone understands you're most likely going to need your ghost gesture ready on the first day. Depending on how quickly you're working through the text, everyone will understand when you'll need extra time for Polonius's death, that you will need the fight director in attendance when you reach the end, etc. Everyone can anticipate when complicated or time-consuming moments are approaching and will make the appropriate preparations and adjustments to time and expectations.

This approach is not so simple with a new play. Similar steps can and should be taken, but it is much more difficult to predict the shape of a new play tech process. There may be moments of stage action that—in rehearsal, in design meetings, and in dry tech—seem very complex on paper but are not in practice, and moments no one expected to be challenging can consume an entire afternoon. With an established play, one can reasonably assume everyone working on the production knows roughly what to expect. With a new script, however, it is likely not everyone was able to attend a run-through, and you cannot assume everyone can predict upcoming challenges. The amount of unknowns, handled by a group with varying knowledge of the play, can cause confusion and delays. Stage and production management must use the first few days of tech to learn how quickly or slowly you are working so that you can adjust your schedules and expectations. If you are working through about twenty pages a day, for example, you must make certain everything you need for the next twenty pages is prepared for the following day, and so on until you are ready to stumble-through.

Actor–Designer Collaboration

That not everyone can work on the piece at the same time also applies to the designers and the cast. Not only will the rehearsal room version need to expand and change during tech, the designers will have technical needs and creative ideas that an actor may feel infringes on their work.

I once collaborated with a lighting designer on a project that had a complicated set. There was a solid ceiling overhead, among other challenges, so there were not many locations for lights to be hung. The designer kept asking the actors to move a few steps upstage or downstage, stage left or stage right, so they could be in strong positions to look their best. To a lighting designer, that is a very reasonable request, but to the actors it felt as though he was casually throwing away deeply considered staging choices.

The designer is serving the play and their vision, but in doing so, their work may conflict with acting choices. This can trigger conflict, which a director must mediate. Both artists need to understand each other's good intentions and be open to change in the spirit of collaboration. Actors can sometimes feel like props during tech or as though their hard work is disposable. Designers can feel like actors are shutting down their ideas and impulses, as though they are only there to serve the actors. These feelings and disagreements will inevitably arise when some of the artists have been working for a long time in a very deliberate way while others are only just joining the process. These situations are resolved by the director making creative decisions: are you comfortable with adjusting blocking to accommodate design? How does the story change as a result? Can or should the designer make an adjustment? Remain open to and empathetic with both artists and let what you observe onstage inform your decisions. Your ability to find resolution rests in your prioritizing the choice that makes the most dramaturgical sense, not in choosing sides. If the best version of the story is for the blocking to remain the same, for example, the lighting designer must find an alternative.

On another occasion, I was working with a sound designer who was very busy, and who joined us in tech having not been able to spend much time in the rehearsal room. He came in with a lot of ideas I had not heard, and he proceeded to play underscoring through many of the scenes. The actors were upset. They felt underscoring undercut their work. That their performances were overshadowed, buried under music, and they were angry with me because they felt I was allowing their work to disappear. I had to explain to the cast that the designer needed his own process: he needed time to learn and to be free to experiment. If this underscoring was going to get cut (and it did soon after), it is best for the designer to find their way to that decision on their own. That requires grace and patience. I could have immediately defended the actors and told the designer this music was all wrong, that he couldn't even try it. That would have appeased the actors in the moment, but would have shut down the designer's process before it even began. The designer would no longer be a collaborator but our employee, doing what I or the actors told him to do, and would never have another opportunity to find his own way into the project.

Ending Day One

By the end of the first day of tech, everyone will have accumulated a massive amount of new and useful information. How quickly or slowly you are working through the play, the degree to which you and your designers have fallen into a rhythm, which departments are behind, how soon you may be able to stumble through a draft, what technical elements need changing, fixing, or other support, and most critically: whether or not you can see the play clearly among all the many moving parts.

After the cast has been released for the day, you and your designers, the heads of each department, and your stage and production managers will meet in the space for a production meeting. This is a chance to combine individual needs into one master worklist and to schedule work calls based on it. Management will ask each department to describe what worked well for them, what did not, and what changes and adjustments need to happen before actors are onstage again. There is only so much work that can happen and only so many crew people to do it, so how everyone chooses to prioritize will profoundly impact the next day's work.

If you feel something is necessary or urgent, this meeting is the time to make it known. Everyone will have their needs, will feel their list is most urgent, and will all be correct: the lights *do* need to be refocused, the sound designer *does* need a few hours of silence to build cues, the set designer *does* need a wall repainted, and all right away. It will be your responsibility to articulate what you need to see tomorrow, as priority will be given to those elements the director needs in place for the next rehearsal.

Share with the group what you hope and expect to accomplish the next day so everyone is clear about where you want to begin and how many pages you expect to cover. Where you expect to begin is a key piece of information: because so much work will happen onstage, the crew will need to know how you expect the space to look when you begin. Do not presume everything will be ready for you without being explicit.

Subsequent Days

The first day of tech will be the slowest one: the second and every day following will not have the same tentative feeling, so you and your designers can begin working with a bit more confidence. You are building a shared language as a group as well as a cohesive visual language onstage. The designers are watching and learning from what they are seeing and from each other, you are learning to communicate more effectively, a natural rhythm to the work is forming, the actors are becoming more comfortable onstage, and you can see glimpses of harmony. Slowly, the piece should begin to come together, a little more quickly and easily every day.

As you get further into the play, your designers will use the discoveries of the first few days to inform present choices. This means the second half of your rough draft may be in better shape than the first. It is very common for those sections of the play that were teched on a second, third, and fourth day to be far stronger and clearer than everything that was built on the first. Your impulse may be to go back and fix or change the first day's work, but that is not time well spent. Continue pressing on to the stumble with the understanding that the beginning will just have to be particularly messy while later sections may feel more refined. The stumble will teach you how to work backwards: to apply to the beginning of the play what you learned from working on the end.

Rough Draft/Stumble-Through

You will be ready to stumble through the rough draft as soon as every moment from beginning to end has a cue, all of the blocking has been recreated onstage and adjusted as necessary, all of the quick changes rehearsed, and all of the transitions staged. The hope for this stumble-through is to give everyone a sense of overall shape, so the goal should be to continue without stopping. If anything feels unsafe, you must, but if there are mistakes or if some transition or stage business is taking longer than expected, the stage manager should pause, let the actors and crew sort out the obstacle, and then continue. Even the messiest stumble-through will provide you and your team with clarity about what sections and elements need immediate attention. As was true in rehearsal, this stumble-through is an opportunity to experience the piece just as it is, and to build your next worklist based on what you observe.

The stumble-through is a teaching moment for everyone, not only the creative team. The crew needs to understand transitions, prop and scenery tracking, costume changes, backstage movement, and the general shape of the production. How much time they have between tasks, how difficult setting up a transition will be, how quickly they can reset for the top of the play: these pieces of information are necessary for the crew as they prepare to run the show at full speed later. The stage manager also needs this stumble-through to practice "calling" the show, meaning giving light, sound, and other cues. Think of this stumble as three simultaneous rehearsals: the cast onstage, the crew backstage, and the stage manager in the booth. Each group needs practice, even at this early stage.

This stumble-through can be, and usually us, humbling. Some actors will play each scene fully while others will mark it, some will be preoccupied with props, costumes, or the space itself. Transitions will take far longer than you want them to, and crew may forget their tracks or what they are expected to do. In short, what you will see is a jumble of elements colliding.

Your job is to locate the signal within the noise. To identify what ideas have potential even if they are far from their performance-level form. You are not looking for what works, but what *could* work, and what you suspect *will* work. As you have many times before, clear away any distractions, and note only those moments you want to discuss and consider with the group later. Do not concern yourself with acting notes: they cannot be addressed until you have recaptured the rhythm of the play. Challenge yourself to see the stumble-through as it is. This can be particularly difficult because of the amount of stimuli: concentrate on being present, on noticing, and on being aware of your reactions. Huge sections will not work, and that is to be expected. What you must do is be aware of your experience so that you can identify *why* the section was unsuccessful. To get mired in notes is to focus on the problem without any insights about solutions. Sit back and watch: what have you made? How does it feel to watch it again with all of these new elements? What feels the same? What feels new? In what ways do the design elements elevate the story? In what ways do they obfuscate it?

Post-Stumble-Through Meetings

After the stumble-through, make a list of reactions, feelings, thoughts, and notes. This will become your worklist. Divide your observations into three categories: what may work, what does not work, and what remains unclear. Remember that many problems will resolve themselves with practice. A brutally long transition may not need restaging, it may just need to be run a few times. Do not judge everything too quickly: those items on your "does not work" list should focus only on moments that need to be completely rethought. Everything else can be considered a work in progress.

Meet with the cast to tell them what you saw, and to ask them how it felt. Actors are usually exhausted and stressed at this point in the process. They are very aware that an audience will be there soon and that the production has taken a step back. Even if intellectually they understand that this part of the process is necessary, they may still be frustrated. Remind them that the work ahead will focus on tightening and returning the music of the text to the performance. The stumble-through marked the moment in which all the elements finally came together: now the work is about pace, timing, refinement, and specificity.

Convene a meeting with your designers and ask them to talk about what they saw and how they reacted. Ask what is working for them, what they think has potential, and what was a failed experiment that needs a new direction. Cross-reference their observations with your worklist: there should hopefully be a considerable amount of overlap, which is always a good sign that you are in creative alignment. Under your guidance, each designer should be encouraged to talk about the piece as a whole, not only their specific contribution. Now that you have had the shared experience of watching the entire piece, it is not possible—nor should it be—to return to siloed work.

Post-Stumble Rehearsals

Begin work from the top of the show, focusing your attention on the most significant changes you and your designers have decided to make. If there is not enough time to work through the entire play again from the beginning, make a worklist of ten things, then another, then another until you run out of time. Like the rehearsal process, implementing changes after the stumble-through should happen faster. Everyone is able to work in more detail and with greater confidence, everyone understands each choice in context, and everyone has a clearer grasp of what the other artists are doing. The work onstage should be technical: design changes, transition rehearsals, and tightening the pace of both performance and cues. No matter how slow or disorganized the stumble-through was, everyone on and off-stage now knows the play can be done, that it has made the journey from the rehearsal room to the stage intact, and knowing that can buoy spirits and add a positive urgency to your work.

As you create each day's worklist, discuss it with your stage manager as they will have a better understanding of how much time each item will take. Everything you want to look at onstage will require some amount of set-up and strike. If your stage manager tells you that working on a transition toward the end of the play will take twenty minutes to prepare, do you feel that is time well spent? If you wanted to run through the show again, how long would it take to set up for the top? Collaborate with stage management to maximize your time: it is possible you can work on one section while another is being prepared, but that takes planning and coordination. Lean on your stage manager to help you create the most efficient schedule possible. You are working toward a run-through, or if time will not allow it, preparing for the dress rehearsal.

Sunk Cost Fallacy

In the business world, "sunk cost fallacy" describes the scenario in which someone has invested a significant amount of money and time into a failing project, and yet they continue to pour resources into it. The "fallacy" is believing that because they have already devoted so much time and money, it would be wasteful for them simply to give up. The correct next step would be to cut one's losses: to stop putting more time, energy, or money into the project. The sunk cost fallacy is human nature: we do not want to give up on something we have spent so much time cultivating, even well after it has proven to be a failure. Sometimes we cling to unsuccessful things out of pride, spite, fear, or devotion. This is true in business, in relationships, and in art.

Luckily, theater is a relatively easy environment to make a change for the better. Some call this process "killing your darlings," but parting ways with elements that no longer serve your production is not about destruction, it is about finally seeing with clear eyes, about being honest with yourself, about admitting what is and is not effective, and about having the bravery to let go of that which is no longer useful. If you continue to struggle to make some element of the production work without any progress, you are being offered a lesson. If the same item appears on your worklist day after day and you cannot seem to make it work, you must stop asking yourself why it is unsuccessful and start asking why you continue to try. Only you can answer that question truthfully, but frustrating yourself and your collaborators, losing time and/or money trying to force something into existence is a sign that the idea must be parted with.

These items are often brilliant ideas that existed long before tech began. A coup d'theatre at the end of the play, a big visual gesture, a special effect, a shocking reveal. Maybe the idea was expensive to realize, took a significant amount of time to build, or required the hiring of a specialized artist to create. Maybe your determination to keep it relates to how hard you fought to get it, or how much money you spent to make it possible. How can you cut something that was supposed to be the centerpiece of the design? Your directorial signature? The big moment that would make the production a success?

Think of these ideas as creative scaffolding. They were constructed first and offered stability to the rest of the project as it was being realized. They were great ideas, and probably still are: the problem is that they no longer fit. They are not integral to the whole, and need to be taken away. This can be difficult because of your emotional attachment. The release of an unsuccessful idea will improve everything around it, but that doesn't make parting with a cherished idea any easier.

The Design That Ate the New Play

I have heard writers say, after watching a run during tech, that they can no longer see their play. The amount of visual and sonic stimuli is so overwhelming that the play itself—the language and performance of it—has disappeared behind the design. While a writer will naturally be protective of their words and sensitive to any additions they feel compromise them, they often make a salient point. Your subsequent passes through the play during tech may reveal that you and your designers have done too much.

Everyone arrived to tech with an abundance of ideas, and all of them were promising and worth exploring. You and the designers have been imagining how the play could be realized for months, and only have a few days together in the space to experiment. You owe it to yourself to try as much as you can, to include as many ideas as possible, to fill the production with months' worth of experiments. There will come a time, though, when you must ask which design elements best serve the story, and scale back on those that might be fun, beautiful, or interesting, but that are not supportive of or relevant to the play.

This is particularly necessary with a new play. A big gesture in an established work will highlight the director and designers' cleverness and singular point of view: how you realize Hamlet's ghost, how you stage the final exit in A Doll's House, etc. With a new play, the audience is listening closely, absorbing the text for the first time. That requires an enormous amount of concentration, and you must highlight the language or an audience may not follow. Too many design flourishes will pull an audience's focus or telegraph the play's meaning in a way that either distracts or does the audience's work for them. If the production is overwhelming, the play will become difficult to hear: an audience will begin to ask the wrong kind of questions, or will stop asking them altogether. Even the most beautiful design, if it's not in service of the text, can be an obstacle to the audience's experience. It can answer the "good" questions before an audience has the opportunity to ask, it does the work for them, and encourages them to be passive.

As you create your second and third drafts in tech, consider what elements need to be scaled back. Be the audience and notice what holds your attention: is it the actors and the text? Music? Bits of stage business? Are the costumes so elaborate you spend more time looking at them than the actors inside them? Is the lighting so dark you cannot see the actors' faces? You've created so many wonderful images with your design team: now differentiate between those choices that elevate the production and those that may obfuscate the text.

Actor Care

The physical toll of tech on actors should not be overlooked. The cast is coming into tech after weeks of rehearsal, so it's likely they will arrive exhausted. The long hours, the emotional strain, and the nervous energy of tech can have a negative effect on enthusiasm and morale.

The worst way to begin a preview process is with an overworked company, which is often how actors feel at the end of tech. A director should be mindful of when a company needs rest. Exhaustion is a safety issue. If you are working your actors too hard, they will get fatigued, and if you continue to push, you risk illness or injury. Do not wait until that moment arrives to take action. If they need more breaks, offer them. A pleasure of tech is that there is always something else to work on, to fix, to change without the full company. Even if exhaustion were not a safety issue, a cast will turn on you if they feel their time and energy are not being respected. Prioritize the cast's health and well-being: it is the generous, ethical, and professional thing to do.

Leading by Example

Tech rehearsals can often become fraught, tense, or stressful. The ways in which a tech rehearsal can fall apart are infinite, but the reason is usually unexpected, which can lead to confusion, frustration, and panic. In those moments of heightened emotions, a director's primary responsibility is to set the tone for the room through example.

When you are on a turbulent flight, you naturally look to the flight attendants to see how they are responding. If they appear calm, they are teaching you something through their behavior. We are naturally soothed by their reaction, or lack thereof, and we worry less. A relaxed flight attendant is an emotional guide, showing us what an appropriate and reasonable response looks like, and helping us understand that, while the turbulence we are all feeling may be dramatic, it is not cause for alarm.

Sometimes, the most significant contribution a director can make to a process is to project a sense of calm and composure. A director cannot fix a piece of broken scenery, and a director cannot heal a crew person who called out sick at the last minute. What a director can do is understand that everyone is nervous, and everyone is looking to the leader to understand what is an appropriate reaction. A director does not need to pretend that everything is fine when it is not, but they can teach a group that everything will be fine, that it will work out, and that this moment, like turbulence, will pass. There will be moments of crisis when a serious, but not panicked, response will help the group understand how to respond. Sometimes that is all a director can do, and it is often enough.

Ending Tech

Your worklist will always require more time than your tech schedule can provide. Decide what you feel must be changed or fixed before the dress rehearsal, and what you feel can wait until after previews begin. You want to avoid time running out because of poor management. Aim to end tech deliberately, on your terms, so that you can proceed to the dress rehearsal with clarity: you have separated the urgent items on your worklist from those that can be rehearsed after performances begin.

Ask yourself what must be changed or fixed before you put the production in front of an audience. Begin with moments that are potentially unsafe: they are your priority. Moving scenery, stage violence, or complicated transitions must be addressed first. Then identify the moments that could stop the show if they are not executed properly. Finally, ask yourself which moments would you like to improve before an audience arrives. Performance notes, design, or technical changes, even, possibly, rewrites.

It is a natural impulse to try to cram everything you want to work on into the last day of tech. A moment looks so sloppy to you, for example, that you cannot stand the idea of an audience seeing it. Rushing is a mistake. Changes implemented during panicked moments always appear underdeveloped, and hurried changes during tech can be potentially dangerous. Having to watch a moment you know doesn't work one more time is far better than rushing a change into the play that actors and crew are not ready to execute confidently. A careless change is never a significant improvement over the current version no matter how much you may hate it. Make an achievable top ten list and complete it. Your goal for the end of tech is a performable version of the play that you can learn from by sharing it with an audience. The dress rehearsal can feel like the end of rehearsal: that everything must be "perfect" or "complete," as if there could even be such a thing. If you have a draft that is safe and reliable, you and the company are ready for the next step.

22
DRESS REHEARSAL

A dress rehearsal is a complete, uninterrupted performance of the production. It is an opportunity for the crew to set for the top of the show, the cast to begin building their preparation and warm-up rituals, and stage management to get accustomed to making their show calls and announcements, all as they will for actual performances. A dress is also the last time your production will be performed without a paying audience.

Preparation

A director cannot go backstage after the stage manager has called half hour (thirty minutes to places). No notes, no conversations, no hanging around dressing or green rooms. You must respect the actor's space and empower them to prepare on their own. Even an actor who has a question or wants to discuss a note must wait: breaking the half-hour rule will cheat the cast out of their first opportunity to practice what their backstage pre-show process will be like throughout the run.

This distance is also necessary for your stage manager. The clearest and strongest way for you to show your trust in the stage manager is, ironically, through your absence. If anyone in the company has a question or concern, they must get accustomed to going to stage management. Once the show opens, you will be around rarely if at all, so helping everyone in the company understand that stage management is now the leader of the production is how you can best support them in this moment of transition.

This can feel counter-intuitive, especially after so many weeks of working closely with the company. How can it be that a director's absence is useful? What a cast needs most from a director during the dress rehearsal is trust and empowerment. What you are doing by giving them space is handing the play over to them. It is now their story to deliver to the audience each night. Your giving the company space is your telling them they are ready for the task and the responsibility.

Invited vs. Closed

Some producers have preferences about whether or not to invite an audience to the dress rehearsal, but when the decision is yours to make, you must consider the circumstances of your production. The virtue of an invited audience is that you can experience the play in front of a crowd before the first preview. If you have had a smooth tech process and the cast is so ready they cannot stand the idea of doing the play again to an empty house, invite an audience. One potential drawback is that the invitees are customarily friends of the company, so the response you will get is not authentic. Is it useful for the cast to experience a reaction they may not get in front of a public audience? The value of keeping the dress closed is that you are giving yourself and your designers one final chance to watch the play without any outside input. If tech has been rocky and the cast is feeling vulnerable, keep the dress rehearsal closed. The theater will be full soon enough, and you and the cast will receive a massive amount of new information then. Would it be best to have one last clean performance of the most recent version before that moment?

The circumstances of every production are different, and every process will arrive at the dress rehearsal in its own psychic and emotional state. Ask yourself exactly what you hope to learn, and what effect an open or closed dress may have on the company.

Photos

Often, a theater will bring one or more photographers to the dress rehearsal. This is because they need production photos as soon as possible for press and publicity purposes. This can be distracting, but it is necessary. Make certain you know in advance if and when they are coming, and make sure stage management alerts the cast. Actors' union rules dictate that there must be a notice posted on the callboard backstage, but you should not assume everyone will pay attention. Ask stage management to give everyone a verbal reminder so there are no surprises.

Before the dress begins, introduce yourself to the photographers, and let them know if there are any moments in the play that should not be photographed. Nudity, moments of intimacy, or anything that would spoil the plot. Do not be too precious about keeping visual elements secret (a big reveal, a special effect, a scenic transformation): a director may want to maintain the element of surprise, then regret it later when the production photos are not as exciting as they could have been. A reliable choice is to restrict only those moments that protect the actors and the plot. Visual spoilers may seem like a problem, but they are always worth sharing as a marketing tool.

Watching the Dress

This is the first moment in the entire process in which you are simply an observer of the proceedings. You will sit in the audience (empty or not) and the performance will begin when the stage manager calls it, not when you let them know you are ready. You cannot yet "hold" or "stop," as only the stage manager has the ability to pause the performance. The tech tables, where the designers and production staff sat during tech, will be put away, revealing the house as it will look for an audience. The dress can be a surreal experience for a director after having poured over every detail for so long, but this moment is a gift: you are being given the opportunity to step all the way back from the canvas and see what you've made in its entirety. All you have to do, all you *can* do, is watch and listen.

It is very easy in this moment to let anxiety take over. To notice only those moments that still need work, to flag the notes the actors did not take, or the detailed work from the rehearsal room that has been lost during tech. The loss of control during a dress can lead a director to focus on what is wrong, what isn't playing how it was rehearsed, what doesn't look at all like it did during tech. That way of thinking is a lost opportunity to watch the piece one last time before you begin integrating everything you will learn from the audience. This is a time to savor your accomplishments before your next step.

If you choose to take notes during the dress, keep them simple. There will be very little rehearsal time, if any, between the dress and the first performance, and building up the morale and confidence of the company should be a higher priority than any change you may want to insert before the first audience. You are about to receive a massive new set of information after watching the play among an audience, so any notes you take now will be all but irrelevant the next day. Burying your head in a notepad or whispering to an assistant will rob you of the wonderful opportunity to reconnect with months' worth of thoughts, notes, and ideas. Encourage the writer to do the same: this is the end of the process as a private collaboration. Tomorrow the play enters into a dialogue with the public.

Post-Dress

A cast may be nervous, they may despair, or they may feel confident and eager for an audience after the dress. Keep your notes simple and brief: focus on encouragement and on helpful reminders, avoid any drastic new thoughts or ideas. Your primary task when meeting with the actors is to assure them that they are ready for an audience. This readiness has nothing to do with the quality of the dress itself but because you have all learned as much as you can without input from an audience. Only new perspectives will teach the group what needs attention and consideration. Remind them that the arrival of the audience is not the end of rehearsal, only a new phase of your work. Your most influential and consequential collaborator arrives tomorrow. Reiterate your trust and faith in the company: it is time for the actors to claim ownership of the production, as they are ready to deliver the story to an audience.

PART SIX
THE AUDIENCE

In this section, we will discuss previews: what they are, how a director learns from them, and how to transform observations into a rehearsal worklist. We will also look at how to insert rewrites, make changes, and give actors notes once performances begin. Finally, we will step through opening night, the process of maintaining a show during the run, and closing.

It has been said that a work of art is only half finished until a viewer sees it. The audience's experience completes the work. Everything you and your collaborators have created will get you to the halfway point: when an audience sees the work, your partner has arrived. The story unfolds for the viewer, and the endeavor is complete.

Inviting an audience in to see your work can be euphoric, terrifying, frustrating, humbling, and affirming. Until now, your process has been private. Now a dialogue between performer and audience will begin, and you will learn so much about what you've made from that interaction. A director in previews is an observer and student: watching the play and gathering information from the experience and reactions of the audience.

During preview performances, the audience will be your teacher. They will not lie because they do not know how they are "supposed" to behave or react. They will not laugh at something that isn't funny (even an audience of enthusiastic friends will eventually fall silent if the jokes aren't landing), they will not pay attention to something that doesn't naturally hold it. They will tell you what does and doesn't make sense, and what is and isn't clear. You cannot force an audience to respond a certain way, and you cannot push them to experience something they are not. The audience is the perfect teacher because they are always honest—sometimes brutally—and while you may disagree with them, they are never inherently wrong. Audiences reveal moments you had forgotten about or never noticed, they will hear jokes you didn't know were there, react to profundities you missed, and delight in moments that had frustrated you for weeks. An audience will reintroduce you to your own work, and they will teach you more about what you've made than you could ever hope to discover alone. While you can never expect unanimity, if you can stay present and pay attention, an audience will share with you a consensus. You can get upset or deny them, but they are only telling you the truth. All you can do is listen, learn, and choose whether or not to make an adjustment.

Imagine choreographing a duet. Your goal is to guide the dancers into such effortless synchronicity that you cannot tell who is leading and who is following. There is no separation between the two: they move in unison, both feeding off the cues and energy of the other. It is a generous, playful communion of two parties. This is your task during previews: to coax the production out over the edge of the stage and into the audience, and to draw the viewer in so close that there is no gap between them. The audience is neither left behind nor too far ahead, they are never pushed or pulled: they are guided by the director through the experience of the play.

23
PREVIEWS

The preview process is a series of public performances that take place while rehearsals continue in the afternoons. You and the creative team are still working on, and making changes to, the production throughout. A director will watch a preview and, based on what they see, will create a rehearsal worklist. They will implement those notes, rewrites, and changes the next day, which will then go into the performance that night. This process will repeat itself until preview rehearsals end and the production opens.

A producing organization advocates for previews because they can begin to generate income from ticket sales before the rehearsal process officially ends. Previews are an asset to a creative team because they provide an unparalleled opportunity to learn from an audience in real time. No waiting, no hypothesizing: you make a choice in the afternoon, receive feedback from the audience that night, and continue your work tomorrow.

The Third Time a Play Falls Apart

A tightly rehearsed play is a well-oiled machine, flowing briskly from moment to moment. What it does not yet account for is the experience of someone who has never seen it before. An audience needs to be welcomed in, to be taught the rules of the world, to be told the story in a clear way, and to be guided toward the most intriguing and engaging questions. The actors must open their performances up once again to make room for this last group of collaborators. This means disrupting the flow of what you've built one final time.

It will be thrilling for your cast to perform for an audience. The excitement of feeling their responses, of finding new moments to explore, of learning to play off their energy: the company will finally experience what they have been imagining for so long. It can be a challenge, however, for them to know how to pace their performances: that will take practice. You cannot force an audience to understand a story that moves too fast, and you cannot ask them to remain engaged if it takes too long to get where it needs to go. A director's job is to help the cast find a rhythm that honors both the music of the text and the ideal momentum for an audience experiencing the story for the first time.

That a cast must relearn the rhythm for a third time can be jarring, in no small part because it must happen in public. Lines that were spoken in the same way for weeks can suddenly feel wrong in front of an audience. Moments that were consistently funny in the rehearsal room can be met with silence in performance. Dramatic pauses that seemed powerful during tech can be filled with the sounds of rustling programs. Conversely, a line no one thought was funny can elicit such a loud reaction that the audience doesn't hear the next three lines because they were laughing so hard, or a powerful moment is rushed through because the company did not realize what a profound impact it would have.

The music of the play, which you found around the table, at the end of rehearsal, and at the dress, must be recaptured with the addition of the audience's participation. The only way to achieve this balance is by listening to their reactions, understanding when they are and are not engaged, and then assessing why. The cast will naturally begin to feel when laughs will come, when silence is helpful, when critical information is being received, and when picking up the pace is a virtue. Because audience responses will vary, especially during the earliest previews, you must be patient and listen for patterns in their reactions: an audience will tell you what they want and need, and you must take that information into account to find the ideal rhythm one more time.

Watching a Preview

Previews require a director to observe three things at once: the performance, the audience, and the interaction between the two. They must be honest with themselves about what they notice. It can be easy, when watching an audience fall silent during a comedy, to hope for a more enthusiastic crowd the following night. But because audiences do not lie, a director must respect the information they are being given. A quiet audience does not mean everything should change, but hoping audiences will suddenly get "better," or blaming them for not responding the way you would like, is to ignore the lesson. When an audience tells you something, believe them. If you listen and trust them, they can not only be your teacher but also your strongest creative ally.

The preview process can feel particularly hectic. It can feel as though everything must happen all at once, with the added stress of having an audience watch your work at the end of every rehearsal. To understand what a director must do during a preview, we must break down the basic tasks into four steps:

Step One: Listen to the Audience

A director's observations will center on the gap between the response you expect and the one you get. You must pay attention to clues that the audience is engaged, as well as when they seem lost, confused, or bored. Some basic prompts to ask yourself are:

- Is the audience following the story?
- Are they attentive?
- Are they emotionally engaged?
- Are they particularly invested in some characters over others?
- When are the exact moments they become passive or disinterested?
- When do they seem confused?
- When do they seem ahead of the story?

In general, when an audience does not respond to a moment as you had hoped, there are two basic causes: they either didn't understand it or they *did* understand but didn't like it. The former is confusion, the latter is a conflict of taste. Your task is to identify the difference: if the audience is confused, there is a flaw in the delivery of the given circumstances (who, what, where). Consider the ways in which you can clarify what is happening onstage. If the audience doesn't like it, you must ask yourself if you are open to changing your choice to suit their taste.

Remember that your production is site specific. Choices that you may not have even considered before will become suddenly relevant when an audience arrives:

- How long is the space open before the performance begins?
- What is the audience's experience during that time?
- Is there pre-show music?
- Does it set an appropriate tone for the play?
- Who chose it?
- Is there a pre-show announcement?
- Who wrote it, and what tone does it set?
- How quickly do the house lights go out?
- How soon after does the performance start?

These gestures may seem small, but they will have a profound impact on the audience's experience. They must be considered as thoughtfully and intentionally as anything that happens over the course of the performance itself.

Notice how the audience responds to the first moments of the show. This is their introduction to the world: how are they being invited in? What have you chosen as the first impression of the world of this play? This moment is a welcoming: it can be a joke, a quiet moment on an empty stage, an explosion, anything you can imagine. You are making a statement about everything that will come after: what would you like an audience experience first? Pay attention to how they take in the first few moments: if an audience is immediately confused, if they are working too hard to understand where they are, you are putting them at a disadvantage.

- How is each character introduced to the audience?
- What are the first pieces of important information?
- Do you sense the audience hears it?

Listen for pacing. A cast will customarily begin previews by speaking too quickly for the audience. They are moving at the pace of the rehearsal room, which an audience cannot follow. The phrase "keeping pace" means "to make progress at the same speed": the cast must keep pace with both the natural rhythm of the text and with the audience's ability to keep up. Too slow, and the company is not honoring the momentum. Too fast, and the company is leaving the audience behind. Pace is not about going as quickly as possible, it is about traveling at the optimal speed for both the play and for the audience. The correct pace will take time and practice to discover.

Listen to the moments in which important information is shared throughout the play—plot points, reveals of character, irrevocable change, foreshadowing. Every scene will have an event: is each of them clear? There is no need to overemphasize any of these moments (do not do the audience's work for them), but strive always for clarity: you can always identify a confused audience by their lack of engagement.

Often, you cannot tell if an audience has understood a moment until much later in the play. Many writers introduce plot points early that pay off later: if a moment doesn't seem to land, be aware that the moment itself might work well: the confusion may be caused by something the audience missed much earlier in the play. Any time a moment does not seem to work, consider that the cause may be far from the moment itself.

Listen for laughter. You and the cast have assumed where moments of humor may be, but the audience has the final say. Previews are when the cast will learn to ride the waves of audience responses (not only laughter). Allow the audience to offer input and suggestions, but do not let them overtake and reshape the rhythm.

Rarely watch from the same seats. You need different perspectives, both for sightlines and to understand how the experience of the play changes depending on your seat.

- What is the emotional experience of the play in the front row?
- Is it the same as from the back rows or from a balcony?

- How is it different?
- Where would you like the critics to sit?
- Have you watched a performance from those seats?
- What makes them especially good?

When you sit in the seats that are held for you and the designers ("production seats"), you are surrounded by people who already know the show. They may laugh at familiar moments, but is anyone else?

Some actors naturally understand the dimensions of a theater and scale the size of their performance to fit. Others need guidance, and in order to help them, you must be able to speak from experience: what did an actor's performance feel like from the last row, or the balcony, or from the farthest house left or right seat?

Different perspectives can influence your thoughts on potential changes. A moment may not make sense from one part of the house but is very clear from another. Had you not watched from multiple locations, you may have advocated for a rewrite or given an acting note when a staging change was the solution.

Learning from an audience is not the same as surrendering your creative agency to them. A director maintains their taste and vision by knowing when to stand firm for a choice they believe in. Audience responses will provide a wealth of useful information, but a director must not let the audience control their work. Choices you stand behind are how you display your taste, your perspective: it is where you exist in the production. Make sure that in your effort to clarify and dispel any confusion, you do not compromise your vision in the process.

Step Two: Identify Patterns

Unexpected or undesirable reactions can be the best teachers of all, but only if they are given the time to be understood properly.

I once directed a very dark drama about a murder. In the rehearsal room, we were all very serious, fully ensconced in the tone of the play, but during a climactic moment at the first preview, the audience burst out laughing. I was horrified and confused. How could they make light of such an intense moment?

That moment of laughter triggered a series of events that temporarily caused more problems than they solved. In my shock at the audience's response, I demanded the actor to cut the unintentional "laugh line" (with the writer's permission). The actor was confused, then offended: he thought I was blaming him for the audience's reaction. The truth was that I made an impulsive decision because I could not stand to hear that laughter again. It was a purely emotional response: there was no artistic reason for the change. The next performance they played the scene without the line, and the audience laughed on the following one. It was then I began to realize the problem was more significant.

We eventually learned, after a few previews, that we had made our production so relentlessly dark that the audience was desperate for relief and found it where they could. The problem was the tone, not the text. As painful as it felt at the time, their reaction helped us identify our mistake.

In rehearsal, you could let a moment not "work" so you can see it over and over until a solution revealed itself. This tactic remains the same during the preview process. Impulsive decisions based on audience's reaction will leave you with unconsidered choices that are rarely successful and sometimes difficult to reverse. You must wait until you can identify a *pattern* of audience behavior, then strive to understand why it exists. Making changes quickly and frequently will frustrate and confuse a cast and will make it more difficult for you to identify exactly what is not working. Constant changes will lead you away from the root problem and will take up a huge amount of rehearsal time: the same moment should not appear on your worklist every day. You may have enough previews to identify a pattern, but no director has enough time to untangle the damage caused by inserting a new and unconsidered version of a scene every day. A preview process will be positive and productive if changes and rewrites come from observations over time and not from reactionary responses based on single performances.

There's an old story about a comedy writer who would bring in new jokes for every preview. Any line that didn't get a laugh was immediately cut and replaced the next day. If an audience member coughed on the line, it was cut. If someone rustled their program: cut. This is a questionable approach for two reasons. First, it can destroy an actor's confidence. The writer is teaching the company they are not trusted to deliver the line effectively. The second is that you cannot reliably evaluate text that changes every day. You will not be able to tell if the new line was unsuccessful because of the delivery, because it was an under-rehearsed moment, because it was new to your ears, or because it just wasn't a great line. A director cannot know if new text works unless it is given time to settle in and for the actors to get comfortable playing it. Seeking success by rewriting the same moment every day is to rely on luck over wisdom.

A writer I once worked with chose a different approach. Any time she wanted to implement a change, she wrote it down but gave herself twenty-four hours to consider it. That way, she could hear the old text one more time in performance, and if she still wanted to make the change, it would be rehearsed the next day for the following preview. Working this way provided her with a sense of confidence: she felt certain the new text was an improvement. Asking the writer to wait, to resist impulsive choices, to see the moment again in front of an audience, and only then to proceed with the new pages will provide the cast with rewrites that are thoughtful and thorough. This way of working may feel like it takes a lot of time, but it is much faster to make one change with assuredness than many reactionary changes with no end in sight.

Step Three: Disassemble the Audience's Reactions

In the rehearsal room, you conducted experiments to see how a single choice would affect the entire piece. In previews, that process happens in reverse: the audience will offer a response to the whole, and you must figure out how each choice contributed to it. An audience cannot grasp each choice individually or understand how every part affects their experience: they are simply listening and reacting. It is the director's responsibility to find out why. You must disassemble a moment like a mechanic would take apart an engine: do all the pieces seem to work separately? Is there a problem with how they are assembled that is leading to an undesirable result? Only through deconstructing a moment, separating it back down to its individual elements—text, performance, design, staging, timing, delivery, clarity, pace, etc.—can you transform an audience's reaction into a workable note for rehearsal.

Begin with a moment that continues to elude your desired response. Identify the problem: let's say the audience seemed disengaged during a dramatic scene. Consider all individual components that could have influenced the audience's experience:

- Are there gaps in narrative logic?
- Is the pace too fast or too slow?
- Does the audience have all the information they need?
- Has the audience seemed to follow the story until now? Can you pinpoint the moment their attention wanes?
- What events led up to the scene? Plot, character development, dramatic tension, momentum: are they contributing as you need them to?
- What acting decisions were made in rehearsal about the playing of the scene?
- Is the actors' behavior in alignment with the action, and is that action supported by the text?
- What are the design elements in this scene: how do they impact the dramatic tension?
- How is the scene organized spatially? Would a change to the staging tell a different story?

By asking these questions, you are dismantling the moment to see what could be causing confusion. Once you have an idea of what the problem could be, put it on your rehearsal worklist.

Step Four: Create a Top Ten Worklist

Your list should be a mix of both complex and simple changes. Remember that you will have time to address most of your changes and ideas, just not all at once. Divide your notes into two groups: items you need to work onstage and verbal notes you can share with the cast and designers in conversation. Only those items you need to see onstage will go onto your list of ten: verbal notes will be given whenever you can find the time. Identify one or two sizable design notes, one or two significant acting notes, one or two rewrites, and then four or five smaller adjustments that need to be worked onstage. A varied worklist will allow everyone to maximize their productivity. A well run preview rehearsal is one in which many different things are happening at once: some actors should be reviewing new lines offstage while others are onstage working on acting notes. The backstage crew is setting up for the next item on the worklist while the lighting and sound designers are rewriting cues to be seen and heard later that afternoon. If only one group is working at a time, you should reexamine how you are building your list.

Meeting with the Cast Post-Preview

Your interactions with a cast during previews require optimism and total honesty. Actors always know if an audience is engaged: if you go backstage and tell the cast they loved it when they did not, you are breaking the pact. You can be encouraging, you can explain what you loved about the performance and why, but you cannot pretend a disengaged, quiet, or distracted audience wasn't any of those things. If you betray an actor's trust during previews, they will immediately stop listening to you. You must find a way to be supportive that is also completely honest.

Any notes you give immediately after a preview should be simple observations: what you saw, what you noticed, what you experienced. Your thoughts may not yet be fully developed, particularly when it comes to identifying solutions to problems, so do not share impressions you don't yet understand: the wrong note has the potential to reverberate for days. Offer your perspective, make yourself available for questions, and preach patience, especially if the performance did not go well: letting something be wrong can be difficult for a director, but it can be brutal for the actors tasked with doing it. Have compassion for their struggle and remind them that solutions will come.

Post-Preview Production Meeting

The designers, stage management, and department heads will convene after preview performances for a production meeting. All the work that will happen before your afternoon rehearsal will be scheduled now, so make clear any changes or adjustments to the design that need to happen before the actors are back onstage. Do not assume your priorities are shared: even if there is a technical disaster during a performance, you should not presume it will be addressed by the next day. Make clear to the group if you want to see the cast in costume, if you need to use props, if anything on your worklist will require full lights and sound. If you anticipate rewrites (even if you don't know yet what they are), prepare the group for that possibility.

Reconfirm what time the actors are called, what time you can begin work onstage, and when you have to finish. Crew calls can change for many reasons, which can affect what you can do and when. If your time onstage will be shortened because of a work call, for example, or a piece of scenery will not be available to you, you need to know that ahead of time to plan accordingly.

After the meeting, share your potential worklist with stage management. It should be arranged roughly by priority. Stage management will want to stagger actor calls, and they will want to strategize the order of work so you don't lose time by asking the crew to jump from scene to scene. Share how much time you anticipate needing for each item on your list. If not everything on your list will fit in your allotted rehearsal hours, swap out a complicated item for something easier and move the complicated one to the top of the list for the following day. If you plan to work on an emotionally delicate scene, or anticipate a rewrite that may involve a lot of discussion, give yourself ample time so you are not rushed. In spite of how quickly you must work, your task is to end each rehearsal with a cast that is prepared to perform for an audience: everything must be clear and finished for the day so they can perform safely and with confidence that night.

Meeting with the Writer

End your post-preview meetings with the writer. This conversation should take as long as necessary to find common ground on what you both felt worked, what needs changing, and which of those changes should involve rewrites. Of all the adjustments you can make during preview rehearsals, new pages are the most time consuming, complex, and difficult to implement: you and the writer must be in alignment about what to change, why it must, and how to do it.

First preview can be an emotionally complex and unpredictable experience for a writer. They have imagined this moment — seeing their play in front of an audience — for months or years, and the event can be euphoric, confusing, or galvanizing. Begin your meeting simply: ask them how they felt it went. Encourage them to describe their feelings, there may be many and some could be contradictory. It may take time to guide this conversation toward the creation of a worklist: that is normal, and everything they are willing to share is useful information.

Once they have described their experience, begin to ask them about specifics:

- What did they feel was successful?
- What did they feel was unsuccessful?
- What would they like to change?
- What do they imagine are the solutions? Modifications to performance, design, staging, or text?

Encourage the writer to offer you some notes, including and especially ones that do not pertain to the text. Ask them to articulate their thoughts about performance, design, staging, tone, and pace. You must understand their holistic view of the production so you can evaluate any rewrites through their point of view. A writer in previews may try to "fix" problems through revisions, including those you feel should be addressed a different way. The better you understand their perspective about what works and what doesn't, the more successful you will be at guiding them toward helpful or necessary rewrites and away from those that you suspect will not remedy the problem.

Share your observation about the preview and then debate the differences. Conflicting perspectives will help sharpen your point of view and will push you to solidify your arguments about what should change and what should not. If you cannot come to an agreement, let the issue under discussion remain untouched in rehearsal so you can watch it again in performance with each other's perspective in mind.

Discuss rewrites. A writer needs the freedom to experiment, but you need clarity about what new pages to expect and when to expect them. Ask the writer for any details they can provide: what scenes they expect to change, what those changes could be and how extensive, and when you can anticipate seeing them. A writer may change their mind, hit a dead end, or get a new idea that takes them in another direction: do not schedule rehearsal time for rewrites unless you are certain they are ready. Only after you have seen the pages should they go onto a schedule.

Performance Reports

Once previews begin, stage management will pivot from distributing rehearsal to performance reports: similar documents with a few significant differences. They will include a brief synopsis of the performance, and some stage managers will comment on the audience's reaction. They will also describe the quality of the performance (high or low energy, for example). Compare your experience of watching the play with how stage management describes it in the report. If you do not agree with their assessment, ask them to elaborate on what they wrote and offer suggestions about how they might also see the performance from your point of view. Once the show opens and you are no longer watching the show regularly, this report is your only window into the quality of the performance: you should encourage stage management to be mindful of those aspects of the production you feel are important. Previews are an opportunity for you and stage management to get into alignment about what you are seeing so you can leave the production with confidence that the reports are accurate and reliable snapshots of each show.

The key information in a performance report is the running time. Over the course of a run, a play may slow down (rarely does it speed up). Actors hold for laughs or for dramatic effect, natural pauses become elongated, and cues are not picked up at the same rate. This is natural, and you will know when it is happening by changes to the running time. During previews, notice the running times of those performances you think are particularly well-paced: that should be the rough number the cast should aim to maintain. A few minutes faster or slower is normal, but when the number begins to increase regularly, ask stage management to note where the cast is adding time and request that a pacing note be given to correct it. The running time is the single best barometer of how the show is going: identify your ideal number and then pay close attention to how it may change.

The (rough) Shape of Previews

In spite of its intensity and seeming volatility, the early preview process has a very predictable shape. Knowing this can help you decide when is best to make changes, when to wait, and how to understand your own emotional experience.

1st preview: Will be euphoric and full of adrenaline, on and off stage. Even if there are technical problems, forgotten lines, or any other snafus that plague the performance, the dominant reaction from the company will be the profound excitement and satisfaction that comes from performing a play for the first time. Surrender to the emotional experience: technical notes can wait. You will learn more about the piece by communing with the audience and watching it through their eyes.

2nd preview: Will be similar to the first but without the adrenaline. It will feel like a step back. The problems and errors that were overlooked during the first preview will become glaring here. The cast will expect a similar emotional high and will not get it, which can lead to confusion or worry. Was the performance lacking? Why was it so good the first night and so off the second? These reactions are the result of trying to recreate the energy of the first preview, which cannot be done. You and the company are not responding to the quality of the preview itself, but to the distance between how last night felt compared with tonight. A dip in energy is inevitable: it is neither a sign of trouble nor a source for concern. It is a common impulse to take an enormous amount of notes during the second preview. So many moments can feel sloppy, the energy will seem off, the mistakes are too many, and your worklist may seem endless. Remember that this is primarily an emotional reaction and rarely a reflection of what you are seeing onstage. Rushing into a long notes session after second preview will not be to your or the company's benefit.

3rd preview: Will display early evidence of an equilibrium. The adrenaline of the first performance is behind you, as are the doldrums of the second. The shock of doing the play in front of an audience is beginning to abate, and now the cast can perform without a strong emotional current pulling them in either direction. They are beginning to understand how to work in concert with an audience. Useful patterns are emerging, influencing your work in rehearsal. You are able to separate the signal of a lesson from the noise of pure emotion. Your worklist will become more reliable and organized.

4th preview: Will be the one in which you will understand what you have built. You have now experienced a high, a low, and an even-keeled performance. By now you will have seen a similar performance twice in a row, energetically speaking, and you can make changes with confidence. You will be able to prioritize your worklist easily and go into rehearsals with clarity about what needs attention, and why.

Outside Opinions

Among early preview audiences will be plenty of familiar faces. Friends, partners, rivals, family members, agents, managers, actors who auditioned but didn't get cast, writers and other artists who come to support, writers and other artists who come to judge, and future collaborators … all of them will see the show throughout the run, but their presence has the most impact and influence during previews.

Directors observe audiences as a group, but not everyone in the crowd is a stranger. The cast will have guests come early, and they will inevitably share their opinions. An actor may go out with their agent after, who may say the actor's costume isn't flattering, or the second act doesn't make sense, or some other actor is miscast. These comments can shake an actor's confidence to their core: not only are they receiving outside feedback for the first time, it is coming from people they trust and want to impress. This can pose a problem for a director. How can you disagree with an actor if their agent told them they look terrible in their costume?

Your task in these moments is to listen and give the actor your full attention. Do not underestimate the power of these observations. Even ridiculous or nonsensical notes need to be heard because of the emotional power of the source. Dismissing them is telling an actor their feelings do not matter, so taking these thoughts seriously will do much to assuage the actor's feelings of vulnerability or concern. Provided the actor-director pact is strong, you are still the person the cast looks to for perspective, so their coming to you with questions, concerns, and ideas are usually requests for clarification and assurance.

How these outside opinions are shared with you will depend on the actor. Some may call you in a panic, others may find you at the start of rehearsal. Some might casually share a "new" idea and ask for your thoughts. We can call this phenomenon a phantom note. You will know the idea came from outside of the group because overnight an actor will have a strong but random idea about how to play a scene, or suddenly believe their character needs something like a wig. If you do not want to entertain the note or idea, articulate why quickly and completely. Otherwise, the actor may think they have discovered a significant flaw in the production, and the longer you entertain an idea, the more convinced they may become that they were right: there is a problem. But most outside opinions are not egregious. They are only serious because they can shake an actor's confidence. They are emotionally charged not because of the validity of the note, but because of the actor's relationship with the person who gave it.

24
PREVIEW REHEARSALS

Time moves very quickly during preview rehearsals. The pressures of making changes in the afternoon, knowing they will be attempted for the first time in front of an audience that night, can elevate adrenaline, excitement, and tension among all of your collaborators. Brilliant work can happen during preview rehearsals when everyone is focused, decisive, and fully committed, but tempers can flare, frustrations can mount, and time can evaporate.

Preview-Day Structure

A typical preview day unfolds as follows: in the morning, the crew will have a work call, where they will address the notes from the previous night's production meeting. Sometimes designers are at these calls to rehang or refocus lights, to listen to sound cues, or to work alongside the crew to implement changes. Like you, the crew will have a worklist longer than the amount of hours they have to complete it. This is why you must continue to articulate your priorities: because they will not get everything done overnight, you must make certain they at least make the changes you feel are necessary for rehearsal.

In the afternoon, you and the cast will be onstage. Because your worklist will include items for everyone, stage management should print out and distribute your worklist so that everyone can understand the plan for the day and begin their work without waiting for further instructions.

When the afternoon rehearsal is over, the cast and crew will break for dinner, then reconvene for the half hour call. After the performance, you will meet with the cast, then the designers and production team, then the writer. The cycle is repeated.

Putting in Rewrites

In the morning, the writer should send you any new pages. As always, you must review them yourself before you share. Ask yourself if the changes are a noticeable improvement from the previous version and if they address and solve a specific problem. Sometimes writers want to do too much. In their well-meaning effort to make improvements, they will produce changes that are different, but not significantly better. Changes for the sake of changes are too much to ask of an actor who is preparing for a performance: if the quality of the rewrite is debatable, delay putting them in until you have communicated your feelings to the playwright. If you can articulate your reservations, they may be open to taking another pass.

The natural resistance to the new can grow during previews. Actors will become more attached to the text once they start performing it, and may be increasingly less enthusiastic about changes. Not only will new pages rearrange their character's psychic trajectory, but the actor will be forced to spend the performance remembering their lines and cannot be fully present. The resistance begins with you: when reading new pages, ask yourself if you are favoring the older version because there is comfort in the familiar, because you don't want to throw out all the work you've already put into it (sunk cost fallacy), or because you genuinely feel the old version is superior to the new pages. It can be difficult to know the answer immediately, so do not rush. The changes can go in (or not) the next day, after you have had time to reflect.

If you read new pages and cannot make sense of them, you need to wait until there is time to have a more in-depth discussion with the writer. If you have a creative or narrative objection to the new pages, do not bring them into rehearsal until the matter is settled. New pages you read once and then decide to use can be confusing to a company, so while you and the writer need the freedom to try changes, your ability to experiment is not limitless. This is a question of quality over quantity. You cannot predict how an actor will respond to a rewrite, but know that at a certain point, you will exhaust their ability to incorporate new text. Only present new pages to a cast that you feel confident they should perform that night.

This confidence is important because an actor may push back on a rewrite, or pose a question that can be difficult to answer in such a short amount of time. If you cannot articulate the reason for making the change, the cast may feel you are favoring the writer over the actors. Previews are a vulnerable time for a cast: part of your preparation for delivering rewrites is in your confidence in knowing they are worth trying.

Consider the amount of pages the playwright has given you and the amount of time it may take to rehearse them. If a writer brings in twenty new pages (yes, that has happened) and you have not budgeted enough rehearsal for such a large change, you need to consider your options:

- Can the rewrite be divided into parts that can be inserted over a few days and still make sense in performance?

- Would breaking the rewrite up be more confusing for a cast than to do it all at once?
- Can a company memorize that many pages in a day?
- If not, should you give them a few days to memorize (while performing the older version at night), then make the change?
- Is that the most confusing scenario of all?

Preview rewrites will be your first experience with script changes that affect all departments simultaneously. Do not assume that because you are rewriting a scene without any technical elements that it will be easy for a backstage crew to adapt: that could be their busiest time as they prepare for an approaching sequence. Cutting scenes, reordering sections: these can be incredibly complex changes for the crew and designers. Conversely, even a small rewrite could mean cutting a prop, adding one you don't have, changing a costume, rearranging a transition. All changes can impact the production so all rewrites must be treated as logistical changes in addition to creative ones.

Rehearsing Rewrites

Of all the changes you will present a cast with, rewrites take the longest to learn and to metabolize. As thorough as you have been in the planning of a rehearsal day, it is still impossible to predict what questions, challenges, and concerns rewrites may bring up, or exactly how long it will take to stage them. This is why you must begin with them: once you start putting in rewrites, you cannot stop halfway to move on to another item on the list. It will take as long as it takes, and other items will have to be postponed. Rehearsing something in part, running out of time, asking the cast to revert to the old version for that night's performance, then finishing the next day can be enormously confusing. It is putting the actor in an unfair position and will not give you or the writer any sense of what is and isn't working: you're simply watching actors trying to remember which version of the play they have been asked to perform.

Small changes can be more difficult to implement than large ones because they can be much harder for an actor to remember. I once worked with a writer who said they did not have any rewrites, then arrived at rehearsal with a few dozen one-word changes scattered throughout the script. The cast was not pleased. A writer and a company may have drastically different opinions on what counts as a "small" or "large" rewrite, which is why decisions about what changes happen and when are left to the director.

Noting Actors

After distributing rewrites, share your verbal notes. Focus primarily on observations and adjustments: this is what I saw, this is what I would like you to try tonight, and this is why. If a note evolves into a deeper conversation about character, story, behavior, etc., pause the discussion, tell the actor you will add the moment to your worklist, and move on. Entire preview rehearsals can be devoured by the discussions prompted by verbal notes.

When noting a preview performance, a primary concern is to avoid confusing an actor. In the same way there are no small changes to a script, there are no minor thoughts, ideas, and observations. Generally speaking, preview notes concern pace, staging, underplaying, overplaying, and behavior: notes that affect the music of the text, the stakes or dramatic tension of a scene or moment, and the clarity of the action. Challenge yourself to be as simple, clear, and brief as possible: the goal is to give a note that is so easy to understand that the actor can take it and try it that evening.

Because rehearsal time is so valuable, consider writing out notes to share with actors to read on their own time. The value of this approach is twofold: it gives you the chance to edit and choose your words very carefully. It also gives the actors time to read the notes and consider them before rehearsal. The downside is that you are not present when the notes are read and cannot correct misunderstandings or misinterpretations. This approach is not for every company or process. Some actors prefer the time to process and reflect, and others can be very put off by it. When writing out these notes, if you find any observation difficult to articulate or too complicated (or risky) to share in this way, you need to give the note in person.

Working Onstage

The goal of your onstage rehearsal work is to make choices that the cast will feel comfortable trying in performance that night. This way of working mirrors the end of your time in the rehearsal room: you watch a run, you put in changes, then you see them in context during the next run. The difference here is that the "run" happens every night in front of an audience. Because of the higher stakes, preview rehearsals are less about experimentation and more about inserting changes, making certain everyone is clear on what they are and how to implement them, and building up the actor's confidence to try them. There is very little time for discussion and even less for trial and error. Time for reflection and consideration happens as you *prepare* for rehearsal. Coming in not-knowing will waste time and rattle nerves. If there is an experiment to conduct, it will not happen in rehearsal, it will happen in front of the audience.

Because of this dynamic, your ten-item worklist should be clear, concise, and achievable. It should not include questions to ponder or experiments to conduct. As you work, your stage manager should be looking ahead toward the next item so the crew can prepare. The further everyone can plan ahead, the faster you can move through your afternoon.

While the goal is a smooth and orderly rehearsal, heightened emotions and a lack of time can derail an afternoon: there will continue to be sections you find troublesome, confusing, or frustrating. Avoid putting them on your worklist every day: the repetition can be counterproductive. Only add items to your worklist after you have a clear idea of what you want to do with them. Rehearse a moment because you have a proposed solution, not simply because you're unhappy with it and feel it *should* be rehearsed. Working the same moment over and over without a plan only reinforces the problem. Hoping that a solution will suddenly appear puts an unfair amount of pressure on you and the cast: no artist can be expected to find an answer with such limited time and so much outside pressure. It can feel counter-intuitive not to schedule a scene that doesn't work, but rehearsing without a plan or a goal can frustrate or demoralize a cast.

If you bring an idea into rehearsal that doesn't work, set it aside for more contemplation and do not put it back on your worklist until you understand why it was unsuccessful. Repeat your process of disassembly and consider other elements that could use revision. If you tried to restage it, maybe it's an acting adjustment. If acting adjustments don't seem to work, maybe a rewrite is necessary. Consider as many options and combination of options as possible: the broader the search for answers, the faster they will come.

"The Cement Hardens Faster on Broadway"

Not all processes move at the same rate. Some writers work slowly, some casts adapt to changes easily, some productions preview for weeks and some for a few days, some audiences are excited to see a work in progress, while others expect something polished.

A producer once told me that "the cement hardens faster on Broadway," meaning I didn't have as much time as I thought to make changes during previews. This was not because I didn't have a lot of rehearsal time (I did), but because the *nature* of that time was different from what I expected. In a smaller space with cheaper tickets and a more adventurous audience, a company may feel more daring and open to rewrites, drastic changes, and experimenting in performance. A larger space (like a big regional theater or, in this case, a Broadway house) has a different energy: the audience arrives with certain expectations regardless of whether it's first preview or a year into the run. Actors can feel this—the audience teaches them—and they may not want to experiment very long: they will want decisions to be made, and quickly. Keep this in mind when budgeting your time in rehearsal. The space and circumstances can influence how open to changes and brave a cast may be. If the cement hardens fast, you must work quickly.

25
FINAL PREVIEWS AND FREEZING A PRODUCTION

Late Previews

The difficult truth of previews is that there will always be more you'll want to do, to change, and to refine. This is the nature of any creative process: the time to work ends while the ideas keep coming. Be realistic about your worklist and the amount of rehearsal you have left: it will help you prioritize your final days. A director's impulse, as they realize the end is near, can be to push for more rehearsals, more notes, and more rewrites. Knowing that you will never cross everything off your list, you must make some decisions about what changes are possible and most worthwhile. The company is beginning to find a reliable and repeatable rhythm: is that last change worth upsetting that dynamic? Serving the greater good of the production must be the priority over any one note.

Above all, late previews are about empowering the cast. That can mean winding down rehearsals, giving fewer notes, and generally letting go. If the cast is ready to begin the run of the show without your advice or perspective, it is proof you have done your job well: you have coaxed the production toward the audience and the audience toward the production, and now all the information they need is being passed directly from one to the other. There is real power in that exchange; and while it may be difficult, you should encourage it by stepping aside.

Final Days with the Writer

Like you, the writer may worry about the lack of time, and that feeling can generate a sudden burst of new pages. This behavior comes from fear: that the script isn't ready or good enough, that the text is somehow unclear or incomplete. Remind the writer that they have done strong work and that now boosting actor confidence matters more than any last minute text change. Writers may disagree with that sentiment, or merely hate it, but you must protect the production from rewrites that are an emotional reaction to the end of the process. I have had to tell writers that they can make further changes in subsequent productions, but that they could not keep rewriting for this one. Even a brilliant change needs to be weighed against the difficulties and interruptions of inserting it at the last minute. A cast needs to settle into a rhythm and experience the confidence that can only come through repetition. Anything that upsets their assuredness is an obstacle, and that includes rewrites.

Last Rehearsals with the Actors

As performances become more predictable and relaxed, the company's awareness of the audience increases: they can make adjustments to pace and momentum in the moment. They can listen, feel, and respond in real time. The byproduct of this wonderful development is that a cast will become naturally less reliant on the director's observations of a performance: they are beginning to trust their own perspective and experience.

Some actors will continue to rely on the director's feedback, but more often a company will begin to listen only to their proverbial dance partner. As a result, actors may become resistant to notes, which can be frustrating, but it is proof you have prepared them well to take ownership of the story. Focus your remaining notes on adjustments that will clarify moment-to-moment storytelling and on those observations the cast still cannot sense from the stage. At the end of previews, you are preparing the cast not for the next performance, but for them to do the entire run without your presence.

Last Meetings with the Designers

As previews stretch on, especially if you have a process that can be measured in weeks and not days, fewer people will attend the production meetings. Department heads will send assistants if they have them, designers may move on to other projects. You must know well in advance when you will start to lose collaborators. Do your designers need to leave for another project before previews are over, and when exactly? Is there a date when the crew will no longer be available for work calls or afternoon rehearsals? You should not assume everyone will be at the space every day until you freeze. Gather as much information as possible and let it inform your worklists. If you only have a few days with your lighting designer, for example, you need to prioritize that work. These are scheduling concerns, but they will have a direct and significant impact on your process.

On Amateurism

There is a theory that the most complex problems in math or science can best be solved by someone who doesn't know anything about either. Since they do not have the clutter of training or expertise interfering with their vision, they are able to see what is right in front of them and provide a simple—and accurate—solution. Amateurism argues that it is precisely this lack of knowledge that allows them to be brilliant: they can provide answers to the most puzzling questions and offer insights an expert cannot locate from so deep inside their work. This is why the audience is such a flawless teacher: because they are not an expert on the play, they can see it just as it is.

The simplest, most profound, and most useful observations will come from people who have just seen the show. As you get deeper into previews, invite friends to watch your work and ask them questions afterwards. They should not be professional colleagues but people who know very little about how theater is made: they will have the most honest, unencumbered perspectives.

In addition to the people you invite, ask the opinions of those who work at the theater but are not a direct participant in your production process—staff members who are in the space but not in rehearsals, who haven't heard you describe your vision, and who haven't read the play. In my experience, the most useful input comes from ushers. They have seen as many previews as you, they have eavesdropped on the audience as they've left the theater, and they have witnessed all the changes throughout the process. They will tell you the truth (why wouldn't they?), and they will tell you what the audience really thinks. If you have created a hit, they will know before you do. If you have not, they will know that, too. You'll never find a more illuminating and unbiased opinion: they can help you see your work in way you never could otherwise.

It can be alarming when the play is described back to you in a way you had never considered. A friend might casually share a thought or offer a perspective that upends your point of view about the entire play. This can induce panic: after all these months of deep reading and rigorous work, how can you have missed something so profound? So important? And what can you do about it now, when there is so little time left for changes?

When you are offered a new way to look at the play, that is a testament to the strength of the text, not a criticism of your work. If the play is good, there will be many ways to see and understand it. Like any great work of art, it is open to many different interpretations, and all of them will be valid. When someone shares their perspective, especially an insightful one that makes you doubt your work, you are simply learning that your suspicions those many months ago were correct: the play is fantastic.

Freezing a Show

The freeze date is the official end of the rehearsal process. The script you perform that evening is the production draft of the play and there will be no further changes to design or staging: your production is "frozen." A text is frozen out of necessity: the press office needs to share it with critics, the stage manager needs the cues in their calling script locked, and the understudies (if you have them) need to start memorizing lines.

Your final notes session with the cast should focus on simple and holistic thoughts: what you would like them to remember about their roles, the world of the play, and how to keep their performances engaged and fresh throughout the run. Ask yourself which two or three thoughts you'd like the cast to remember before every performance: those should be your final notes.

After the last rehearsal, meet with your stage manager to highlight what you want them to pay attention to during the run: moments you think may continue to change, tonal issues, scenes that were inconsistent during previews, an actor who likes to improvise. Any element you suspect may drift over time. Ask them to remain aware of changes and to check in with you about them over the course of the run.

That evening will be the cast's first time performing without rehearsal the next day. This is a significant psychic shift, and while some actors will be relieved to no longer rehearse, there are some that will still want to ask questions and will seek out your perspective. Make yourself available to the company, but do not offer any more notes. They need time to acclimate to the new normal.

Press Performances

Critics will be invited to the production after the show is frozen. The production is not open to review while changes are still being made, but a producing organization will be eager to host critics quickly in hopes their reviews will boost ticket sales. You can expect the reviewing press to come almost immediately after the freeze date.

Enforce a strict rule against discussing the attendance of critics, especially in front of the cast. They should not know who is coming, or when, or where they will sit. Some actors will claim not to be bothered and ask: do not tell them anyway. An actor cannot know how they will react to that knowledge until they have it, at which point it is too late. The only way to avoid troubling an actor about the presence of the press is to not discuss it. Let the cast perform unencumbered by concerns outside of their control: you owe it to them and to your work.

Avoid tinkering with the production. Do not go backstage and give an actor one last note, do not go backstage and say "it's an important night!" Treat it like any other performance.

It is often the producing organization who will interfere during press performances. I once directed a play that froze just before a day off. The artistic director felt the cast should meet for a line speed-through the next afternoon to keep them "fresh." Two problems emerged: the first was that a member of the company became irate that he was asked to come in for an afternoon and run lines for a show that just froze. His negative attitude made the line-through tense and uncomfortable. The second problem was that, because the cast had spent the afternoon speeding through lines, they unintentionally rushed through the first scene in that evening's performance. A review that came out a few days later said the opening moments were so frantic it was impossible to follow. In hindsight, I should have trusted the actors and pushed back against the artistic director's wishes. You will know and understand the needs of a company better than anyone: suggestions that can compromise their work must be rejected.

A common way producers tinker with press performances is through "papering." Free tickets are offered to specific people (friends of the company, staff members, etc.) in hopes that they will create a vocal, energized audience and a packed house. Even if you have already been enjoying enthusiastic responses, papering ensures a positive atmosphere: it leaves nothing to chance, which is why producers like it. This tactic is not without risk. Critics are smart, and they know when they've been surrounded by friends of the company. If a papered house feels inauthentic, a critic will know they are being manipulated.

I once directed a very dark comedy that the producers feared would be too intense for the press without a positive and vocal audience. Even though the audience response during previews had been fantastic, they were nervous and so they papered. The theater shook with laughter the night an influential critic was in attendance, and the audience leapt to their feet for the curtain call. Three days later, the review came out and the critic destroyed the play. He said it was a tasteless comedy that aimed for cheap laughs over depth and complexity. Was the critic responding to the production, or to the roar of the audience surrounding him? What I do know is that he did not experience an authentic audience-actor relationship. The producers had manufactured an atmosphere by asking the audience to perform for the critic instead of to engage with the play.

I could only contextualize both of these reviews because I had watched the press performances. Some directors stay as far away as possible on press nights, but I find watching useful. Seeing what a critic sees will help you understand the review and how your work is perceived by a critical eye. It is also helpful to see the performance in case an actor reads a review and has any questions. You should be able to provide an actor with counsel and context, and you can provide neither if you were not there to see the same performance as the critic.

26
OPENING, THE RUN, AND CLOSING

Opening Night

Opening nights can be perplexing for a director: there is so little to do. You can't rehearse, you can't work or make changes, and now there you are, dressed up, waiting for the reviews.

An opening night audience can be a tricky dance partner. Because the company has friends, family, agents, or managers in the house, the performance can feel pushed or tentative, or somehow off-rhythm. The rest of the audience will be producers, donors, investors, board members, or guests of the producing organization. This combination can make for an overly responsive crowd or a more scrutinizing one. You can trust the company will feel the pressure and significance of the occasion (who doesn't want to deliver a fantastic performance for opening?), and that they understand this is their last performance before the reviews are made public.

What a director can do on opening night—perhaps the only thing they can do—is express gratitude for the opportunity to work, for all your collaborators, and for the producing organization's support. Display your pride, as it will be contagious. Even if all you see as you watch the performance is what you still want to change, put that feeling aside and recognize the enormous collective effort that went into creating this production. Everyone will look to the director on opening: you owe it to yourself and to all of your collaborators to celebrate what you have made together.

The Reviews

Some time during the opening night party or the following day, the reviews will be published. You may know because you'll see the scattered glow of phones, or because the energy will shift: it will get louder and more celebratory, or much quieter. Nothing can clear out a party quicker than rumors of bad reviews.

The great actress Estelle Parsons once told me "I always read my reviews because I always learn something." While I would not give this advice to an actor, directors must know what the critics have said about the work. Reviews can have an effect—sometimes a profound one—on both the company and the audience. Outside influences impacting your work so significantly can be frustrating, but knowing what was written will help you mitigate a review's effect on your production.

Most reviews of new works focus on the play itself: criticism as a referendum on the text. The production is a secondary consideration. When articulating their thoughts—what they believe the play is about, if they think it is successful as a work of art—critics are teaching audiences not only about the play's merit, but about its meaning. You may or may not agree with the critic's assessment, but you cannot stop the review's influence on future audiences. Because of this, the response will change in the days after opening night. If your preview audiences have been reluctant or disengaged and the critical consensus is rapturous, you can expect suddenly enthusiastic (and larger) crowds. Conversely, vocal and engaged houses can become quiet (and smaller) if the reviews were negative. Regardless, this trend does not last. You can expect audiences to forget reviews over time and have their own experience, not the one they've been told to have. And while you can count on this course correction over time, a company can be thrown by very different audience reactions immediately after opening.

Reviews can have a profound effect on ticket sales, and they can also influence the work itself: one critical observation can alter an actor's performance, and a good review is just as likely to cause changes as a negative one. I once worked on a play that was widely acclaimed off-Broadway and transferred to Broadway later that season. In the Broadway review, the same critic who raved about the production off-Broadway praised the lead actor, saying he was "even better." The actor felt that his performance had not changed, and so the critic's comment sent him into a spiral of self-doubt. Was his performance that different? Was he doing something on Broadway he hadn't done before? Was his off-Broadway performance lacking somehow and no one told him? Even unqualified praise made the actor anxious, and he struggled with self-consciousness during the Broadway run.

Another play I worked on was well received by the critics, and the cast was pleased to perform for enthusiastic houses. A week after opening, the stage manager called and explained that one of the actors had completely changed how they were playing a scene. I watched the next performance, and a section that in previews had been very subtle had transformed into one actor screaming through tears at her completely stunned scene partner. After the show, I asked the actor why she had made such a character and scene-altering change. She confessed that she had read a review and was troubled to see her performance described as "understated." She was so embarrassed by the criticism (which was actually a compliment), she made a decision to "fix" it.

In both cases, the actors' responses were unrelated to the quality of the review. What suffered was the actor's relationship with and confidence in their work. This is why you must familiarize yourself with the reviews: you cannot predict how they might affect an actor or a production. Go to the theater the night after opening and make yourself available to the company. If an actor has a thought, question, or concern about the reviews, they will find you. These conversations should happen privately, as you must assume the rest of the company has not read them. Help the actor remember why they made the choices they did, and how much thorough trial and error went into choosing the strongest option. You are leading them back to their choices in hopes they can reclaim ownership of it. A cast cannot be shielded from reviews entirely, and an actor cannot predict how they will respond, but a director can be empathic and offer perspective to guide an actor back to their best work.

Inviting Potential Colleagues

One of the great professional obstacles a director must face is that their work is ephemeral. A writer has the script, an actor can work on film, designers can photograph their work, but the director's art disappears on closing night. You must learn to be your own promoter. Invite producers, artistic directors, literary managers, agents, actors, designers, writers, and stage managers to your productions. Anyone you admire and would want to collaborate with, invite all of them to see your work.

Send out invitations as early as possible to give your potential guests enough time to plan. Be proud of your work: do not include apologies or disclaimers. Be specific about why you thought to invite this person: is there a reason why you have singled them out? If you are simply inviting anyone you can think of, colleagues can tell. Articulate the reason why you want them to see this piece, why their work resonates with you, and why you want to collaborate in the future. That is the best way to expand your professional circle and to generate your own opportunities.

Maintaining a Show

Your contract ends on opening night. Your work is done, your obligations are complete. Stage management has taken over the daily maintaining of the production and noting of the cast, but even the most attentive ones cannot keep a production from drifting over the course of the run. This is especially true for new plays, as it is likely there were rewrites throughout previews, and some moments can go into the run relatively under-rehearsed. Those sections leave ample room for change, and this is why, if you are able, you should return occasionally to watch performances.

The first time you watch the production after a period of time can be shocking. It can appear completely different from what you rehearsed. This is because shifts in timing and performance are inevitable, and because a director's memory is imperfect. A gap will exist between what you are watching and how you remember it. Identify exactly what feels different: is it altering the meaning of the scene, character, or story? Is it damaging to the production? Give yourself time to reflect: are you reacting strongly to the change itself, or to the surprise of not seeing exactly what you remember? Your impulse may be to go backstage and give pages of notes, to try to steer your production back to your memory of the "frozen" version. Since drifting is inevitable, consider which changes compromises the story, and which are simply different. The former requires you to take action, the latter does not. Notes should go through stage management: do not undercut their authority to communicate with the company about their performance.

Occasionally, you will be informed of creative conflict among the cast. An actor may reach out to you and tell you their scene partner has changed how they play something, or the stage manager will tell you they've noticed a change. Ask your stage manager to resolve the dispute. If they cannot, watch a performance if you are able, and speak with both actors. You need to let the performance itself guide any conversations: you cannot mediate a cast conflict if you haven't seen the work. Choosing a side without an informed perspective will exacerbate the problem. Remember that conflicts that arise after opening are often rooted in personal issues, but your responsibility is exclusively to your production. Any argument that is more personal, a director cannot and should not get involved.

Closing

Saying goodbye to your work and to the people you made it with can conjure a bittersweet combination of emotions. Closing night can be a complicated occasion for a director because you have not been an active participant in the day-to-day machinations of the production for some time. A new set of rituals and a new group dynamic will have taken shape during the run, and closing marks the end of that as well.

Closings, like openings, are occasions for gratitude. You all came together to build a difficult and complex thing that now exists only in memory. The temporal nature of theater can be exhilarating but also heartbreaking: take this occasion to honor the time, work, effort, talent, and generosity of everyone who came together to bring the piece into existence. A closing night is an acknowledgment that it happened.

For the director of a new play, a closing night can be particularly special. You helped birth the play. You coaxed it off the page and brought it to life for the first time. Saying goodbye to a work of art that you spent months or years developing is a specific type of loss. There is no way to avoid the sadness of parting with something that occupied such a large space in your creative life, but hopefully you can take enormous pride in knowing that your talent and wisdom were instrumental in bringing the play into existence. Hopefully, because of your production's success, the play will be performed again. Even if you don't participate in future productions, the play is being seen by more audiences, and you made that possible. The world needs good art, and if you can bring more of it into the world, then your work was an unqualified success.

Success, Failure, and Next Steps

Like any artistic undertaking, directing a new play will mean losses and triumphs, clarities and confusions, and all of them should be reflected on. Every project is an opportunity to learn, to grow, and to accumulate wisdom to apply to the next one.

Evaluating your work can take a very long time: you may find yourself reflecting and ruminating on a project years after it closes. Sharing a work of art is risky and requires bravery: everyone who sees it will have an opinion, and absorbing the public's response can be a challenge. If you had not determined for yourself what you hoped to achieve, if you did not begin with a clear vision for the thing you wanted to make, a director can be easily swayed by unreliable points of view. Believing a good or bad review over your own taste, for example, can lead you away from yourself and your art, and the longer you follow what others say about your work, the more difficult it can be to find your way back to yourself. Understand how you feel about what you make, every time, and trust that feeling. Then outside influences cannot pull you away.

Take the time to sit with your feelings and observations after every project. That's how the work becomes a lesson, and then wisdom. There can be a temptation—if the reviews were wonderful, or if you won awards—to tell yourself you have it all figured out, and then go into the next process certain you are an expert. If you haven't identified why *you* think the work was a success, you will have learned little, and you may find yourself humbled by the next one. Conversely, when you work on a production that is not a success, you may want to forget what happened and move on as quickly as possible. In both cases you are depriving yourself of hard-earned wisdom.

Ask yourself about your process:

- What made you passionate about the play the first time you read it?
- Do you still feel the same way about it? Why or why not?
- Do you believe that feeling made its way to the audience? Why or why not?
- How did you first imagine the production would look and sound?
- How was it the same and how was it different?
- In what ways did you feel you served the play and your emotional connection to it?
- In what ways could you have improved?
- How would you describe your experience with each collaborator?
- What were the ways in which those collaborations were or were not successful?
- How was your relationship with the producing organization?
- Did you feel supported, understood, and respected?
- Would you want to work with them again?
- Will you approach your relationship with a producer differently next time?

Questions like these will help you see your own process: every part of your experience is a potential lesson.

If you deem a project a failure (your *own* definition of failure), you must give yourself time to mourn. If the process was difficult and the creative team is parting on strained terms. If the audience response was negative. If a production was poorly received. If you were not able to make the art you had hoped to. Mourning a creative disappointment is critical. Without time to reflect, a director can bring negative or defensive energy into their next process. Sit with your feelings, listen to and respect them, and then find peace within them: otherwise they will remain, and fester, and subconsciously become part of your future work. Only by understanding difficult experiences can you begin every new process with the necessary openness and optimism.

A play that is poorly received does not automatically mean that a producer will not be excited to work with you again. Those relationships have more to do with respect, trust, and artistic quality than with box office. The same goes for your writer, and for your cast. The nature and success of your collaboration will have far more influence over your future with these colleagues than any public or critical reception. The opposite is also true: directing a hit will not guarantee future work at an organization if you treated the crew or the staff poorly. The reception of a piece and the experience of making it are never in perfect alignment: while successes will do wonders for your career, they can mean little if producers do not want to collaborate with you again.

Eventually, you will direct a play that will be an enormous success. You will earn well-deserved attention, offers to direct more work, invitations to take meetings with writers, producers, and actors: you will be in demand. This moment of hard-earned success usually comes after many years of struggle. Because of all the time you've spent fighting for a moment of relative ease and opportunity, it can be easy to forget that the reward lies in being able to make the art you want. Success means you have a responsibility to yourself and to your work to focus only on those projects that excite and inspire you. It can feel risky or counterintuitive to pass on all of the many offers coming to you after so many years of struggle, but you must: for the quality of your work, your mental and physical health, and for your nourishment as an artist. Your hard work and talent have earned you success and positive attention: honor your art by pacing yourself, by choosing work that speaks to you, and by having the self-knowledge and confidence to know when to say yes.

CONCLUSION

Praxis is a key to learning how to direct, but how can one practice when there are so few opportunities for a new or aspiring director to be in a rehearsal room? While overseeing a process is the best education, a director can continue learning about their work, their taste, their point of view, and their art by observing and refining their tools of observation. Reflect on how you move through your day. Are you remaining open to what is happening around you? Are your senses engaged? What do you notice? How do you react? When and how is your imagination triggered? Are you curious about the people in your life? Your relationships? Strangers on the street? How well do you listen to others? Can you challenge yourself to listen with greater attention? Millions of reactions, thoughts, and ideas will pass through your mind every day: which do you consider, observe, and value?

Remaining engaged with your tools—awareness, taste, vision, curiosity, and communication—will allow you to strengthen and refine them. How you choose to move through the world is how you will be in a rehearsal room.

I've never been a firm believer that an artist's life must be their art and vice versa, but it is undeniable that art/life boundaries are porous, especially for those of us who work in the theater. This is because we are an art of human beings: our bodies in space, our presence, our behavior, our language, our relationships, our feelings, our beliefs, our lies and our truths, and our endless complexities. Theater is the experience of artists and audiences in a room together, sharing a live, ephemeral moment that can never be repeated. This is why theater is timeless and primal, like drawing a picture of an animal on a cave wall. Standing before a group and telling them a story is just something human beings do. It is inside of us, like song or sport or spirituality. That is why even though theater's epitaph has been written and rewritten for generations, we are still compelled to make it and to see it. There is something necessary beyond intellect or even language that calls on us to come together and watch someone say, "This is what it's like to be alive. This is my experience." We feel less alone for a while, we understand ourselves better, we see something new or see something old in a different way. We are reminded of parts of ourselves we had forgotten. There is comfort in acknowledging that we are human beings, that our experience is shared, that we may not be as different as we thought or feared. This is nourishment for our hearts and our minds. We will always need theater and the artists who make it to hold a mirror up to nature. To ask, over and over, "What is it to love, hate, fear, embrace, reject, doubt, and adore?" These are the questions we will wrestle with our entire lives. As people and as artists.

Directing a production is an incredible achievement, but it is the repetition, the ritual, the act of coming together again and again to see and to perform plays that will always be a necessity. Directors guide not only a single production, we help uphold an ancient form that was gifted to us, and that eventually we will pass on. We are stewards, links in a very old chain, and to be a part of that tradition is an honor and responsibility. What we create in rehearsal rooms may be ephemeral, but our contributions are timeless. The world always needs new perspectives: share yours.

ACKNOWLEDGMENTS

When I began this book, with the encouragement of the great playwright and my dear friend Christopher Shinn, I had no idea how many people it would take to bring it into existence. This book is the product of decades spent in rehearsal rooms: watching, listening, trying, and trying again, and so I must express my deepest gratitude to all of the directors and artistic directors I've worked with and for. There are too many to list here, but I must acknowledge the late Jim Houghton and Todd Haimes, who continue to have a profound impact on my life. Thank you to Andre Bishop, Adam Siegel, and the entire staff of Lincoln Center Theater for their support. Thank you to Di Glazer at CAA for her help and guidance, and to Jennifer Chang, Jane Steinberg, and Angelina Burnett for reading early drafts and for offering their insights. Thank you to Alex Kilgore, Jen Frasher, Ari Graynor, and especially Andromache Chalfant for giving me space to write. Thank you to Ajahn Pesalo and everyone at the Temple Forest Monastery. Thank you to Blair Singer. And thank you to my family: my parents, Michael and Susan; my wife, Rocio; and my children, Clara and Jonah.

INDEX

abstraction 96
actor/director pact 148–9, 162, 166, 177, 190, 232, 237
actors 145–58, 192, 232
    challenges 150–8
    communication 149–50
    new work 146–7
    ownership 169
    tablework 127–32
adaptation 7
amateurism 246
answers 10
art object 6, 147–8, 161
art-by-committee 6, 12, 113
artistic directors 101–2, 194–5
artwork (Marketing) 106
assistant directors 68
audience 47, 114–16, 148–9, 161, 223–43
auditions (*see* "casting")
awareness 8–9, 43, 80, 189

backers audition 26
benefit of the doubt 130–1, 149, 173–4
blocking 137
blurbs 105–6
brainstorming 88–90
budgets 98–9, 111–2

calendars 109–11
casting 72–87
    adjustments 81–2
    breakdowns 75
    callbacks 83–5
    decisions 85–6
    directing 83, 84–5
    memorization 77

offers 73–5, 86
readers 78–9
readings 26–7
scheduling 78
sides 76–7, 84
space 77
writers 82
casting director 72–3
closing 252–3
commercial theater 100
communication 8, 10–1
    actors 23–4, 42, 44
Company Management 104
composers 66
conflict 122, 128, 151–2, 173, 252
conflict resolution 177–9, 210
consciousness 8–10
contracts 102–3
costume design 65–6, 95–6
critics 247–8, 250–1
curiosity 8, 10, 47, 114, 130

deadlines 98–9
decisions 164
democracy 122–32, 140
design process 88–99
designer runs 193–4
designers 62–6, 245
development 23–55
dialects 66–8
dictatorships 140
directing 5–6, 13
dramaturgs 68–9
dress rehearsal 219–22
    open vs. closed 220
    photos 220

editing 58, 165
empathy 8, 12
ensemble building 128–9
entrances and exits 92
established play 3
ethics 8
event (peripety) 60
experimentation 37–8, 43

failure 134, 253–5
falling apart 133–4, 204, 225–6
Fiddler on the Roof 190
fight direction 66–8
first rehearsal 117–21
fittings 65–6
freeze date 110, 247

General Management 102–4
genres 20
gossip 22
gratitude 8

harmony 6, 197, 207, 212

"I Don't Know" 134–5, 139, 153, 164
intellectual property 103
intimacy direction 66–8, 142–3
invitations 55, 251

laboratory 37
lighting design 63–4, 94
literary offices 14

maintaining a show 251–2
marketing 105
marking 172–3
meet and greets 117–18
meetings
    actors 86–7
    artistic director 51–3
    casting directors 73
    designers 61–6, 88–99
    general 53–4
    producers 51–3
    stage management 141–3
    writers 18–22, 120–1, 162–4, 233–4

method 151–2
miscast 176–7
momentum 48, 131, 137–8, 152, 162–3, 165

new plays 3
not-for-profit 100–7
notes 149–50, 166–9, 189–90, 194–5, 232, 241, 247

objective truth 115–16, 124–7, 131, 189
obstacles 54–5
off-book 173
opening night 249
opinions 236–7
optimism 15, 254
over-analysis 152–3
over-design 96, 216–17
over-development 47–8
over-rewriting 183
overplaying 170–1

papering 248
paradoxes 6–7, 127, 129, 147
paraphrasing 173–4
patience 8
performance reports 234–5
play definition 3
playing space 93
playwrights
    established 15, 20–1
    finding them 14
pre-production 57–112
press 107
press performances 247–8
preview rehearsals 238–43, 245
previews 225–37, 244–8
priorities 59, 190–1
producers 101
producing organizations 100–12
production 3
Production Management 104
production meetings 107–12, 199–200
pursuing a production 50–5

INDEX

questions 10, 24, 27, 47–8, 87, 114–16, 129, 216, 225

read-throughs 118–20
reading texts
    development 23–4
    first read 15–17
    pre-production 58–60
    rehearsal 114–16
    taste 14
readings 25–36
    acting notes 32–3
    audience 28
    casting 26–7
    intermissions 32
    listening 33–4
    location 28
    preparation 28–30
    private 25
    programming 25, 54
    public 25
    rehearsal 30–2
    scheduling 27–8
    stage direction reader 32
    stage directions 30
    writer meeting 35–6
realism 96
reflection 192–3
rehearsal reports 143–4
rehearsals 113–96
    challenges 170–7
    preparation 141–4
    rewrites 184–5
relationships 197
    actor/designer 210–1
    actor/director 148–9
    producer/director 53–4
    set/light designers 64
    writer/actor 131, 151, 184–5
    writer/director 18
reviews 249–51, 253
rewrites 35–6, 41, 45, 87, 143, 180–5, 192, 230, 238–40
rhythm 137–8, 141
Robbins, Jerome 190
rough draft 133–58
royalties 103
rule breaking 127

rules 42, 124–7, 131, 151–2, 153, 188, 225
run-throughs 186–9, 196

scene breakdowns 59
set design 62–3
setting 91–2
shadow directors 153
site specific 96
sound design 64–5, 94–5
space 96–8, 197
specialists 6
stage business 174–5
stage management 41, 70–1, 141–3, 252
staggered calls 142
staging 133, 136–7
story 4
strong and wrong 43
stumble-throughs 159–64
sub-rights 103–4
subconsciousness 9–10
subjective Interpretations 115–16, 124–7, 131
submissions 50–1
success 253–5
summaries 59
sunk cost fallacy 215–16, 239

tablework 122–32
taste 8, 9–10, 14, 27, 53–4, 63, 134, 148, 207, 227, 229, 253
tech 199–218
    actors 217
    crews 205–6, 213, 240
    dry tech 200–2
    first day 205–6, 211–2
    leading by example 217–18
    preparation 199–200
    rough draft 206–13
    stumble through 212–14
    writers 204–5
tools 8–12, 256
top ten lists 190–1
transitions 93–4, 201–2
translation 7–8
trial and error 41, 43, 95, 133–9, 153

under-rewriting 182–3
underplaying 172–3
ushers 246

video designers 66
violence 67–8, 142–3
vision 7, 8, 10, 21, 58, 83, 87, 120, 192, 229, 246
vocal "notes" 175–6

worklists 43, 190–1
workshops 37–47
    casting 40
    location 40–1
    preparation 38–41
    producers 40
    scheduling 39
    stage management 41
writers groups 14